D1559838

THE FUTURE OF

INSURANCE REGULATION
IN THE UNITED STATES

THE FUTURE OF

INSURANCE REGULATION
IN THE UNITED STATES

MARTIN F. GRACE

ROBERT W. KLEIN

editors

GEORGIA STATE UNIVERSITY
Atlanta

BROOKINGS INSTITUTION PRESS
Washington, D.C.

Library of Congress Cataloging-in-Publication data
The future of insurance regulation in the United States / Martin F. Grace, Robert W. Klein, editors.
        p.   cm.
    Includes bibliographical references and index.
    Summary: "Enhances research and informs the debate on restructuring the framework for U.S. insurance regulation. Evaluates proposed legislation to create an Optional Federal Charter for insurance companies and agents. Also goes beyond discussion of OFC and lays out the broader context and need for regulatory reform in the insurance industry"—Provided by publisher.
    ISBN 978-0-8157-0286-3 (cloth : alk. paper)
    1. Insurance—State supervision—United States. 2. Insurance—Government policy—United States. 3. Insurance law—United States. I. Grace, Martin Francis, 1958– II. Klein, Robert W. (Robert Warren), 1953– III. Title.
    HG8535.F88 2009
    368'.0190973—dc22   2009011150

9 8 7 6 5 4 3 2 1

Typeset in Adobe Garamond

Composition by Circle Graphics, Inc.
Columbia, Maryland

Printed by R. R. Donnelley
Harrisonburg, Virginia

Contents

Preface

The issue of whether the insurance industry in the United States should be regulated by the states or by the federal government has been the subject of considerable debate over the last century and a half. The states have successfully defended the primacy of their authority, but an increasing number of insurers have come to favor an optional federal charter. The debate over an optional federal charter is lodged within a broader discussion of who should regulate insurance and how it should be regulated. The current financial crisis and calls for restructuring the framework for overseeing financial institutions and markets have drawn further attention to insurance regulation.

The importance and currency of these issues led Georgia State University, the American Enterprise Institute, and the Brookings Institution to cosponsor a conference on the future of insurance regulation, with funding support from the Risk Foundation. The conference was held on July 9, 2008, in Washington, D.C. Several papers were presented and discussed by prominent insurance and regulatory experts. These papers, subsequently revised, form the primary content of this book. We believe that the book will be a valuable reference for those policymakers and other stakeholders charged with considering the merits of an optional federal charter and other policy reforms in insurance.

We wish to acknowledge the efforts of a number of people who made the conference and this book possible. Richard Phillips, Robert Litan, and Peter Wallison were closely involved in the planning process. Ellen Thrower served as the principal liaison with the Risk Foundation. Karen Dubas coordinated the logistics for the conference at the American Enterprise Institute. Mary Kwak acquired the book, and Diane Hammond edited the manuscript. The views presented in the chapters are those of their authors and are not necessarily those of the participating institutions.

1

The Future of Insurance Regulation: An Introduction

Martin F. Grace and Robert W. Klein

The question of who should regulate the insurance industry has been debated in the United States since the time of the Civil War. Insurance continues to be regulated by the states despite several challenges to their authority over the years. The states' authority over insurance was supported in various court decisions until the *Southeastern Underwriters* case in 1944.[1] In that case, the Supreme Court determined that the commerce clause of the Constitution applied to insurance and that insurance companies (and agents) were subject to federal antitrust law. The Court's ruling caused the states and the industry to push for the McCarran-Ferguson Act (MFA) in 1945, which delegated the regulation of insurance to the states.[2]

At that time, the majority of insurance companies favored state over federal insurance regulation. However, since the passage of the MFA the bulk of insurance is now written by national (and international companies) operating across state borders. Many of these insurers have come to view state regulation as an increasing drag on their efficiency and competitiveness and now support a federal

1. 322 U.S. 533 (1944).
2. 15 U.S.C. secs. 1011–15.

regulatory system. This is reflected in recent proposals that would establish an optional federal charter (OFC) for insurance companies and agents that would allow them to choose to be federally regulated and exempt from state regulation. However, there is fierce opposition to an OFC among the states and state-oriented segments of the industry.

Since the Gramm-Leach-Bliley Act (GLBA) was enacted in 1999, there has been increasing interest in Congress and significant sectors of the insurance industry to establish some form of federal insurance regulation. The GLBA provided the opportunity for banks, insurance companies, and other types of financial intermediaries to be owned by the same holding company. In addition, each type of firm was still subject to regulation by the particular intermediary's regulator. Although the GLBA was a significant step forward, a number of experts have criticized the division of regulation among various agencies and levels of government. In this sense, insurance is marked as the area most out of line with a modern, integrated system of financial regulation.

The demand for federal regulation arises from not only the high cost of state regulation but also other problems associated with it. The high cost of state regulation derives from the fact that insurers must comply with the specific regulations in each state in which they do business. Insurers are burdened by duplicative yet often inconsistent regulation of many aspects of their operations, including solvency, products, prices, and market conduct.[3] While solvency regulation is relatively uniform (albeit enforced by each state), the regulation of insurers' other activities (that is, market regulation) varies greatly among the states. Many insurers are concerned about the hurdles they must overcome in getting prices and products approved and the constraints and mandates imposed on various aspects of their market activities, which they view as excessive and unnecessary.[4] These concerns have grown as the industry has becoming increasingly national and international in its scope of operations and as financial convergence has spurred competition between insurance companies and other institutions in the sale of certain financial products with similar attributes. The U.S. system of state insurance regulation is viewed as substantially undermining insurers' efficiency and ability to compete in national and international markets.

At the same time, any move to federal insurance regulation is strongly opposed by certain stakeholder groups, including state officials, state and regional insur-

---

3. Grace and Klein (2000).

4. For a series of case studies on the effects of automobile insurance price regulation, see Cummins (2002).

ance companies, and many insurance agents. Opponents of federal regulation raise concerns about the possibility of weakened regulation, reduced consumer protection, and lack of proper attention to local issues. State regulators, understandably, also may fear significant erosion of their authority if large segments of the industry become subject to federal regulation. Additionally, state-oriented insurance companies and agents may be concerned about the competitive advantages that would be gained by national insurers and agents that opt for federal regulation. Hence proposals to establish some form of federal insurance regulation, principally an OFC, have been mired in a fierce debate that has thwarted decisive legislative action.

Still the push for federal insurance regulation shows no signs of abating and may very well intensify in the context of the current problems in financial markets and efforts to restructure the regulatory framework for all financial institutions. The U.S. Department of the Treasury issued its blueprint for financial services regulation reform in March 2008, before conditions in financial markets reached crisis proportions and contributed to cascading problems in the overall economy.[5] The Treasury blueprint acknowledged an important federal role for insurance regulation and advocates an insurance OFC similar to that conceived in pending federal legislation. The 2008 Treasury plan will likely be revisited by the new administration and Congress that took office in January 2009, but many of its components, including an insurance OFC, may be incorporated into the reform measures advocated by this administration.[6]

With the financial crisis of September 2008, the significant financial failure of a noninsurance subsidiary of the American International Group (one of the largest insurers in the world), and the resulting federal bailout of the financial services industry, the interconnections among various financial institutions and markets became apparent, increasing the pressure for overhauling the regulatory structure. Insurance will likely be a subject of considerable discussion as reform efforts move forward, but how and when it might be incorporated into a federal regulatory framework remains uncertain. Views differ as to how recent events will affect the prospects for federal insurance regulation. However, the issues underlying the

---

5. U.S. Department of the Treasury (2008).

6. In testimony before the Senate Banking Committee, the new Treasury secretary, Timothy Geithner, stated that OFC proposals had merit and that his personal view is that a federal charter is likely to be an important part of the administration's regulatory reform plan. See "Geithner: Federal Insurance Charter 'Important Part' of Financial Plan," BestWire, February 10, 2008.

need for examining the structure of insurance regulation have remained largely unchanged even as market conditions have changed.

This brings us to the purpose of this book. In July 2008 Georgia State University, the American Enterprise Institute, and the Brookings Institution sponsored a conference on the future of insurance regulation in Washington, underwritten by the Risk Foundation. The following chapters are based on papers presented at the conference and address a number of issues surrounding the structure of insurance regulation and its policies. Although the papers were presented in July 2008, in the chapters that follow the authors reflect on subsequent events and their significance for the future of insurance regulation.

The conference addressed a number of important issues surrounding the future of insurance regulation and the different paths it might take, primarily the question of state versus federal regulation, specifically the merits of an OFC and how it might be designed. Beyond the questions involved with the institutional framework for insurance regulation, the conference also considered how insurance should be regulated from a policy perspective and the implications of financial convergence and the internationalization of insurance markets for an optimal regulatory structure. Arguably, current OFC proposals leave a number of unanswered questions, and other reform scenarios are possible. Hence, the purpose of the conference was to look beyond the merits of an OFC and to ask broader questions, such as

—What is the right administrative apparatus for insurance regulation?
—What areas should be regulated and how?
—How does deregulation affect markets and consumers?
—How does financial convergence interact with changes in regulation?
—How does regulation affect insurance markets internationally?

This is an appropriate time to examine these questions. Recent events have exposed further vulnerabilities in financial markets and cracks in the regulatory structure for financial institutions. Policymakers must tackle a host of issues in charting a future course for financial regulation generally and insurance regulation specifically. The following chapters put the OFC proposal in context and examine various aspects of its design and implementation as well as a broader set of questions associated with insurance regulation. This book provides policymakers and academics with insights into the implications of a number of the policy choices that are likely to be considered.

An Overview of the Insurance Industry and Its Regulation

In chapter 2 Robert Klein provides an overview of the insurance industry and its current regulatory structure that establishes a context for the following chapters. He reviews the considerable growth and evolution of the U.S. insurance industry and its principal sectors: life insurance and annuities, accident and health insurance, and property-casualty insurance. Since the enactment of the MFA, the industry has grown substantially in size, scope, and complexity. Most of the insurance in a given state is sold by insurers that are domiciled in other states. Insurers also now underwrite a wide variety of exposures, and their financial structure and risks have become much more complex. The states have been challenged in keeping pace with the industry and its growing scope and complexity.

State insurance regulators have responded to these challenges by substantially increasing their resources and improving their methods in overseeing the industry. They have made substantial changes in many areas and have embarked on various initiatives to harmonize their regulatory requirements, eliminate unnecessary constraints, and ease the compliance burdens of insurers. Still these efforts have fallen far short of what national insurers would consider satisfactory, and it is questionable whether a state-based system could ever achieve the efficiencies of a federal regulator. Nonetheless, the vision of federal regulation may not be realized any time soon, which makes reforms at the state level all the more relevant.

Klein also outlines alternative frameworks for insurance regulation. An OFC has received the greatest attention and support, but other structures have been proposed. Other proposals include federal standards for state regulation and the creation of a single-state regulatory system in which an insurer would be subject solely to the oversight of its domiciliary jurisdiction regardless of where it did business. While these other proposals have not attracted strong constituencies, their relative merits may surface as the debate over insurance regulation progresses. Indeed, if history is any guide, the pattern of incremental changes in federal and state roles may continue for some time before a more fundamental restructuring of insurance regulation occurs.

The Pros and Cons of Federal Insurance Regulation

In chapter 3 Martin Grace and Hal Scott examine the legal structure of regulation proposed in OFC legislation and compare it to current state practice and current federal regulatory practice. The chapter starts with an overview of the economic argument for an optional federal charter approach to insurance regulation. In the last few years a number of researchers have attempted to document the costs of the state system of regulation. Evidence exists that the insurance industry is an interstate business. Thus duplicative regulation is costly, and the states themselves are not necessarily efficient regulators. The average property liability company has sixteen state licenses, and the average life company has twenty-five licenses. Grace and Scott pose several questions. Is there any social value in having sixteen or twenty-five different regulators looking at each company? Is there any value in duplicative regulation or inconsistent regulation? Does each state have the proper incentives to regulate when it knows there are other states looking at the firm? Evidence suggests that small states might free ride on bigger states' regulatory apparatus. A federal regulator might be able to reduce these types of costs to the benefit of the insurance consumer.

Grace and Scott also look at the response of the National Association of Insurance Commissioners (NAIC) to the issue of duplicative regulation by examining the commonality of regulatory approaches for a number of model acts promulgated by the NAIC. Few of the model laws in their (admittedly nonrandom) sample were uniformly adopted by the states: there not only seems to be a natural limit to the number of states that might adopt a model act but, in addition, some large states have adopted their own version of the model.

Grace and Scott also find that there are significant questions left unaddressed by the current proposal. For example, it is still feasible for firms in a group to expose the market to significant systemic risk and be outside the scope of systemic risk review. In addition, because of the competitive nature of various markets and the various sophistication levels of consumers of these products, what gets regulated needs to be examined. Further, how state solvency funds interact with an OFC warrants more thought. Finally, in a point that is often overlooked, the authors stress that a national and international industry needs the regulation that will allow it to thrive in its chosen markets.

In chapter 4 Robert Detlefsen takes a critical look at an optional federal charter style of regulation. He summarizes several criticisms of an OFC, including the likelihood that a dual system would create inequities among firms competing within the same markets; the potential that an OFC would confuse consumers as to who is responsible for regulating their insurer; and the possibility that an OFC would require the establishment of a new federal bureaucracy on top of the bureaucracies that exist in each state. Detlefsen also takes on the question of whether federal regulators would be more competent than their state counterparts, given the recent performance of federal regulators responsible for overseeing financial institutions and markets.

Detlefsen also points out that the demand for an OFC style of regulation is different for each sector of the industry. While both are concerned about uniformity of licensing and the speed to market for new products, property-casualty companies are interested in reducing distortions caused by rate regulation and underwriting restrictions. In contrast, life companies are more interested in avoiding the costs of duplicative and inconsistent regulations, which hamper their ability to get new and innovative products introduced in the market.

Detlefsen examines the dual-charter option in the banking industry in a practical light. He asserts that an OFC is not really optional, as competition between state and federal regulators is illusory. First, companies may choose a federal regulator, but the costs of reversing such a decision would likely be high. Second, there will not really be regulatory competition between the states and the federal government due in part to the high costs of switching as well as the possibility of significant federal preemption of state regulatory authority. Restricting state authority to what the federal government decides is proper takes away the states' ability to compete. This is important in Detlefsen's view because Congress could take an interventionist approach to insurance with the goal of fairness in mind. However, fairness is likely to socialize private risk sharing by prohibiting the use of risk-related underwriting criteria. While this could happen in the states, the comparison between markets can provide evidence to other states regarding the desirability of such policies.

Regulatory Policy Reform

In chapter 5 Martin Grace and Robert Klein tackle the issue of policy reform. They believe that proponents of a federal charter approach envision that federal regulators will diverge significantly from the restrictive policies enforced in a number of areas by the states. Thus even if an OFC could achieve significant structural efficiencies, its ultimate effect on insurers and insurance markets will greatly depend on the policies adopted by federal regulators. Also, to the extent that the states continue to be the predominant regulators, their policies will have significant implications for how insurance markets function. Hence Grace and Klein outline a set of principles and discuss needed reforms in key areas of insurance regulation that are relevant in either a state or a federal framework.

Grace and Klein argue that insurer solvency regulation is mired in an antiquated paradigm that relies too heavily on accounting valuations of insurers' financial condition and their compliance with extensive prescriptive rules and too little on insurers' management of their financial risk. The U.S. approach is being

eclipsed by the development of principles-based regulation of insurance companies in other large markets throughout the world. Principles-based regulation is
also being implemented for other financial institutions in the United States and
internationally. The current system also performs poorly in terms of prompt intervention when insurers encounter financial distress and managing the receiverships
of failed companies. The costs of managing the receiverships of insolvent insurers
are high relative to other financial institutions, in part due to the current structure
of state insolvency management. Grace and Klein contend that there is a strong
need for U.S. regulators to move to a principles-based approach to solvency regulation that employs the best methods to assess an insurer's financial risk and the
management of that risk.

Grace and Klein also call for substantial reforms with respect to the regulation
of insurers' prices, products, and market practices. They recommend that prices
be fully deregulated, given the competitive structure of insurance markets and the
problems created in states and in lines of business in which prices are still subject
to significant constraints. They also argue that the regulation of insurers' products
should be rationalized and streamlined to foster innovation and to speed the introduction of new products to meet consumer needs. Other areas marked for reform
include excessive constraints and mandates in the underwriting of insurance policies, the mismanagement of residual market mechanisms, and the inefficient
methods used to police insurers' market conduct.

Focusing on one of the proposed benefits of an OFC, Robert Litan and Phil
O'Connor look at state insurance price regulation and deregulation in chapter 6.
This is an important issue to the property-casualty insurance industry. Price regulation is specifically precluded in current OFC proposals, which would allow federally regulated insurers to charge rates based on the cost of risk as well as other
competitive considerations. The competitive market would discipline insurers
and, as in other sectors, would keep premiums in line with claims, other expenses,
and a reasonable profit, given the risk of the line of business.

Historically, automobile, homeowners, and workers' compensation insurance
have been subject to considerable price regulation by the states. Presumably this
has been motivated, in part, by concerns that insurers charge excessive prices, but
other factors also may play a role, such as keeping insurance "affordable" and limiting the premiums paid by high-risk insureds. Litan and O'Connor assess the
empirical evidence on automobile insurance specifically to determine how consumers have fared under different regulatory policies. This question is particularly relevant to the proposed OFC legislation, which explicitly eliminates price
regulation.

Litan and O'Connor examine prior research on rate regulation in auto insurance as well as conduct their own tests of the effects of changes in states' regulatory polices. A large body of evidence suggests that rate regulation has been ineffective in what it set out to do. The regulated lines are generally quite competitive, which raises questions as to the need for or the benefits of price regulation. Overall, the effect of regulation on average premiums appears to be negligible. However, the prior research also suggests that price regulation distorts the market, subsidizing high-risk drivers at the expense of low-risk drivers.

Litan and O'Connor further assess the effects of deregulation in two states (New Jersey and South Carolina) and the impact of increased regulation in a third (California). They look at prices before deregulation and after deregulation to assess the effect of an OFC prohibition on price regulation on auto insurance markets. They find that average auto insurance consumers paid no more after deregulation than before deregulation. Indeed, they suggest that regulation may cause consumers to pay higher prices than necessary in the long term, as insurers may be more reluctant to lower rates in a highly regulated environment. In addition, they find that residual markets (populated by the highest-risk drivers) shrink after deregulation, thus providing additional evidence that deregulation reduces subsidies to high-risk drivers. They conclude that current OFC proposals that would deregulate insurance pricing would offer significant benefits to consumers.

Financial Convergence and Global Insurance Markets

In chapter 7 Peter Wallison examines the effect of convergence (cross-industry competition) on the insurance industry. Convergence comes in two forms, each of which affects the structure of regulation. One convergence is the agglomeration of banks, insurers, and other intermediaries within a holding company structure. Another convergence is the group of individual financial intermediaries that provide financial products that overlap with financial products provided by other sectors of the financial services industry. Both types of convergence are, potentially and unnecessarily, constrained by an antiquated regulatory system. The Treasury's blueprint for reform also noted that outside forces put pressure on the U.S. regulatory structure. Convergence has occurred in other parts of the U.S. financial system to some extent as part of the GLBA, but it is more common in other markets internationally. The GLBA is just a partial response to the market pressure for increasing convergence. In fact, Wallison observes there are more than a hundred state and federal regulators for banks, insurers, and securities firms. So while there is some convergence in the financial services industry, there is little interest in changing the overall regulatory approach despite the long-term market trends.

The important long-term trends are the growing productivity benefits from information technology and the growth of interindustry competition. Banks and securities firms are competing, as are banks and insurance companies. The latter competition is especially important given the recent financial crisis. This is, in part, due to the varied types of industry competition. Banks and insurers are developing products that compete as substitutes for capital market contracts. Banks and capital markets are able to produce substitutes for traditional insurance products. Corporate consumers are also looking to many types of providers for their risk management products, and sophisticated savers are looking to both banks and insurers for annuity-like products. Finally, securities firms are competing with insurance producers in markets for mutual funds and other products with similar characteristics.

One of the reactions to the convergence phenomena is regulatory resistance; the turf battle between the Securities and Exchange Commission (SEC) and the Commodity Futures Trading Commission (CFTC) over derivatives markets is a classic example of how things might evolve in other markets if a given agency attempts to provide benefits to firms within its jurisdiction at the expense of others. Wallison argues that an optimal regulatory structure should provide a level playing field in terms of how different financial institutions and their activities are regulated. Firms would not receive arbitrary benefits from chartering with a given agency, so which regulator oversees a firm would become immaterial in terms of its ability to compete in various markets. Wallison concludes that a reasonable way to accomplish this objective is to treat banks, securities firms, and insurance companies as a single industry and regulate them according to the objectives of regulation rather than the particular way that their products and services were structured or delivered in the past.

In the final chapter, John Cooke and Harold Skipper examine the international dimension of the structure of regulation in the United States. On the surface, to enter the U.S. market in its entirety, a firm would need fifty-six licensees from fifty-six regulatory bodies. Cooke and Skipper argue that the costs of entering the U.S. market as a result of its state-based structure constitute a significant entry barrier. Further, other countries may use this structural barrier as a means of justifying barriers for U.S. insurers. International banks can obtain a national charter, which raises questions as to why insurance companies are treated differently.

Like Peter Wallison, Cooke and Skipper point to the forces of convergence and the fact that other countries have responded to this convergence differently. Some countries have adopted a single-regulator system for all financial services, while others use functional regulatory schemes with mechanisms to promote coherence among the various regulators. For example, Australia uses two regulators, one for consumer protection and one for market conduct.

Cooke and Skipper also point to the EU's approach to federalism as a possible example for the United States. Each EU country has, by treaty, agreed to harmonize regulations and use similar standards in regulation. In addition, a company licensed in any country is allowed to sell in any other member country. The EU approach theoretically promotes a high degree of coherence for solvency regulation and at the same time leaves market conduct to the member states. This approach has a close U.S. analog in the Interstate Insurance Product Regulation Commission (IIPRC), which was set up to provide a centralized clearinghouse for product approvals. However, while important to the life industry, the IIPRC covers only a narrow aspect of insurance regulation, and only thirty-three states have become members to date.

Insurance is becoming more important internationally: insurers sell their products through cross-border sales, through the establishment of country-specific subsidiaries or branches, and through the reinsurance market. A well-functioning competitive insurance market needs international insurers. To the extent that regulatory structure limits competition, social welfare is reduced. Cooke and Skipper point to a number of aspects of U.S. insurance regulation that have been identified as trade barriers for both interstate and foreign entry. Important barriers include multiple state licensing requirements, government entities that are either monopolists or direct competitors in the market, compulsory reinsurance requirements, extraterritorial application of state laws, and significant state-imposed exit costs. Government-owned foreign insurance companies seeking to enter the U.S. market also face problems if the states have certain restrictions, requirements, and trade laws (such as restrictions on a foreign-owned firm obtaining a license, citizenship requirements, seasoning requirements, trade laws that allow states to retaliate against insurers for their home country's laws or regulators, and requirements that foreign insurers maintain surplus funds with a state trustee).

Cooke and Skipper believe that an OFC would be similar to the regulation of other large markets by not only providing the benefits of additional competition in the United States but also allowing U.S. companies to enter international markets at lower costs. In addition, it is presumed that a national regulator would be able to remove the barriers to entry that hinder legitimate insurance competition. The states and the NAIC have been aware of these international trade issues for many years, but little has been accomplished: the federal government cannot speak on behalf of the states for insurance regulation, and the states have no incentive to agree on international trade provisions. However, an OFC approach would offer competitive advantages to U.S. insurers, provide a single regulatory voice for international trade issues, and promote competition.

Conclusion

Insurance regulation has historically been focused on state markets. However, state markets are no longer dominated by local firms. This has been true for some time; the industry is becoming more of an interstate and international business with each passing year. In addition, insurance companies are competing with other types of financial services firms, such as consumer and corporate product firms. The U.S. regulatory system for insurance was designed for a world that no longer exists, and the United States is at a crossroad in terms of resolving this dilemma. The following chapters provide valuable insights on various questions associated with the future of insurance regulation in the United States and how it might evolve.

References

Cummins, J. David, ed. 2002. *Deregulating Property-Liability Insurance: Restoring Competition and Increasing Market Efficiency.* Washington: AEI-Brookings Joint Center for Regulatory Studies.

Grace, Martin F., and Robert W. Klein. 2000. "Efficiency Implications of Alternative Regulatory Insurance Structures." In *Optional Federal Chartering and Regulation of Insurance Companies,* edited by Peter J. Wallison, pp. 89–131. Washington: American Enterprise Institute.

U.S. Department of the Treasury. 2008. *Blueprint for a Modernized Financial Regulatory Structure.*

2

The Insurance Industry and Its Regulation: An Overview

Robert W. Klein

Insurance regulation in the United States has been steeped in controversy over its 200-year history. In its early years, industry and regulatory failures prompted reforms and the coalescence of insurance oversight into a state regulatory framework. Beginning in the mid-1800s both the industry and its state regulators have been subject to a series of federal challenges. The states' regulatory authority was reaffirmed in these challenges, most recently with the passage of the McCarran-Ferguson Act (MFA) in 1945.

However, as the insurance industry has evolved, its support for state regulation has eroded, and large segments of the industry now support the creation of an optional federal charter (OFC) for insurance companies and agents that would preempt state regulation for federally chartered firms. An OFC is strongly opposed by the states as well as certain industry groups, and a fierce debate continues over establishing a federal regulatory system for insurance. This debate has taken on added importance in light of the current financial crisis and calls for reforms in the regulatory framework for all financial institutions.

In considering the merits of an OFC, it is important to understand how the insurance industry and its regulation have evolved, the structure of the current system of state regulation, and how it has been affected by the interplay of economic and political forces. Both the structure of the industry and the current system of regulation have significant implications for reform proposals and the arguments of their proponents and opponents. Other frameworks for insurance regulation also have been proposed and warrant some brief discussion. Further, it is helpful to articulate some basic economic principles for efficient insurance regulation and review the rationale for various areas of regulation and associated policies in evaluating proposed reforms.

The Structure of the U.S. Insurance Industry

The U.S. insurance industry has changed dramatically since its inception in the late 1600s.[1] In its early years, small local and regional insurance companies writing fire and life insurance dominated the industry. The relatively narrow geographic scope of these companies led to a state-based regulatory framework. Since then, the industry has grown substantially in terms of the amount and variety of insurance products. Insurers of various sizes selling a vast array of products across state and national boundaries now populate the industry. Economic opportunities and competitive pressures have caused insurers to widen their geographic scope and assume increased risk. Over time, a broad range of insurance services have become available to buyers in response to the growth of the national economy and the diversity of buyers' needs and tastes for insurance coverage. The evolution of the industry has compelled changes in its regulation; regulation, in turn, has facilitated the industry's development.

The significant growth of the private insurance industry in the United States is reflected in figure 2-1, which plots the insurance industry's contribution to the nation's GDP in current dollars and as a percentage of total GDP for the period 1980–2006. The industry's GDP increased from $53 billion in 1980 to $281 billion in 2006. Its portion of the nation's total GDP also increased, suggesting that the industry grew somewhat faster than the overall U.S. economy. The financial assets of property-casualty and life-health insurers grew from $149.7 billion in 1960 to $6.3 trillion in 2007.[2] The industry's development also is reflected in the rise in industry employment, from 1.5 million in 1970 to more than 2.3 million in 2007.[3] However, the number of property-casualty and life-health insurance companies decreased from 4,580 in 1970 to 3,913 in 2007 as a consequence of industry consolidation. This figure does not include 3,860 other firms in the

1. See Hanson, Dineen, and Johnson (1974).
2. Figures on the insurance industry's assets, employment, and number of companies were obtained from the Insurance Information Institute (2008).
3. Insurance Information Institute (2008).

Figure 2-1. *Gross Domestic Product in Insurance, by Decade, 1980–2006*

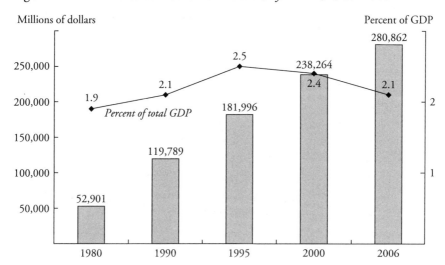

industry, including health maintenance organizations, fraternal insurance companies, title companies, and risk retention groups.

The industry also has become globalized, with growing international trade in insurance and related services. Foreign companies are making increasing inroads into the U.S. domestic market, while some U.S. insurers are establishing a significant presence overseas.[4] In 2004 affiliates of U.S. insurers posted $100.4 billion in sales in foreign countries, and foreign-owned insurers recorded sales of $109 billion in the United States.[5] International trade in insurance services has significant implications for U.S. regulatory institutions and policies (see chapter 8, this volume).

Property-Casualty Insurance Markets

The nature of the property-casualty insurance business is very different today than it was sixty years ago. In the industry's infancy, local stock companies and mutual protection associations formed to provide fire insurance to a particular community.[6] Over time, property-casualty insurers expanded the types of insurance they

---

4. U.S. insurers contend that their regulation places them at a competitive disadvantage relative to foreign insurers. International trade in insurance is discussed in greater detail in chapter 8.

5. Insurance Information Institute (2008).

6. Hanson, Dineen, and Johnson (1974).

offer and the geographic area of their operations. These firms now cover numerous kinds of exposures, ranging from residential property to product liability. This has increased the complexity of the business and its risk.

One of the significant factors causing increased risk in property-casualty insurance is the long payout pattern for commercial liability lines, which makes proper pricing and reserving difficult and subject to error.[7] Shifting legal doctrines also increase the margin for error and insolvency risk. Cyclical pricing and periodic crises, prompted by severe loss shocks, have plagued the industry.[8] Significant cost inflation in certain commercial lines has induced some buyers to purchase coverage from alternative sources, such as surplus-lines insurers and risk retention groups, or to become self-insured, which increases competitive pressure on traditional insurers. Adverse weather patterns, earthquakes, and extensive building in high-exposure areas also have increased catastrophe risk in property lines. Indeed, climate change poses a new set of threats to property-casualty insurers. Additionally, the industry must cope with man-made perils, such as terrorism and crises in financial markets. Greater risk and its impact on earnings will continue to challenge property-casualty insurers.

Table 2-1 presents historical data on the portion of the property-casualty insurance sector represented by traditional or standard insurers. There are still a significant number of small, independent companies selling property-casualty insurance in a limited geographic area. However, large national carriers now account for a bigger share of many markets, relegating other insurers to niches they are better positioned to serve. The top ten property-casualty insurers accounted for close to 50 percent of direct premiums written in 2006, compared with about 35 percent in 1960. Fierce competition has forced insurers in all sectors to streamline their operations and abandon unprofitable lines. A number of insurers appear to be selling off marginal segments of their business and concentrating on areas where they believe their core competencies and best opportunities lie. This is contributing to industry consolidation and increased market concentration in certain lines of business.

The growth and increasing financial strength of the property-casualty insurance sector also are reflected in table 2-1. The assets of property liability insurers

---

7. Insurers are required to set reserves (liabilities) for unpaid losses (claims).

8. See Cummins, Harrington, and Klein (1991). The alternating pattern of soft and hard markets in certain property-casualty insurance markets has been labeled the *underwriting cycle* and is a subject of continued academic inquiry. Arguably, it is not a cycle in the conventional understanding of this term but rather a pattern of falling and rising prices that reflects insurers' responses to various developments, such as changes in interest rates, loss shocks, and shifts in profits.

Table 2-1. *Property-Casualty Insurance Trends, 1960–2006*
Percent unless otherwise noted

Item	1960	1970	1980	1990	2000	2006
Companies (number)	n.a.	2,800	2,953	3,899	3,215	2,648
Assets ($M)	30,132	55,315	197,678	556,314	1,034,090	1,483,013
Revenues ($M)	15,741	36,524	108,745	252,991	341,590	501,106
Net premiums written	95.1	94.3	89.6	86.9	87.7	89.3
Investment income	4.9	5.7	10.4	13.1	12.3	10.7
Ten-firm ratio (largest insurer groups)	34.4	36.8	38.2	40.3	43.7	48.5
Premiums, surplus	125.5	210.2	183.4	157.6	75.6	89.7
Return on net worth	n.a.	11.6	13.1	8.5	6.5	13.4

Source: Insurance Information Institute (2008).

increased from $30.1 billion in 1960 to $1.5 trillion in 2006. Commensurately, total premium and investment income increased from nearly $16 billion to $501 billion over this same period. Concurrently, the industry's leverage reflected by the ratio of net premiums to surplus declined from 210 percent in 1970 to 89 percent in 2006.[9]

One can see the conditions that are contributing to the restructuring and consolidation of the industry. The increasing capitalization of the industry, coupled with soft pricing, is prompting insurers to reassess their capital allocation. The number of insurance companies began to decline in the mid-1990s, and mergers and acquisitions have increased dramatically. Some insurers and financial holding companies are bulking up to compete with other financial giants on a global basis. Other insurers are shedding marginal business segments and concentrating on areas where they believe they have a comparative advantage. Although the industry is consolidating on the whole, this has not prevented the emergence of some new players targeting niche opportunities, such as property insurance in coastal states.

Figures reflecting the structure of property-casualty insurance lines on a countrywide basis are provided in table 2-2. Personal auto and homeowners insurance represent approximately 45 percent of total property-casualty premiums. In excess of 1,270 insurer groups (including stand-alone companies) sold property-casualty insurance in 2006, with several hundred insurers competing

9. In insurance accounting terminology, *surplus* refers to an insurer's capital or equity.

Table 2-2. *Property-Casualty Insurance, Market Structure, 2006*
Units as indicated

Line	Number of insurers	DPW (% of sector)[a]	CR10 (%)[b]	HHI[c]	Since 1997 (%) Entries	Exits
Personal auto	389	33.2	64.1	651	29.4	48.9
Commercial auto	389	6.2	44.4	272	33.4	46.2
Homeowners	438	12.3	64.2	784	27.9	41.2
Fire and allied	544	4.2	53.7	502	24.8	41.6
Commercial MP	365	7.4	49.0	318	24.1	45.6
General liability	697	12.2	57.7	595	36.8	42.8
Medical malpractice	225	2.5	45.8	295	112.4	57.2
Workers' compensation	312	9.5	54.2	487	32.1	48.0
Other	715	20.0	43.1	255	26.2	45.8
All lines	1,270	100.0	48.6	318	43.5	43.4

Source: Data from National Association of Insurance Commissioners and author's calculations.
a. DPW is direct premiums written.
b. CR10 is the ten-firm ratio.
c. HHI is the Herfindahl-Hirschman index.

in each major line.[10] The principal measures of market concentration, the ten-firm concentration ratio (CR10, or the market share of the top ten insurers), and the Herfindahl-Hirschman index (HHI, or the sum of the squared market shares of all insurers) also indicate competitive market structures in these lines. The top ten insurers accounted for less than 65 percent of the premiums in any given line and 40–50 percent in many lines. Similarly, HHI values ranged from 255 to 651, with most lines falling between 300 and 500. These levels of concentration are considerably below levels that most economists consider necessary for firms to begin acquiring market power.[11]

Entry and exit barriers also appear to be low. Regulatory capital requirements are relatively modest compared to the standards set by rating agencies and the

10. Many insurance companies are affiliated in groups and holding companies. Within a group, companies tend to specialize in particular lines of insurance and geographic areas. Also, it is common for insurance groups' companies to vary in terms of the stringency of their underwriting standards. "Preferred" companies insure exposures that meet the most stringent underwriting standards; "standard" and "nonstandard" companies insure exposures that meet less stringent underwriting rules.
11. The Department of Justice's merger guidelines consider markets with HHIs in excess of 2,000 to be highly concentrated. Mergers in such markets are subject to closer scrutiny by the DOJ.

levels of capital that insurers actually hold.[12] Information and the cost of establishing distribution systems likely have a greater impact on entry and exit, but these factors do not appear to impose significant barriers to many insurers.[13] The ease of entry and exit is revealed by the high percentage of entries and exits in and out of these lines since 1997. These figures do reflect some industry and market restructuring, as exits have exceeded entries in all lines shown except medical malpractice. This is consistent with the general consolidation of the industry and with insurers' increased focus on markets in which they believe they can be most successful. It should be noted that entry and exit barriers can be somewhat higher at the state level than the national level, as insurers must apply for a license to write insurance in a particular state and incur additional costs to enter a state market.

Table 2-3 provides some interesting information on the relative shares of premiums written by domiciliary and nondomiciliary insurers in each state in 2006. In most states, nondomestic companies (that is, insurers domiciled in other states) write 60–90 percent of total property-casualty premiums. This figure is 75 percent for all states combined, which indicates that most property-casualty insurance transactions cross state boundaries. The interstate nature of the insurance business is a major driver of the interest in federal regulation and plays a prominent role in the arguments for offering insurers a federal alternative to the current state regulatory system.

Figure 2-2 compares profitability (as measured by the rate of return on net worth) in the property-casualty insurance industry with diversified financial services and commercial banks for the period 1985–2007. Over the entire 1985–2007 period, property-casualty insurers' average rate of return on net worth was 8.8 percent, which is below the rate of return earned in other industries. This reflects the highly competitive nature of the industry and suggests that insurers generally have not been earning excessive profits. While the industry's subpar performance stems primarily from its competitiveness and other economic factors, many insurers would argue that the current regulatory system also undermines their efficiency.

Accident and Health Insurance Markets

Dramatic changes also have occurred in the health insurance industry. Severe medical cost inflation and competition have led buyers to search for savings in

12. Klein and Wang (2007).

13. Information and expertise are arguably the most important resources to insurance companies. To be successful in penetrating any market, insurers must have a good understanding of risks and costs.

Table 2-3. *Nondomestic Property-Casualty Insurers, Market Share, by State, 2006*[a]
Percent

State	Share	State	Share
Alabama	85.4	Nebraska	87.9
Alaska	86.9	Nevada	94.7
Arizona	90.7	New Hampshire	87.1
Arkansas	94.2	New Jersey	71.1
California	69.1	New Mexico	94.0
Colorado	95.9	New York	75.2
Connecticut	83.6	North Carolina	84.5
Delaware	87.6	North Dakota	87.5
Dist. Columbia	97.7	Ohio	62.1
Florida	72.6	Oklahoma	85.7
Georgia	89.0	Oregon	74.6
Hawaii	68.7	Pennsylvania	75.2
Idaho	84.6	Rhode Island	81.4
Illinois	56.1	South Carolina	94.4
Indiana	84.0	South Dakota	94.8
Iowa	74.9	Tennessee	86.0
Kansas	89.3	Texas	57.5
Kentucky	83.0	Utah	86.9
Louisiana	81.0	Vermont	89.0
Maine	76.8	Virginia	96.9
Maryland	86.2	Washington	81.5
Massachusetts	55.9	West Virginia	71.1
Michigan	53.0	Wisconsin	54.2
Minnesota	89.3	Wyoming	92.7
Mississippi	88.0	Guam	14.8
Missouri	87.9	Puerto Rico	12.1
Montana	98.2	U.S. Virgin Islands	58.3

Source: Data from National Association of Insurance Commissioners and author's calculations.

a. *Nondomestic* means that the premiums were written by insurers domiciled in other states.

their health insurance bills. The standard indemnity policy has declined as insurers have been compelled to redesign their products and services to allow buyers more cost-containment options. Many carriers now offer managed care programs and integrated service networks that involve alliances with doctors and hospitals. Insurers also have tightened their underwriting standards in order to reduce prices for low-risk groups, which has decreased availability and raised premiums for high-risk groups. This transition of health insurance markets has been bumpy, as some insurers have suffered from both significant cost inflation and strong competitive pressures. Further, the quality, price, and availability of health insurance

Figure 2-2. *Net Income after Taxes, Three Industries, 1985–2007*

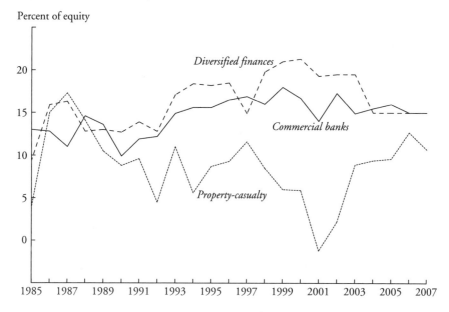

Percent of equity

have become significant political issues and have sometimes led to additional regulatory constraints and mandates.

The sharp escalation of medical costs over the last two decades has prompted a number of alternatives to traditional health insurers as sources of medical coverage. These options include health maintenance organizations (HMOs) and preferred provider organizations (PPOs), among others. A number of employers have taken advantage of federal Employee Retirement Income Security Act (ERISA) preemptions of state regulation to set up their own group health plans and contract with various providers and vendors for certain services to help them administer their plans.

A number of HMOs have been consolidated in the face of fierce competition and large losses.[14] Some multiline insurers also have sold their health care operations because of poor performance. State governments have tightened enforcement of standards for quality of care. Hence a shakeout is occurring, which will result in a more concentrated and a more efficient group of health care financing entities. As pressures increase to provide health coverage for uninsured Americans,

14. Economies of scale are particularly important for HMOs that must provide health services for their enrollees within a given community.

the plans and programs that are eventually established could have significant implications for health insurers.

The markets for disability income and long-term care (LTC) insurance have grown, but their development has been hampered by certain challenges. With the aging of the population and increasing longevity, the need for custodial care is rising rapidly. However, insurers have encountered difficulty in developing, pricing, and selling attractive long-term care products. Many older Americans are reluctant to pay for LTC insurance. Still financing custodial care will become an increasingly important issue over time, and its resolution will be of great interest to LTC insurers. In addition, the fact that states guarantee LTC contracts against insolvency will put pressure on the regulation and pricing of these contracts.

Life Insurance and Annuities Markets

For many years, life insurers' products were confined primarily to standard term and whole life policies, which emphasized death benefits and offered a modest savings component (for whole life policies). That environment has dramatically changed, as life insurers now offer an expansive menu of life insurance policies, annuities, and other interest-sensitive contracts with various risk-return characteristics, many of which may compete with other noninsurance financial products. This shift is reflected in the fact that life insurers' reserves for retirement-related products (individual and group annuities and supplemental contracts with life contingencies) grew from 27.2 percent of life-health insurance reserves in 1960 to 65 percent in 2006.[15]

The increased significance of interest-sensitive products and insurers' greater exposure to disintermediation (that is, policy loans, surrenders, and lapses) have increased the importance of appropriate asset-liability management strategies. At the same time, competitive pressures have induced insurers to maintain high crediting interest rates on their policies. A number of life insurers have been stressed by their holdings of mortgage-backed securities, mortgages, contract loans, and other assets (stocks and bonds) that have suffered losses due to the current financial crisis and its rippling effects on the economy. Still most life insurers hold portfolios of relatively conservative assets and are unlikely to suffer the severe financial distress that has struck other financial institutions.[16]

Financial convergence is another significant development affecting life insurers, as various types of financial institutions offer both insurance and noninsurance

15. American Council of Life Insurers (2008).
16. Willis Ltd. (2008).

Table 2-4. *Life-Health Insurance, Market Trends, 1950–2006*
Percent unless otherwise noted

Item	1950	1960	1970	1980	1990	2000	2006
Companies (number)	649	1,441	1,780	1,958	2,195	1,268	1,072
Assets ($M)	64,020	119,576	207,254	479,210	1,408,208	3,185,945	4,882,884
Ten largest insurer groups	n.a.	62.4	57.7	52.5	36.7	41.7	n.a.
Income ($M)	11,337	23,007	49,054	130,888	402,200	826,660	883,597
Life insurance premiums	55.1	52.1	44.2	31.2	19.1	15.8	16.9
Annuity considerations	8.3	5.8	7.6	17.1	32.1	36.7	34.3
Health insurance premiums	8.8	17.5	23.2	22.4	14.5	12.8	16.0
Investment income	18.3	18.7	20.7	25.9	27.8	25.2	27.1
Other	9.5	5.8	4.4	3.3	6.5	9.5	5.9
Policy reserves ($M)	54,946	98,473	167,779	390,339	1,196,967	2,711,420	3,607,743
Life	n.a.	71.9	68.8	50.7	29.1	27.4	30.8
Annuities	n.a.	27.2	29.1	46.5	68.1	69.1	65.0
Health	n.a.	0.9	2.1	2.8	2.8	3.5	4.2
Investment income, net rate[a]	3.1	4.1	5.3	8.1	9.3	7.1	5.4
Capital ratio[b]	n.a.	n.a.	9.7	9.2	8.5	11.1	10.0
Return on equity	n.a.	n.a.	n.a.	13.9	10.7	10.0	12.0

Source: American Council of Life Insurers (2008); Insurance Information Institute (2008).

a. Net investment income divided by mean invested assets (including cash) less half of net investment income.

b. Capital plus surplus plus asset valuation reserve divided by general account assets.

products in competing for households' savings and investments. The implications of financial convergence (see chapter 7, this volume) for the life insurance industry are likely to be more significant over the long term than fluctuations in asset values. Indeed, competition with other federally regulated financial institutions further motivates life insurers' support for an OFC.

Some general information on the development of the life-health insurance sector is provided in table 2-4. Since 1950 the number of life-health insurance companies increased from 649 to 2,195 in 1990 and then fell to 1,072 by 2006. Sector assets increased from $64 billion in 1950 to $4.9 trillion in 2006. Total annual income increased from $11.3 billion to $883.6 billion over this same period. The dramatic shift from traditional life insurance to annuities is evident in the relative shares of income and reserves for these two segments. Due to the aging of the U.S.

Table 2-5. *Life-Health Insurance, Market Structure, 2006*
Units as indicated

Line	Sector reserves (%)	Insurers (number)	CR10[a]	HHI[b]	Since 1997 (%) Entries	Since 1997 (%) Exits[c]
Life						
Industrial	...	67	93.0	2,970	25.3	51.6
Ordinary	27.4	389	57.1	498	18.1	49.8
Credit	3.3	103	72.8	779	19.5	56.7
Group	0.0	245	72.3	1,160	19.2	55.6
Annuities						
Individual	42.2	258	58.0	425	21.0	53.3
Group	22.4	108	76.5	732	24.8	50.3
Supplemental contracts	0.5	...	...	...	...	...
Accident and health						
Group	2.9	237	65.5	863	20.5	59.1
Credit	1.3	76	78.4	1,099	13.6	56.1
Individual	0.1	262	68.3	791	19.5	53.9
Other	...	2	100.0	8,409	66.7	100.0
All lines	100.0	460	46.6	308	17.8	54.0

Source: Data from National Association of Insurance Commissioners and author's calculations.
a. CR10 is the ten-firm ratio.
b. HHI is the Herfindahl-Hirschman index.
c. Many of the exits may represent mergers and acquisitions of life insurers into large holding companies.

population, it is expected that life insurers will continue to see dramatic growth in retirement-related products.

Table 2-5 presents 2006 data on the structure of various segments of the life and annuity sectors. As in the property-casualty sector, there are numerous insurers selling various life and annuity products. A total of 460 life insurer groups (including stand-alone companies) reported financial data to regulators in 2006; 100–300 insurers offer products in each of the major lines.[17] In general, market concentration is relatively low in these broad lines, and entry and exit activity is relatively high. Exits have exceeded entries, consistent with industry consolidation and the decline in the number of life insurance companies and groups. The data on the relative market penetration by domiciliary and non-domiciliary life-health insurers (table 2-6) also reflects a pattern similar to that for

17. The number of insurer groups selling industrial life and health credit insurance is smaller, but these are small and declining markets.

Table 2-6. *Nondomestic Life-Health Insurers, Market Share, by State, 2006*[a]
Percent

State	Share	State	Share
Alabama	94.6	Nebraska	86.7
Alaska	100.0	Nevada	100.0
Arizona	98.5	New Hampshire	99.8
Arkansas	96.9	New Jersey	85.6
California	99.9	New Mexico	100.0
Colorado	96.2	New York	40.0
Connecticut	43.4	North Carolina	98.3
Delaware	90.4	North Dakota	98.8
Dist. Columbia	99.8	Ohio	88.6
Florida	99.6	Oklahoma	98.2
Georgia	99.1	Oregon	92.9
Hawaii	98.6	Pennsylvania	98.0
Idaho	99.4	Rhode Island	98.3
Illinois	92.7	South Carolina	97.8
Indiana	85.0	South Dakota	99.9
Iowa	50.8	Tennessee	96.3
Kansas	96.1	Texas	87.4
Kentucky	99.0	Utah	93.0
Louisiana	97.1	Vermont	98.0
Maine	98.9	Virginia	81.4
Maryland	99.4	Washington	97.6
Massachusetts	90.5	West Virginia	100.0
Michigan	86.1	Wisconsin	91.5
Minnesota	82.7	Wyoming	100.0
Mississippi	97.0	Guam	98.7
Missouri	96.7	Puerto Rico	70.4
Montana	100.0	U.S. Virgin Islands	100.0

Source: Data from National Association of Insurance Commissioners and author's calculations.
a. *Nondomestic* means that the premiums were written by insurers domiciled in other states.

property-casualty insurers, with an even greater predominance of nondomestic insurers in each state.

The Economic Principles for Insurance Regulation

The economic foundation for industry regulation is based on the possibility (or realization) of market failures.[18] These market failures are judged against the social welfare–maximizing conditions for perfect competition. Perfect competition

18. See for example Spulber (1989); Viscusi, Harrington, and Vernon (2000).

requires many buyers and sellers in a market, free entry and exit, perfect information, and a homogeneous product. Under these conditions, the joint surplus or gains from trade of producers and consumers is maximized. In assessing the need for and benefits of regulation in an imperfect world, markets are often judged against a standard of "workable competition," which reasonably approximates the conditions for perfect competition to the degree that government intervention cannot improve social welfare.[19]

Potential market failures in insurance include severe asymmetric information problems and principal-agent conflicts, which could lead some insurance companies to incur excessive financial risk or engage in abusive market practices that harm consumers.[20] Insurance consumers, particularly individuals and households, face significant challenges in judging the financial risk of insurers and properly understanding the terms of insurance contracts. Consumers also could find it difficult to compel insurers to fulfill their obligations under their contracts. Commercial insurance buyers vary greatly in size and sophistication: smaller buyers may benefit from some regulatory protection, while larger buyers may be better positioned to protect their own interests in insurance transactions.

Beyond market failures, there is a set of circumstances that constitutes market problems. These problems are not failures in the economic sense but are undesirable market outcomes (high prices, unavailable insurance coverage) that result from conditions affecting the insurability and cost of certain risks rather than violations of the conditions for perfect or workable competition. For example, in some markets insurance may be expensive because claim costs are high. While this may cause hardships for consumers, it is a natural result of properly functioning market forces and not a condition that can be remedied by regulation per se. Many existing regulatory polices are motivated by a desire to alleviate market problems rather than to remedy true market failures.

The rationale for government intervention when a market failure occurs is that regulators can remedy the failure and restore economic efficiency. In the case of solvency or financial regulation of insurance companies, it could be argued that the costs of monitoring are so high for consumers that it is more efficient to have the government undertake this task and take action against insurers that incur excessive financial risk. It can also be argued that the scope and stringency of financial regulation can be tempered by reliance on market discipline in sectors in

---

19. Scherer and Ross (1990).

20. Skipper and Klein (2000) articulate principles for insurance regulation in an international context.

which buyers have the incentives and ability to identify financially sound insurers.[21] Regulators can facilitate market discipline by compelling the transparency of insurers' financial condition and risk.

Optimal regulation is based upon an ideal set of policies that attempt to replicate the conditions of a competitive market and maximize social welfare. This theoretical model of regulation is intended to remedy market failures and not market problems caused by other external forces. This may include failures that would otherwise cause insurers to incur an excessive insolvency risk or engage in abusive trade practices (misrepresenting insurance products, refusing to pay legitimate claims, and so on). This assumes that regulators have perfect information and can determine and implement the correct market solutions. However, not all market failures can be remedied by regulation.

Solvency Regulation

The social welfare argument for the regulation of insurer solvency derives from inefficiencies created by costly information and principal-agent problems.[22] Owners of insurance companies have diminished incentives to maintain a high level of safety to the extent that their personal assets are not at risk for unfunded obligations to policyholders that would arise from insolvency. The argument is that it is costly for consumers to properly assess an insurer's financial strength in relation to its prices and quality of service. Insurers also can increase their risk after policyholders have purchased a policy and paid premiums, a principal-agent problem that may be very costly and difficult for policyholders to control.

While this kind of problem may exist in many industries, certain financial institutions with significant fiduciary responsibilities—specifically banks and insurance companies—are viewed in a special light.[23] The fact that they receive and hold funds to fund future obligations to their customers increases the costs of asymmetric information problems and principal-agent conflicts. The long-term nature of many of these obligations and the large amounts of funds involved contribute to solvency concerns. Historically, the adverse consequences of bank and insurer bankruptcies in the absence of government oversight and protections have prompted regulatory responses. Today, the regulation of financial

21. Harrington (2004).
22. Munch and Smallwood (1981).
23. Saunders and Cornett (2003) discuss the rationale for the regulation of financial institutions. While their principal argument is based on externalities (discussed below), other arguments also contribute to the case for government oversight.

institutions is well established in most if not all developed economies with
mature financial markets.

There are other aspects of excessive insolvency risk that may motivate regulatory intervention. Financial regulators are also concerned about "contagion" and
the possibility that a spike in insurer insolvencies could induce a crisis of confidence that may have negative effects on the industry.[24] Further, there may be negative externalities associated with excessive insurer insolvency risk. The costs of
unpaid claims may be shifted beyond policyholders to their creditors. Hence it is
common for the regulation of financial institutions to be coupled with some form
of insolvency guarantees (deposit insurance, insurance guaranty associations, and
so on) that cover at least a portion of the obligations of bankrupt institutions.

The current financial crisis highlights the interdependencies of various types of
financial firms and markets and how their problems can affect national and global
economies. Some of the problems that have occurred might be characterized as
contagion; that is, concerns about the financial condition of one insurance company can lead to concerns about others. Other problems might be placed into the
category of systemic risk, in which problems suffered by one set of financial institutions or a market undermine the proper functioning of other markets and the
economy. With the exception of the problems suffered by the American International Group (specifically its ability to post collateral to cover credit default
swaps) and financial guaranty insurers, it is not clear that the insurance industry
poses the kind of systemic risk to other markets as that posed by banks or other
financial institutions. Still, the issue of systemic risk is likely to be raised in discussions of the need for federal regulation of insurance.

The goal of optimal insurance solvency regulation is not to eliminate insolvencies but rather to minimize the social cost of insurer defaults.[25] This social
cost exceeds the lost equity of the insurer, as it includes losses incurred by policyholders, claimants, and other creditors of insurers. Regulators limit insolvency risk
by requiring insurers to meet financial standards and taking appropriate actions if
an insurer assumes excessive default risk or experiences financial distress.[26]

Price Regulation

There are two potential rationales for regulation of insurance prices. The traditional
explanation for regulation of insurance prices involves costly information and

24. Some might argue that the life insurance industry was on the brink of such a crisis in the late
1980s, when there was a spike in insolvencies due to life insurers' asset problems.
25. Grace, Klein, and Phillips (2002).
26. Cummins, Harrington, and Klein (1995).

solvency concerns.[27] According to this explanation, insurers' incentive to incur excessive financial risk and even engage in "go for broke" strategies may result in inadequate prices. Some consumers may buy insurance from carriers charging inadequate prices without properly considering the greater financial risk involved. In this scenario, poor incentives for safety could induce a wave of destructive competition, in which all insurers are forced to cut their prices below costs to retain their market positions.[28] Historically, the solution offered for this problem was uniform prices developed by industry rating organizations subject to regulatory oversight.

This view essentially governed insurance rate regulation until the 1960s, when states began to disapprove or reduce price increases in lines such as personal auto and workers' compensation insurance. The rationale that some might offer for government restrictions on insurance price increases is that consumer search costs impede competition and lead to excessive prices and profits.[29] It also might be argued that it is costly for insurers to ascertain consumers' risk characteristics accurately, giving an informational advantage to insurers already entrenched in a market and creating barriers to entry that diminish competition. According to this view, the objective of regulation is to enforce a ceiling that will prevent prices from rising above a competitive level. In addition, the public may express a preference for regulatory policies to lower or cap insurance prices consistent with social norms or objectives.[30]

However, the empirical evidence does not support a case for the regulation of insurance prices in the current environment. Studies of insurance markets indicate that they are highly competitive in terms of their structure and performance.[31] As discussed above, entry barriers are generally low, and concentration levels rarely approach a point that would raise concerns about insurers' market power. Further, long-term profits in insurance markets tend to be in line with or below the rates of return earned in other industries, as discussed earlier. We should also note that, over the last fifty years, enforcement of uniform rates has

27. Joskow (1973); Hanson, Dineen, and Johnson (1974).

28. This view likely stems from the periodic price wars (and subsequent insurer failures) that afflicted property-casualty insurance markets during the 1800s and early 1900s.

29. Harrington (1992) explains but does not advocate this view.

30. For example, most states have determined that drivers should carry some form of liability or no-fault auto insurance. Because of this requirement, some policymakers believe that the government should ensure that insurance coverage is reasonably available and affordable for those who are required to purchase it. This argument has been used to justify strict controls on auto insurance rates in some jurisdictions.

31. See Cummins and Weiss (1991); Klein (1995, 2005); and Grace and Klein (2007).

eroded and industry organizations have moved to the promulgation of "advisory" rates or loss costs. Consequently, insurer pricing has become much more independent and differentiated. Hence it is not surprising that studies of the effects of the regulation of insurance rates have not found that it has provided significant benefits to consumers.[32]

Market Conduct Regulation

A stronger case can be made for regulating certain insurer market practices, such as policy forms (contracts), marketing, and claims adjustment. Information problems, constraints on consumer choice, and unequal bargaining power between insurers and consumers can make some consumers vulnerable to abusive marketing and claims practices of insurers and their agents.[33] For example, a number of life insurers were sued and sanctioned in the late 1980s and early 1990s for agent practices that took customers out of safe policies and put them in inappropriate (high-risk) policies. Although prominent insurers were involved in some of these cases, the greater threat probably lies with firms or agents that are not highly motivated to establish and maintain a reputation for fair dealings with consumers. Hence regulators need to be especially vigilant for "bad actors," who seek gains from abusive or fraudulent transactions. Government regulation may be complemented by industry self-regulatory organizations, such as the Insurance Marketplace Standards Association (IMSA), which has been established by life insurers.[34]

Social Preferences and Politics

One can articulate a set of principles that should guide regulation, but it is important to recognize that other factors influence the policies that are established and enforced. These factors include social preferences for market outcomes that diverge from those that would result from a competitive market. Other aspects of the politics surrounding certain areas of insurance and their regulation can result in suboptimal policies. The political economy of regulation is characterized by

32. See for example Harrington (2002).
33. It is true that consumers subject to unfair treatment might seek remedies through the courts and sometimes do so. However, legal remedies may not be feasible for consumers with limited resources and bills to pay. Also, it may be difficult to secure financial damages from some fraudulent insurers.
34. Evidence suggests that IMSA has reduced the costs of market conduct problems while at the same time increasing firm value. See Grace and Klein (2006).

groups vying for policies that favor their economic interests.[35] Some groups may be relatively small but have relatively substantial and concentrated economic interests. They are more likely to prevail on issues that are opaque and not salient to the majority of consumers.[36] Other issues, such as the price of auto and home insurance, may be highly salient to many consumers, and this could lead to political pressure on regulators to force insurers to offer more favorable terms. Thus a number of factors could affect regulatory policies in a given area and the beneficiaries of such policies.[37]

Hence social preferences and interest group lobbying manifested through political choices can influence regulatory and government policies. One example is the attempt to constrain insurance price levels or price differences among different groups of insureds. Such a policy can appeal to consumers if they believe that insurers will otherwise charge excessive prices or if they do not understand the basis of risk-based pricing structures. However, price constraints in insurance markets can lead to problems of adverse selection as well as moral hazard. Other examples include mandated coverages and laws that require insurers to sell coverage to all applicants, which can also have harmful effects. Unfortunately, the negative side of such regulatory policies can be hidden from those who suffer from their consequences. Indeed, there are many circumstances where imperfect public choice mechanisms result in economic outcomes that diminish social welfare and are at odds with voters' long-run economic interests. The tension between economic principles and political realities is relevant to many of the reforms proposed for insurance regulation.

The Current Framework for Insurance Regulation

The current framework for insurance regulation has important implications for proposals that would modify that framework as well the nature of the regulatory policies that would be enforced. The costs and constraints (as well as the benefits)

---

35. Insights from Becker (1983) and related literature are helpful in understanding how interest group politics may play out in government policies regarding insurance. Stigler (1971) and Peltzman (1976) also laid the foundation for an economic theory of regulatory behavior that considers the potential influence of the concentrated economic interests of regulated firms and other groups. Political scientists such as Meier (1988) have broadened this framework to include other factors that might influence regulatory behavior, such as ideology, bureaucracy, the role of political elites, and the complexity and saliency of regulatory issues.

36. Meier (1988).

37. See Meier (1988) and Klein (1995) for discussions of theories of regulatory behavior and how they apply to insurance.

associated with state regulation figure heavily in the debate over establishing an OFC or other regulatory structure. Further, in establishing a new system for insurance regulation, some elements of the current system might be retained while others would be discarded or substantially altered.

A Brief History of Insurance Regulation

The current state regulatory framework for insurance has its roots in the early 1800s, when insurance markets were generally confined to a particular community.[38] The high concentration of risk and the occurrence of large conflagrations led to highly cyclical pricing and periodic shakeouts, when a number of property insurance companies would fail after a major fire.[39] Life insurers became notorious for high expenses, shaky finances, and abusive sales practices.[40] The local orientation of insurance markets at the time led municipal and state governments to establish the first regulatory mechanisms for insurance companies and agents. However, these mechanisms proved to be inadequate, which led to the formation of state insurance commissions in the mid-1800s. These commissions' activities focused on the licensing of companies and agents, approving policy forms, setting reserve requirements, regulating insurers' investments, and administering financial reporting requirements. Price regulation was essentially confined to limited oversight of property-casualty industry rate cartels.

Early on, the states recognized the need to coordinate their insurance regulatory activities. This led to the formation of the National Association of Insurance Commissioners (NAIC) in 1871. Its early efforts focused on the development of common financial reporting requirements for insurers. State regulators also used the NAIC as a vehicle for discussing common problems and developing model laws and regulations, which each state could modify and adopt according to its preferences.

Through the years, insurance department responsibilities grew in scope and complexity as the industry grew and evolved. Arguably, the state regulatory framework has been greatly challenged by the industry's transformation. Every state has had to increase its resources and expertise to oversee a more complex and geographically extended industry. The states' reliance on the NAIC also has necessarily increased its use as a vehicle to pool resources and augment their regulatory

38. See Hanson, Dineen, and Johnson (1974) and Meier (1988) for more detailed reviews of the history of state insurance regulation.

39. Hanson, Dineen, and Johnson (1974).

40. Meier (1988).

activities. Consequently, the NAIC has been transformed into a major service provider as well as a mechanism for coordinating state actions and for centralizing certain regulatory processes. Although the states have substantially increased their resources and the sophistication of their regulatory mechanisms, their critics raise concerns about the inherent inefficiency of a state-based framework and its ability to keep pace with the industry.

State versus Federal Regulation Debate

Tension between the federal government and the states over the regulation of insurance dates back to the mid-1800s. This tension is created by the interstate operation of many insurers and their significant presence in the economy. On several occasions the federal government has sought to exert greater control over the industry, and the states, backed by the insurance industry, have fought back aggressively to hold on to their authority. The economic and political stakes are high for both sides.

The primacy of the states' authority over insurance was essentially affirmed in various court decisions until the *Southeastern Underwriters* case in 1944.[41] In that case, the U.S. Supreme Court ruled that the commerce clause of the Constitution did apply to insurance and that the industry was subject to federal antitrust law. This decision prompted the states and the industry to join forces behind the passage of the McCarran-Ferguson Act in 1945, which delegated regulation of insurance to the states except in instances in which federal law specifically supersedes state law.[42] The MFA also granted a limited antitrust exemption to insurers tied to compensating regulatory oversight by the states.

Despite the passage of the MFA, federal interest in insurance regulation has continued to grow over time, for several reasons. First, the insurance industry continues to play an important financial role in the nation's economy, as financial markets have converged. Second, the performance of insurance markets affects interstate commerce and a number of areas of public policy staked out by the federal government, such as environmental pollution and health care. Third, periodic crises, such as the spike in insurer insolvencies in the 1980s, have fueled concerns about the adequacy of state insurance regulation and have prompted debate about whether federal intervention would be a more efficient mechanism to remedy industry failures. Fourth, considering the vast resources commanded by the industry, it is only natural that some members of Congress

41. 322 U.S. 533 (1944).
42. 15 U.S.C. secs. 1011–15.

might favor a stronger federal role in insurance in order to increase their authority and influence.

Historically, the industry has strongly supported state over federal regulation. However, this has changed as the industry has continued to evolve. Increasingly, many insurers—especially those that operate on a national basis—have come to favor some form of federal regulation, such as an OFC. These insurers have become increasingly frustrated with the additional costs and burdens that they associate with the state system. They perceive that it would be less costly and more efficient for them to deal with one central regulator than fifty-six jurisdictions.[43] Insurers advocating federal regulation have not been satisfied with the states' efforts to harmonize and streamline their regulation. It should be noted, however, that the industry is not unanimous in its support of federal regulation. Many state and regional insurers, along with local agents, continue to support the state framework.

Although the primary regulatory authority for insurance still resides with the states, the federal government has intervened, affecting state insurance regulatory policy and institutions in several ways. In a number of instances, Congress has instituted federal control over certain insurance markets or aspects of insurers' operations that were previously delegated to the states (health insurance, Medicare supplemental insurance, and so on). In other cases the federal government has established insurance programs (crop and flood insurance) that are essentially exempt from state regulatory oversight. Even the threat of such interventions has spurred the states to take actions to forestall an erosion of their regulatory authority.

The federal government also has set regulatory standards that the states are expected to enforce. In the case of Medicare supplemental insurance, for instance, Congress enacted loss ratio standards, which the states were required to adopt to avoid relinquishing their oversight authority to the federal government. Additionally, Congress also has significantly constrained state regulatory control over certain types of insurance entities, such as risk retention groups and employer-funded health plans, in order to increase coverage options in markets where the cost of traditional insurance is high. Finally, federal policies in a number of other areas—antitrust, international trade, law enforcement, taxation, and the regulation of banks and securities—have significant implications for the insurance industry and state regulation.

43. See Pottier (2007); Grace and Klein (2007).

The most recent manifestations of the push for federal regulation are proposals for federal regulatory standards and an OFC for insurers that choose to be federally regulated. The states oppose both proposals, with their strongest opposition aimed at an OFC. They perceive that many insurers would choose an OFC, which would effectively remove a large part of the industry from state oversight. State-oriented insurers and agent groups also strongly oppose an OFC, recognizing that it would reduce state entry barriers and enhance the competitive position of national insurers and producers. The OFC proposal is now the central focus of the state versus federal regulation debate.

Evolution of State Insurance Regulation

Insurance regulation has been greatly affected by—and compelled to evolve in response to—changes in the industry and its economic and financial environment. The reforms begun in the late 1980s were aimed at strengthening solvency regulation. A large increase in the number and cost of insurer insolvencies in the mid-1980s led to an intensive congressional investigation and a number of state regulatory initiatives. These initiatives included the strengthening of insurer financial standards, risk-based capital requirements, improved financial monitoring systems, and a program for certifying the adequacy of each state's solvency regulation.[44] As insurer insolvencies fell, congressional scrutiny diminished, and the immediate threat to the state system seemed to subside.

However, growing industry complaints about the inefficiency and high cost of outmoded state regulatory policies warranted attention. This led to a second wave of state and NAIC initiatives, which continue through the present. The objective of these initiatives has been to streamline and harmonize state regulatory policies and practices to lessen regulatory cost burdens on insurers and coincidentally ease the pressure for federal regulation.

Beginning in the early 1990s and continuing into the present, a number of initiatives have been coordinated by the NAIC and implemented by the states.[45] These include

—Enhanced consumer protection, including the Consumer Information Source (CIS) website.

—More efficient market regulation reflected in guidelines and tools for market conduct oversight.

44. Klein (1995).
45. Klein (2005).

—The Speed to Market Task Force, encompassing the Interstate Insurance Product Regulation Commission (IIPRC) and the System for Electronic Rate and Form Filing (SERFF).

—Uniform forms and processes for producer licensing, including the National Insurance Producer Registry (NIPR).

—Standardized insurance company licensing, reflected in the Uniform Certificate of Authority Application (UCAA).

—Improved solvency regulation, which includes enhanced financial databases, solvency analysis tools, and coordinated oversight.

Other areas have been targeted for reform, including surplus lines, reinsurance, health insurance products, and the system for managing the receivership of insolvent insurers.

While these initiatives are impressive, they have failed to satisfy many insurers' demand for a true national regulatory system. For almost all of the initiatives listed above, each state still retains the authority over licensing applications, rate and product filings, and so on, according to its specific regulations and judgments.[46] While the NAIC has advocated easing regulatory constraints in some areas, in others it has sought—against industry opposition—to strengthen regulatory standards and enforcement. It is difficult to see how insurers' desire for a common regulatory system can be reconciled with the states' desire to retain their individual authorities to regulate insurers and insurance markets as they see fit.

Current Structure of Insurance Regulation

Each state has an official and an agency responsible for regulating insurers and agents (producers) operating within the state. The regulatory framework is not confined to insurance departments but extends to all levels and branches of government. The major authorities in the current regulatory system are state insurance departments, the courts, state legislatures and Congress, and the executive branch at the state and federal levels. Insurance has the additional complexity of having both federal and state government authorities involved in the regulation of the industry.[47]

The state legislature establishes the insurance department, enacts insurance laws, and approves the regulatory budget. An insurance department is part of the

46. The Interstate Insurance Product Regulation Commission differs from these other initiatives in that its state members agree to adhere to a common set of standards for life insurance products.
47. See Klein (1995, 2005) for more detailed reviews of state insurance regulation.

Figure 2-3. *Insurance Regulatory Functions*

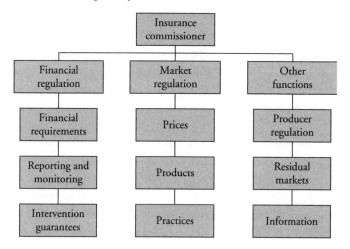

state executive branch, either as a stand-alone agency or as a division within a larger department. Insurance commissioners must often utilize the courts to help enforce regulatory actions, and the courts in turn may restrict regulatory action. Each state's insurance department must coordinate with insurance departments in other states in regulating multistate insurers; these departments rely on the NAIC for advice as well as some support services. The federal government overlays this entire structure, currently delegating most regulatory responsibilities to the states while retaining an oversight role and intervening in specific areas. Regulatory policy is formulated collectively by the insurance commissioner and the administrative branch, the legislature, and the courts.

Regulatory Functions

Insurance regulatory functions can be divided into two fundamental areas: financial or solvency regulation and market regulation. Beyond these two fundamental areas, state insurance departments engage in certain other activities to facilitate competition and to improve market outcomes. Such activities can be important in promoting regulatory objectives and in potentially lessening the need for more intrusive regulatory constraints and mandates. However, the states do not view these activities as substitutes for active regulatory oversight and enforcement. The most important aspects of financial and market regulation are summarized below and are diagrammed in figure 2-3.

Financial Regulation

Protecting policyholders and society in general against excessive insurer insolvency risk is the goal of state-based insurance regulation. Regulators protect policyholders' interests by requiring insurers to meet certain financial standards and to limit their financial risk. To accomplish this task, insurance regulators are given authority over insurers' ability to incorporate or to conduct business in the various states. State statutes set forth the requirements for incorporation and licensure to sell insurance. These statutes require insurers to meet certain minimum capital and other standards and to submit financial reports; they also authorize regulators to examine insurers and take other actions to protect policyholders' interests. Insurance commissioners also promulgate regulations to implement their statutory authority, regulations that are sometimes subject to legislative approval. Solvency regulation encompasses a number of aspects of insurers' operations, including capitalization, pricing and products, investments, reinsurance, reserves, asset-liability matching, transactions with affiliates, and management. It also encompasses intervention with regard to insurers in financial distress, the administration of insurer receiverships (bankruptcies), and insolvency guaranty mechanisms that cover a portion of the claims of insolvent insurers.

The states employ an essentially prescriptive or rules-based approach to the financial regulation of insurance companies. This can be contrasted with the principles-based approach contemplated in the European Union's Solvency II Initiative and currently followed by certain countries such as the United Kingdom. Under a rules-based approach, insurance companies must comply with extensive and specific regulations; compliance with these regulations determines regulatory assessments of their financial soundness. Under a principles-based approach, insurance companies are given broader discretion in meeting regulatory standards if they manage their financial risk according to the standards established by regulators. The NAIC is reconsidering the states' approach to insurer solvency regulation and has established the Principles-Based Reserving Working Group to assess changes in policies and practices. The group is focusing on principles-based reserve requirements for life insurance companies, but the mandate of the group is to expand its study to other aspects of the regulation of life-health and property-casualty insurance companies.[48] Still, it is unclear how far and how quickly U.S. regulators might embrace a principles-based approach to insurer financial regulation.

---

48. See National Association of Insurance Commissioners (2008).

The primary responsibility for the financial regulation of an insurance company is delegated to the state in which it is domiciled. Other states in which an insurer is licensed provide a second level of oversight, but nondomiciliary states typically do not take action against an insurer unless they perceive the domiciliary state is failing to fulfill its responsibility. States use the NAIC to support and coordinate their solvency oversight and compel domiciliary regulators to move more quickly in dealing with distressed insurers, if this proves necessary. This helps to remedy (but may not fully correct) the negative externalities associated with solvency regulation. An insurer's domiciliary state tends to reap the lion's share of the direct economic benefits of its operations (such as employment and payrolls), but the costs of its insolvency are distributed among all the states in which it operates. Such economic and political considerations could cause a domiciliary regulator to be excessively forbearing in dealing with a distressed insurer.

The states rely heavily on a number of reports that insurers are required to file, including annual and quarterly financial statements. Insurer financial reports are subject to statutory accounting principles (SAP), which differ somewhat from generally accepted accounting principles (GAAP). These reports are reviewed in in-house bench audits by regulators; insurers' financial data are analyzed using various automated tools and monitoring systems. Financial monitoring occurs at the state level for all insurers and is also performed by the NAIC for larger companies that write business in a significant number of states. This analysis can trigger further investigation of an insurer if there are concerns about its financial condition. Insurers are subject to both periodic on-site exams (conducted every three to five years) and targeted exams to address particular questions or issues.

Insurers must meet requirements for both fixed minimum capital and risk-based capital (RBC). Fixed minimum standards are set by each state and average about $2 million. Each company's RBC requirement is determined through NAIC formulas, which apply various factors to accounting values. It is essentially a static system; U.S. regulators do not require insurers to perform dynamic risk modeling.[49] An insurer's total adjusted capital (TAC)—its actual capital, with minor adjustments—is compared to its RBC to determine whether any company or regulatory actions are required. The RBC model law adopted by the states specifies authorized or mandatory regulatory actions that are tied to specified TAC-RBC ratio levels. These levels start at 200 percent and become progressively more severe as lower ratio triggers are reached.

---

49. Life insurers are required to perform stress testing of their policy reserves.

Insurers that fail to comply with regulatory financial standards or that are deemed to be in hazardous financial condition are subject to regulatory intervention. Formal interventions typically involve regulators seizing control of a company and can constitute conservation, rehabilitation, and liquidation, depending on the condition of the insurer and its prospects. It is not uncommon for an insurer's financial statement to be39d when regulators step in; hence regulatory measures can progress rapidly from simply controlling an insurer's transactions to an insurer's liquidation if restructuring or rehabilitation is infeasible.

The domiciliary regulator is responsible for administering remedial actions or sanctions against an insurer, including the administration of its receivership; in this the regulator has a fair degree of discretion, with court approval. However, other states in which the insurer is licensed can bring pressure to bear on the domiciliary regulator to act more quickly and decisively. While this dual layer of financial monitoring has likely improved the states' regulation of insurer solvency, there is evidence that domiciliary regulators have been allowed to exercise too much forbearance in some instances.[50]

Each state has separate guaranty associations for property-casualty insurers and life-health insurers. These associations cover a portion of the unpaid claims obligations of insolvent insurers in their respective states. Only certain lines of insurance are covered by these associations, and—with the exception of workers' compensation insurance—there are dollar limits on the amount of coverage for each claim. Generally, insurance products purchased by individuals and small businesses receive greater coverage than those purchased by larger commercial insurance buyers. Guaranty association costs are assessed back against licensed insurers. The ultimate burden of these assessments falls on insurance buyers, taxpayers, and the owners of insurance companies.[51]

Market Regulation

The regulation of an insurer's market practices is principally delegated to each state in which it operates. Hence each state effectively regulates its insurance markets. The scope of market regulation is broad (potentially encompassing all aspects of an insurer's interactions with consumers), and states' policies can vary significantly. State regulation of insurers' prices or rates is a particularly visible and controversial topic. The rates for personal auto insurance, homeowners insurance, and workers' compensation insurance are subject to some level of regulation in all

50. See Grace, Klein, and Phillips (2002).
51. Baresse and Nelson (1994).

the states. The extent of price regulation for other property-casualty lines tends to vary inversely with the size of the buyer. The rates for certain types of health insurance may be regulated, but the prices of life insurance, annuities, and related products are only indirectly regulated through the product approval process.

Insurers' policy forms and products, with the exception of products purchased by large firms, also tend to be closely regulated. Other aspects of insurers' market activities, such as marketing, underwriting, and claims adjustment, generally fall within the area of market conduct regulation. A state may impose some specific rules regarding certain practices, such as constraining an insurer's use of certain factors in underwriting or mandating that they offer coverage to all applicants. Beyond this, regulation tends to be aimed at enforcing fair practices, based on regulators' interpretation of what this means. Monitoring and enforcement typically arise through consumer complaint investigations and market conduct examinations.

Insurance producers or intermediaries (that is, agents and brokers) are also regulated by the states. Producers must be licensed in each state in which they sell insurance and are required to pass tests to demonstrate their competence. They must also comply with continuing education requirements and are subject to regulatory sanctions if they violate regulations governing their conduct. Many insurance producers dislike the necessity of single-state licenses and strongly advocate a multistate or national license. As noted above, the NAIC has sought to make it easier for producers to get licenses in multiple states, but this is not satisfactory to agent groups.

Not surprisingly, market regulatory policies and practices are complex and are also subject to the greatest criticism by insurers and economists. Further, this is an area in which the states most strongly defend their individual authorities and prerogatives. A number of factors influence a given state's policies, including among many others the cost of risk and its political climate. Economists tend to have greater confidence than regulators and legislators in the ability of competitive insurance markets to produce efficient outcomes. Perhaps more important, political interests and social preferences are often at odds with the outcomes that a competitive insurance market would produce, such as risk-based prices. This difference in perspectives is fundamental to understanding the reasons for the fierce debate about insurance regulatory policies and the prospects for their reform.

It should be noted that while financial regulation and market regulation are often discussed separately, they are necessarily intertwined. The regulation of an insurer's financial condition and risk has implications for its market practices, and vice versa. This is an important consideration in discussing alternative regulatory frameworks and policy reforms. Proposed frameworks and other structural options vary in terms of the extent to which financial and market regulatory authority is vested in one entity or divided between federal and state governments. The potential for contradictory financial and market regulatory policies must be evaluated for different regulatory systems.

Alternative Frameworks for Insurance Regulation

Debate continues over whether full oversight of the industry should be transferred to the federal government. Various proposals for some form of federal regulation (or greater federal involvement in state regulation) have been vetted over the years. The concept that is currently receiving the greatest attention and industry support is the establishment of an optional federal charter that would allow an insurer or an agent to choose to be federally regulated and exempt from state regulation. Another concept that has been proposed but that has received less attention is the enactment of federal standards for state regulation that would impose greater uniformity on the current system. These and other possible frameworks are briefly described below.

The Current System

A good place to start in discussing alternative frameworks is the current system of state regulation. To many observers, some form of federal insurance regulation may be inevitable, but the states and some interest groups would strongly disagree. Regardless of what observers think, opponents of federal regulation wield considerable political power, and the prospects for any radical changes in the near future are slim. What might we expect to happen if the states continue to retain their regulatory authority, at least over the near term? We can label this scenario the *current system* of state regulation, with the understanding that it is evolving and will likely continue to evolve.

As discussed earlier, both industry pressures and the threat of federal intervention have compelled the states to embark on ambitious policy and institutional reforms. The stated intent of these reforms is to streamline, harmonize, and rationalize the current system of state regulation while preserving certain state prerogatives. In essence, the states are seeking to reduce as much of the inefficiency associated with the state-based framework as is politically and logistically possible.

This is an important qualification. Fundamentally, if the states wish to retain most of their discretion in how they regulate insurers' market practices, then there is a limit to how far harmonization can go. For example, if a state insists on retaining rate regulation, mandated coverages, or prohibitions on certain underwriting factors, there is no force other than the federal government or market pressures to compel it to do otherwise. Further, the NAIC's centralized systems for filing rates and policy forms, agent licensing, and other processes must accommodate differing state requirements; regulatory approvals and compliance are determined by each state, not by the NAIC. Finally, the policy reforms supported by the majority of states fall short of what the industry and many experts advocate.

There are some positive aspects of this picture. One is that the states have made substantial strides, even if they fall short of what could be achieved under an alternative framework. A second observation is that the threat of federal intervention has tended to push the states in the right direction. Third, while state inertia may thwart or delay beneficial policy reforms, it also can discourage nationwide shifts in the opposite direction. In other words, some would argue that it is better to fight excessive price regulation in a few states than to have a federal regulator establish such a policy in all states. Fourth, state regulators are close to the consumers they are sworn to protect, and this may offer some benefits to the industry as well as consumers.

Looking forward, if the states continue on their present track, it is likely that they will further implement and develop the initiatives aimed at improving the efficiency of state regulation, which would reduce insurers' and agents' compliance costs. It is conceivable that additional initiatives might be launched. Further policy reforms are also likely to occur, although this area is subject to more debate—and states differ on what is appropriate. For example, even though the number of states that have deregulated property-casualty insurance rates continues to rise, others have given no indication that they are willing to take that step. Hence state regulation will continue to progress and will become more efficient, but what is uncertain are the pace and scope of this progression.

It is important to note that the predominance of a state regulatory system has not precluded federal interventions on a smaller scale. Several of these are mentioned earlier. More recently, Congress has considered the establishment of an Office of Insurance Information (OII) within the Treasury. Other federal legislative proposals have been vetted to both ease the regulation of reinsurance and surplus lines insurers and expand the scope of risk retention groups. More of these types of interventions will appear if the states continue to be the principal regulatory authority over insurance.

Hence in the absence of a significant restructuring of the system for insurance regulation, it is reasonable to expect continued incremental changes at the state and federal levels. On the whole, these changes are likely to improve the efficiency of insurance regulation, although not all changes may do so. Pressure from the federal government could expand the scope and accelerate the pace of state initiatives. The states are also subject to pressure from the insurance industry and are conscious of other factors, such as the internationalization of insurance markets and the need to support the competitiveness of U.S. insurers. Still, a state-based system is subject to certain inherent constraints and is fundamentally different from other proposed frameworks.

Federal Standards

One approach to increasing the federal role in insurance involves creating federal standards for state regulation. This concept was embodied in a draft legislative proposal released in 2004—the State Modernization and Regulatory Transparency (SMART) Act—by Representatives Michael Oxley (R-Ohio) and Richard Baker (R-La.).[52] The proposed legislation would establish minimum standards that would govern various aspects of state insurance regulation. Federal rules would preempt state regulations that fail to comply with the minimum standards after specified time periods.

The areas of insurance regulation encompassed by the SMART Act include, but are not limited to,

—Market conduct
—Rates and policy forms
—Insurer and produce licensing
—Surplus lines
—Reinsurance
—Financial surveillance
—Receiverships.

Essentially, all lines of insurance and industry sectors would be covered by the act. A state-national insurance coordination partnership would be charged with determining state compliance with the federal standards and resolving disputes among government agencies.

This proposal has two principal objectives. One, it would compel the states to establish a level of regulatory uniformity that they might not otherwise achieve. Two, it would dictate insurance regulatory policies in a number of areas. The dual nature of the proposal—framework reform and policy reform—is also characteristic of other proposals for federalizing insurance regulation.

52. In June 2006 Ginny Brown-Waite (R-Fla.) introduced part of the SMART Act as H.R. 5637, 109th Cong. 2d sess., June 19, 2006 (NIA sec. 2).

Some might view the SMART concept as less intrusive and ambitious than proposals that would establish a federal regulator, although it is still opposed by the states and consumer groups.[53] Under SMART, the states would still have the responsibility for insurance regulatory oversight and enforcement and would retain some discretion in regulatory policy within the limits of the federal standards. As Scott Harrington observes, SMART would avoid the establishment of a federal regulator and its associated bureaucracy.[54] Further, it could avoid significant policy swings that would undermine market efficiency and harm consumers. The term *could* is an important qualifier, as the enactment of the SMART Act would not preclude subsequent congressional changes to its minimum standards.

At the same time, Harrington identifies a number of potential disadvantages to SMART. From a framework perspective, one of the principal concerns is that SMART could prove to be an administrative, monitoring, and enforcement nightmare. Some states might seek to circumvent the standards, and there would be the prospect of protracted and costly disputes regarding states' compliance with the standards. SMART could be simplified and its scope narrowed, but this would also undermine its objectives of greater uniformity and policy reform. This reflects the fundamental tension between uniformity and the states' prerogative to regulate insurance as they see fit.

The policy changes contemplated under SMART are broad in scope and, arguably, are its principal objective. The thrust of these reforms is to substantially deregulate many areas of insurance and lessen regulatory constraints in others. The states and consumer groups oppose a number of these changes, arguing that they gut essential consumer protections. The proposed reforms are outlined at a relatively high level in the draft document. A comprehensive legislative version of SMART would likely be much more detailed and specific and subject to intensive discussion and modification. At this time it appears unlikely that anything resembling the SMART Act as envisioned by its creators will gain legislative traction, as the industry is placing its bets on OFC legislation. Still, some of the concepts and policies embodied in SMART could emerge in an OFC bill as it proceeds through its legislative gauntlet.

Optional Federal Charter

The current vehicle for the OFC approach is the National Insurance Act (NIA)— S. 40—introduced in 2007 by Senators John Sununu (R-N.H.) and Tim Johnson

53. See Harrington (2006) for a comparative review of options and proposals for federalizing insurance regulation.
54. See Harrington (2006).

(D-S.Dak.).[55] While there are many details that may or may not be in a final bill enacted by Congress, a number of important provisions are likely to be present in any legislation that is enacted. (The OFC is discussed only briefly here, as it is the principal focus of chapters 3 and 4.)

The NIA would set up the Office of National Insurance (ONI) within the Department of the Treasury; it would be akin to the Office of the Comptroller of the Currency. The NIA would permit both life and nonlife insurance companies and agents to apply to the ONI for a charter and license to sell products in all states. It would also permit the ONI to regulate the solvency and market conduct of insurers within its jurisdiction. Additionally, it would authorize the commissioner of national insurance to establish a comprehensive insolvency resolution scheme, to include the state guaranty associations (funds) that meet minimum qualifications.

Thus the ONI would oversee solvency, policy forms, other aspects of market conduct, and insurer insolvencies. It would not regulate prices (except that prices and reserves have to be based upon sound actuarial principles) or underwriting standards. Further, assuming that the states' solvency guarantee systems are adequate, a national insurer would participate in those systems. If a state system did not qualify, there would be a federal plan that would cover insolvent OFC insurers' obligations in the state.

States would not be able to discriminate against federally chartered insurers or agents, but they would still be permitted to tax insurers under current tax law with the qualification that national insurers and national agencies would be taxed the same as insurers and agencies domiciled in the state. This would preserve both states' premium taxes and the special aspects of their retaliatory taxes. Presumably, this provision is intended to mitigate states' concerns about the budgetary implication of an OFC. However, the removal of a significant portion of the industry from state oversight could substantially reduce other state-imposed regulatory fees, which have served as a major source of funding for state insurance departments.[56]

National insurers or agencies would also be allowed, under the NIA, to choose their state of domicile, which could be different from the state in which the company has its headquarters. In addition, the NIA would permit insurers to choose the law under which their insurance contracts are interpreted. Further, the NIA would subject the industry to the antitrust provisions specifically exempted under the MFA, with the exception that insurers would still be able to share information about losses or claim payments.

55. SB 2106, 109th Congress.
56. See Grace and Klein (2008).

It should be noted that there is a distinct possibility that legislation will be introduced for an OFC that would apply only to life insurers. There appear to be fewer legislative concerns about (and perhaps less political opposition to) a life-only OFC. Life insurance products tend to be more standardized across states, and life insurance is subject to fewer state-specific preferences (such as price regulation) than property-casualty insurance. Of course, property-casualty insurers who support an OFC would be greatly disappointed if a life insurance OFC took precedence over an OFC for all insurers. However, this could become a reality.

Proponents of an OFC argue that it would significantly decrease the cost and inefficiency caused by state regulation. OFC advocates also are hoping that it would result in significant policy reforms. Most important, rate regulation would be eliminated for OFC-regulated insurers, a major concern of property-casualty insurers. OFC policies in other areas are more difficult to predict, but additional reforms are possible. These reforms could encompass more efficient and effective solvency oversight and market conduct regulation.

However, there is no assurance that the federal government would establish and sustain the policies that OFC proponents envision. In a number of instances Congress has intervened and required the states to impose additional regulatory constraints on insurers in certain areas (such as health insurance), and other such measures have been discussed. Consumer advocates and economists can debate whether such policies are welfare enhancing, but the federal government is not immune to interest group pressures and excessive and unsound regulatory actions.

Two issues associated with an OFC warrant at least a brief mention here. One issue is the continuing reliance, under an OFC, on the states' insolvency guaranty system. This provision is not surprising, since the removal of OFC-regulated insurers from the system would significantly reduce its financial capacity. On the other hand, to provide a state-regulated guaranty system along with a federally regulated OFC would eliminate the link between financial oversight and insolvency guarantees. There is no easy resolution of this dilemma, but it is an issue that may generate considerable discussion. One potential solution is the creation of something equivalent to the Federal Deposit Insurance Corporation that would cover the claims of both federal and state insurers. The catch in this solution is that a federal insolvency guarantor would need to impose financial standards for both federally regulated and state-regulated insurers.

A second issue associated with an OFC is the ability of a federal regulator to adequately regulate the market conduct of federally regulated insurers and agents. Some might see merit in state regulators' arguments that their geographic proximity to consumers and familiarity with state-specific conditions and issues gives them an advantage in market conduct oversight. Also, it could be argued that the wide variety of insurance products and the complexity of many contracts and transactions make market conduct regulation of insurance more challenging than that of banking, in which federal agencies perform this function for federally regulated institutions. However, nothing would preclude a federal insurance regulator from establishing the necessary infrastructure and employing sufficient resources to adequately police the market conduct of federally regulated insurers and agents. Further, it could be argued that a federal regulator might benefit from certain efficiencies and could deal more effectively with unfair trade practices that extend across a number of states. Hence, although this issue will need to be addressed by federal legislators and officials, it need not torpedo the effort to establish an OFC.

These and other issues have surfaced or will surface in the OFC debate, but they are not necessarily fatal flaws. That said, an OFC faces formidable political opposition from the states and certain industry groups, like independent insurance agents and state and regional insurance companies. The overall framework for the regulation of financial institutions will receive significant attention as the new administration and Congress move forward. It is reasonable to expect that insurance will be an important component of this architecture. What is less certain is where insurance will stand in the queue as legislation is enacted and the regulatory structure for various financial institutions and markets is revamped.

A Single-State Regulator

Another system that has been proposed would allow an insurer to choose one state as its regulator.[57] The insurer would be allowed to operate in any state but would be subject only to the regulation of its domiciliary jurisdiction. That regulator would be responsible for overseeing all aspects of the insurer's financial condition and market practices wherever else it did business. This system has some precedent in the way that risk retention groups are regulated.

This approach has several potential advantages. One is that it an insurer would be subject to one regulator and one set of rules. Second, state insurance regulatory agencies already exist, which would avoid the need for creating a new bureaucracy at the federal level. Third, this approach would give states an incentive to establish good regulatory systems to attract or retain insurers within their jurisdictions.

Some problems could also arise with such a system, however. First, a single-state regulator would deal with, for example, an insurer's market conduct in other

57. Harrington (2006); Butler and Ribstein (2008).

states. Second, consumers may be less informed as to applicable insurance regulations and where to seek regulatory recourse or assistance. Third, insurers competing in a given state market could be subject to many sets of regulations (rather than one or two as with an OFC). Fourth, since insurers could pick their regulator, there may be an incentive to choose the weakest regulator, thus encouraging states to offer weak regulatory standards. While the concept of a single-state regulator might receive some discussion in forthcoming legislative debates, there appears to be no significant constituency (at least at present) that supports this approach. Consequently, it is unlikely to receive serious consideration as an alternative to either the current system or an OFC.

Other Systems

Two additional frameworks for insurance regulation might be proposed. One such system would delegate solvency regulation to the federal government and market regulation to the states. The appeal of this framework is that a single federal regulator might be best positioned to oversee the financial and risk situations of multistate insurers and the states might be best positioned to deal with other consumer protection issues. Further, there is precedent for a federal-state system in the financial services industry in the United States and for insurance in Canada and Australia.

The second framework would impose mandatory, rather than optional, federal regulation of insurance. It is not clear whether proponents of this framework envision that all insurers would be federally regulated or only insurers that have certain characteristics, such as companies that write insurance in multiple states or that would be covered by federal solvency guarantees. However, many might view a mandatory system as extreme and unnecessary, given that banks currently can opt for federal or state regulation.

While these two proposals are not in the forefront of current discussions, some of their elements could appear in future initiatives to reform insurance regulation. Legislation has been introduced that would establish a federal Office of Insurance Information within the Treasury, so it may garner some attention while the industry continues to press for an OFC.[58] It is difficult to predict the

---

58. The political strategy behind the IIO legislation and its implications for the enactment of an OFC are unclear. It could be viewed as a more benign intermediate step to set the stage for an OFC. Some OFC proponents might resign themselves to such a scenario, but others may be concerned that it will undermine the impetus for an OFC. It is possible that an IIO could lengthen the time frame for OFC legislation, but the OFC push will remain strong and an IIO could help pave the way for an OFC in the long term.

exact course of future legislation; a variety of options could come into play as the process progresses.

Summary and Conclusions

A state-based system for insurance regulation may seem somewhat incongruous in a modern financial system, but its historical roots are strong and deep in the United States. Arguably, insurance regulation has many facets and is complex. These characteristics, combined with a well-established state institutional structure and strong political opposition to federal regulation, may cause some legislators to pause in considering "radical" changes to the current framework. Still, the push for an OFC or something like it will continue, along with the debate that surrounds it. The better policymakers understand the context for this debate, the better positioned they will be to evaluate arguments and to make decisions.

References

American Council of Life Insurers. 2008. *Life Insurance Fact Book 2007.* Washington.

Baresse, James, and Jack M. Nelson. 1994. "Some Consequences of Insurer Insolvencies." *Journal of Insurance Regulation* 13, no. 1: 3–18.

Becker, Gary S. 1983. "A Theory of Competition among Pressure Groups for Political Influence." *Quarterly Journal of Economics* 98, no. 3: 371–400.

Butler, Henry N., and Larry E. Ribstein. 2008. "A Single-License Approach to Regulating Insurance." Research Paper 08-10. Law and Economics Colloquium, Northwestern University Law School.

Cummins, J. David, Scott E. Harrington, and Robert W. Klein. 1995. "Insolvency Experience, Risk-Based Capital, and Prompt Corrective Action in Property-Liability Insurance." *Journal of Banking and Finance* 19, nos. 3–4: 511–27.

———, eds. 1991. *Cycles and Crises in Property/Casualty Insurance: Causes and Implications for Public Policy.* Kansas City: National Association of Insurance Companies.

Cummins, J. David, and Mary A. Weiss. 1991. "The Structure, Conduct, and Regulation of the Property-Liability Insurance Industry." Series 117–64, Federal Reserve Bank of Boston Conference.

Grace, Martin F., and Robert W. Klein. 2007. "The Effects of an Optional Federal Charter on Competition in the Life Insurance Industry." Report to the American Council of Life Insurers. Georgia State University.

———. 2008. "The Effects of an Optional Federal Charter for Life Insurers on State Economies." Report to the American Council of Life Insurers. Georgia State University.

Grace, Martin F., Robert W. Klein, and Richard D. Phillips. 2002. "Managing the Cost of Property-Casualty Insurer Insolvencies." Report to the National Association of Insurance Commissioners. Georgia State University.

Hanson, Jon S., Robert E. Dineen, and Michael B. Johnson. 1974. *Monitoring Competition: A Means of Regulating the Property and Liability Insurance Business.* Milwaukee: National Association of Insurance Commissioners.

Harrington, Scott E. 1992. "Rate Suppression." *Journal of Risk and Insurance* 59, no. 2: 185–202.

————. 2002. "Effects of Prior Approval Rate Regulation of Auto Insurance." In *Deregulating Property-Liability Insurance: Restoring Competition and Increasing Market Efficiency,* edited by J. David Cummins, pp. 285–314. Washington: AEI-Brookings Joint Center for Regulatory Studies.

————. 2004. "Capital Adequacy in Insurance and Reinsurance." In *Capital Adequacy beyond Basel: Banking, Securities, and Insurance,* edited by Hal Scott, pp. 87–122. Oxford University Press.

————. 2006. "Federal Chartering of Insurance Companies: Options and Alternatives for Transforming Insurance Regulation." Policy Brief 2006-PB-02. Networks Financial Institute, Indiana State University.

Insurance Information Institute. 2008. *The Fact Book 2008.* Washington.

Joskow, Paul L. 1973. "Cartels, Competition, and Regulation in the Property-Liability Insurance Industry." *Bell Journal of Economics and Management Science* 4, no. 2: 375–427.

Klein, Robert W. 1995. "Insurance Regulation in Transition." *Journal of Risk and Insurance* 62, no. 3: 263–404.

————. 2005. *A Regulator's Introduction to the Insurance Industry.* Kansas City: National Association of Insurance Commissioners.

Klein, Robert W., and Shaun Wang. 2007. "Catastrophe Risk Financing in the United States and the European Union: A Comparison of Alternative Regulatory Approaches." Working Paper. Georgia State University.

Meier, Kenneth J. 1988. *The Political Economy of Regulation: The Case of Insurance.* SUNY Press.

Munch, Patricia, and Dennis E. Smallwood. 1981. "Theory of Solvency Regulation in the Property and Casualty Insurance Industry." In *Studies in Public Regulation,* edited by Gary Fromm, pp. 119–67. MIT Press.

National Association of Insurance Commissioners. 2008. *Principles for the NAIC's Adoption of a Principles-Based Reserving Approach.* Kansas City.

Peltzman, Sam. 1976. "Toward a More General Theory of Regulation." *Journal of Law and Economics* 19, no. 2: 211–40.

Pottier, Steven W. 2007. "State Insurance Regulation of Life Insurers: Implications for Economic Efficiency and Financial Strength." Report to the American Council of Life Insurers. University of Georgia.

Saunders, Anthony, and Marcia M. Cornett. 2003. *Financial Institutions Management,* 4th ed. New York: McGraw-Hill.

Scherer, F. M., and David S. Ross. 1990. *Industrial Market Structure and Economic Performance.* New York: Houghton-Mifflin.

Skipper Harold D., Jr., and Robert W. Klein. 2000. "Insurance Regulation in the Public Interest: The Path toward Solvent, Competitive Markets." *Geneva Papers on Risk and Insurance, Issues and Practice* 25, no. 4: 482–504.

Spulber, Daniel F. 1989. *Regulation and Markets.* MIT Press.

Stigler, George J. 1971. "The Theory of Economic Regulation." *Bell Journal of Economics and Management Science* 2, no. 1: 3–21.

Viscusi, W. Kip, Joseph E. Harrington, and John M. Vernon. 2000. *Economics of Regulation and Antitrust,* 3rd ed. MIT Press.

Willis Ltd. 2008. "Impact of the Credit Crisis on General Insurance Companies." London.

PART ONE

Framework for Insurance Regulation

3

An Optional Federal Charter for Insurance: Rationale and Design

Martin F. Grace and Hal S. Scott

Since the early nineteenth century the states have been the principal authority for the regulation of the U.S. insurance industry. In contrast to other financial services such as securities and banking, Congress has not sought to exercise either concurrent or preemptive authority over insurers on a wide scale.[1] Indeed, the McCarran-Ferguson Act of 1945 explicitly found state regulation of insurance to be in the public interest and provided that no federal law should "invalidate, impair, or supersede" any state insurance regulation or tax.[2] Recently, however, and particularly in the wake of the Gramm-Leach-Bliley Act of 1999, many insurers have proposed a system of optional federal chartering (OFC) and regulation of insurance.[3]

In May 2007 Senators John Sununu (R-N.H.) and Tim Johnson (D-S. Dak.) introduced S. 40, the National Insurance Act of 2007 (NIA), which sets forth a scheme for an OFC for life and property-casualty insurers largely modeled on the National Bank Act of 1864. In July 2007 Representatives Melissa Bean (D-Ill.)

---

1. Congress has preempted state authority, however, in such areas as health and crop insurance. See chapter 2, this volume.

2. P.L. 15, March 9, 1945 (codified at 15 U.S.C., secs. 1101–15).

3. P.L. 106-102, November 12, 1999.

and Ed Royce (R-Calif.) introduced a companion bill, H.R. 3200.[4] In contrast to the state coordination approach taken by the State Modernization and Regulatory Transparency (SMART) Act introduced by Representatives Michael Oxley (R-Ohio) and Richard Baker (R-La.) in March 2004, the NIA would establish a "comprehensive system for the federal regulation and supervision of national insurers and national agencies."[5] State regulation would be preempted except in a few areas, such as taxation and participation of national insurers in state residual market mechanisms and qualified guaranty funds.[6] In March 2008 the U.S. Department of the Treasury endorsed an OFC as part of its blueprint to modernize the federal regulatory structure, much along the lines of the pending bills in Congress.[7]

We first present the arguments for abandoning the status quo and moving toward regulation based on an OFC. We then describe the additional issues that would need to be addressed if the United States adopts an OFC. While the merits of an OFC have been much debated, comparatively little consideration has been given to the matter of how such a system should function if enacted.[8] We consider the proposal by Senators Sununu and Johnson and the issues raised by the need for an appropriate regulatory structure for an OFC. Ultimately, the design of a regulatory structure must turn on the objectives of federal insurance regulation and the areas of insurance to be regulated.

The Economic Rationale for an OFC

Regulatory jurisdictions have strong incentives to utilize their resources efficiently when the benefits of public regulatory services and the public goods they produce are fully internalized within the jurisdiction. In addition to minimizing the social costs of regulation, this further efficiency requirement is added to determine which level of government can best provide insurance regulatory services.[9]

---

4. H.R. 3200, 110 Cong. 1 sess., July 26, 2007.

5. In June 2006 Representative Ginny Brown-Waite (R-Fla.) introduced part of the SMART Act as H.R. 5637, 109 Cong. 2 sess., June 19, 2006. See National Insurance Act, sec. 2.

6. National Insurance Act, secs. 1125, 1601, 1703.

7. U.S. Department of the Treasury (2008).

8. Harrington (2006) provides an overview of options for federal intervention in insurance regulation. He suggests two alternatives to an OFC: federal minimum standards that would preempt inadequate state regulation; or the creation of a system of "primary state" chartering akin to the current system of corporate chartering.

9. Oates (1972); Inman and Rubenfeld (1997).

Efficiency in provision of public goods can also be enhanced by competition among government agencies for their provision, since government regulators can be monopolists and suffer from principal-agent problems of their own. Further, some consumers may value a different bundle of regulatory services from that valued by other consumers, which would generate demand for services not provided by the monopolist. Thus there may be benefits from regulatory competition.

We see regulatory competition in a number of areas. One area is between state and federal banking regulators (even though this competition has been greatly attenuated by the imposition of federal standards on state regulation, like federal capital requirements). In theory, consumers can choose to purchase their banking services from among several types of banks. With their choice of a particular bank, a bundle of terms, which contains the type of regulatory services provided by the particular government regulator, is automatically included. Indeed, in the banking system state regulators can compete with each other (as state-chartered banks operate interstate) as well as with federal regulators.

We also see the states being able to choose to control a substantive area of federal regulation themselves rather than accept a uniform federal regulatory approach in areas such as occupational health and safety. For example, the Occupational Safety and Health Act allows the states to set up their own regulatory apparatus and regulate at a higher level than the federal government if they desire.[10] This is similar in some respects to the proposed SMART Act, which would set minimal federal guidelines upon which the states could build. In addition, various laws, including state corporation codes, provide incentives for businesses to incorporate within a state's jurisdiction. Thus the states compete among themselves to attract companies to their jurisdiction. This latter case forms the basis for the competitive federalism proposal promoted by Henry Butler and Larry Ribstein, discussed further below.[11]

The Status Quo

The current regulatory system for insurance consists of regulators in each of the fifty states as well as in the District of Columbia and all U.S. commonwealths and territories. Thus some fifty-seven regulators regulate insurance within their jurisdictions. The history of this state-based insurance regulatory system is well

---

10. Occupational Safety and Health Act (OSH Act), sec. 18, codified at 29 USC 667.
11. Butler and Ribstein (2008).

documented.[12] However, it has not always been assumed that the states should be the exclusive regulators of insurance. There have been numerous proposals for a federal role in insurance regulation since the time of the National Banking Act, which set up the dual-chartering provisions for the banking industry in the 1860s. Current proposals have their roots in the growing interstate presence of the industry and general dissatisfaction with the state regulatory processes. Despite the current proposals, these causal roots have been concerns for some time.[13]

One can view the status quo as a costly system with significant duplication of costs. These costs reduce the demand for insurance to the extent they are passed on to customers. Further, the status quo regulatory apparatus is not designed to move quickly, as all states must agree to a change if it is to have uniform application. The status quo also suffers (or benefits) from the reality that not all states will agree to various policies since they may view their citizens' need for a proposed policy as higher (or lower) than another state's citizens or than an organization seeking state uniformity, such as the National Association of Insurance Commissioners (NAIC). However, this last reality is a critical aspect of the status quo. Each state can represent what it believes is in the best interest of its citizens. By doing so, new knowledge about regulatory policy effectiveness is created. This new knowledge can be spread to other states if it appears beneficial. One aspect of state regulatory powers is that the federalist's vision of the states being laboratories for good policy is theoretically fulfilled in the regulation of insurance. However, the question still arises as to how quickly good policy can spread throughout the states. Further, as pointed out below, states can impose externalities on others by regulating differently from other states. Also, there may be ways to generate new regulatory ideas without creating state laboratories; after all, federal regulation is constantly changing in response to new problems and ideas.

The Case for Abandoning the Status Quo

While a case can be made for maintaining the current state-based system of regulation, there are a number of reasons to favor an alternative framework. Below we discuss the principal problems associated with state insurance regulation and the arguments for establishing an alternative framework (such as an OFC).

12. Day (1970).
13. Randall (1999).

The Inefficiency of State-Based Regulation

Whether one chooses an OFC or a competitive federalist model, it is clear that the states are costly regulators. What is not clear are the benefits that multistate regulation actually produces. Initially, one can examine the costs of state regulation and compare those to the costs of federal regulation. However, a simple cost comparison between current state and federal financial regulatory systems is only partially informative, because each state agency has a slightly different mission. For example, some states expend a great deal of time on rate regulation and issues related to pricing, profitability, and market conduct. Other states have relatively little price regulation but may spend more resources and time on other issues salient to voters in the state. In addition to mission differences at the state level, there is also mission overlap among federal agencies. This makes comparisons of state and federal expenditures on financial service regulation problematic. For example, the Federal Deposit Insurance Corporation (FDIC) has primary solvency regulatory authority as it is the deposit insurer, but the Office of the Comptroller of the Currency (OCC) and the Federal Reserve also have the ability to assess solvency for their separate purposes. Thus it is not really possible to compare regulatory efficiency by looking merely at summary financial or budgetary information. However, these data do show the relative scale of operations of state and federal regulation.[14]

Table 3-1 shows the budget, assets, and number of employees of various financial service regulators in 2006. The budget per employee ranges from $160,000 for the National Credit Union Administration (NCUA) to $305,000 for the Federal Reserve Board. A high ratio of the budget of the NCUA is in assets under its supervision, while for the budget of the Federal Reserve Board this is a relatively low ratio. There is also a great deal of difference among the agencies in budgets per regulated firm under its authority (a high of $292,000 for the OCC and a low of $22,375 for the Federal Reserve Board).

Some of the state insurance regulatory cost indexes are more useful than some of the indexes for federal financial service agencies, but it is difficult to determine based on this information whether regulation should be performed at a higher (federal) level of aggregation. First, it is difficult to make comparisons across financial service regulatory functions. For example, complaints about insurance are likely more numerous than, say, complaints about credit cards or deposits. And

---

14. This mission overlap is also a type of regulatory competition, as each agency may be able to check the other agency's behavior.

Table 3-1. *Financial Service Regulation, Budgets, Employees, and Assets, 2006*
Units as indicated

Organization	Budget ($M)	Employees
Office of Thrift Supervision	199,497	918
Federal Reserve Board[a]	173,000	567
Federal Deposit Insurance Corporation[b]	998,000	4,476
National Credit Union Administration	150,800	939
Office of Comptroller of the Currency	579,401	2,886
Securities and Exchange Commission[c]	960,800	3,764
Addendum		
Sum of federal regulators	2,100,698	9,786
State insurance departments + NAIC[d]	1,196,677	12,335

Source: Based on Grace and Klein (2007), table 3.3.

a. Includes the number of state member banks and the number of separate banks belonging to bank holding companies. The FRB has overlapping jurisdiction with the OTS and the OCC.

b. The FDIC has financial regulatory authority over insured banks.

c. SEC budget numbers reflect total program costs. The SEC oversaw approximately 5,300 broker dealers, 5,000 investment companies, and 8,550 investment advisers.

d. Includes property-liability and life, health, and annuity companies.

even if they are not more numerous, the technology and effort needed to resolve the complaints may be different. Second, it appears that closing down a failed insurer is much more expensive than closing down a bank. Some argue that a part of this difference in cost is due to the fact that banks' liabilities are generally easy to determine relative to insurers' liabilities, whose long-tail liabilities take time to resolve. Either way, insurance insolvencies are different from bank insolvencies, as they likely have different costs of resolution.[15] Thus other indicators of cost efficiency are needed in order to discuss which level of regulation is appropriate.

One of the major rationales for federal regulation is the economies resulting from the elimination of duplicate actions by the states: if insurance regulation is aggregated to a higher level of government, it is thought, these duplicate costs would be eliminated. The outcome would be lower regulatory costs to the government and lower compliance costs to the regulated firms. For example, every state undertakes regulation of insurance agents. According to Laureen Regan, the average life agent has about nine state licenses.[16] This cost is borne by the agents, their employers, and their customers. Further, every state licenses the companies

15. Grace, Klein, and Phillips (2007).
16. Regan (2007).

operating within its jurisdiction. In addition, the average property-liability company holds sixteen state licenses and the average life-health company holds twenty-five.[17] Two questions thus arise: Is there a social value for multiple states to undertake similar or identical licensing? And is there an alternative regulatory system that would impose less cost and provide greater benefits?

There is not a great deal of evidence regarding the social value of duplicative regulation, but there is some evidence regarding the costs. Martin Grace and Robert Klein, in their attempt to determine the effect of multiple state licensing requirements on insurers, find that the elasticity between the ratio of total expenses to premiums written and an additional license is about 10 percent.[18] This is fairly significant. Steven Pottier, using a different technique, finds that the total additional costs of having multistate regulation of the life insurance industry is about 1.25 percent of net premiums annually.[19] This translates into approximately $5.7 billion each year. Thus the evidence suggests a large dollar cost to multi-state regulation. While these figures are for the life insurance industry, one would expect a similar result for the property-liability industry.

To answer the second question—whether there is an arrangement that will provide a higher social value—we can see whether insurance is regulated at the proper level of political authority. A framework exists for determining whether aggregation of regulatory power is appropriate. The ideal level of regulatory power should be exercised at the jurisdictional level best able to capture all the costs and benefits of regulation within its limits. Thus it is appropriate for county governments, for example, to regulate sanitary conditions at restaurants and swimming pools and for the federal government to regulate the allocation of broadcast frequencies or passenger air routes. This is the essential argument underlying the proper level of regulation. So in addition to cost economies from the aggregation of insurance regulation from the state level to the federal level, one might need to see evidence regarding the interstate nature of the industry or the presence of interstate externalities. The more interstate the business, the stronger the argument is for federal regulation.

Table 3-2 shows the premiums written by domestic and foreign companies in each U.S. state. The data show three facts. First, the domestic market share is small compared to the interstate share: the weighted mean domestic market share for all states for both sectors in 2006 was only 18.93 percent; in other words, out-of-state insurers provided over 80 percent of all insurance.

17. National Association of Insurance Commissioners (2006).
18. Grace and Klein (2000).
19. Pottier (2007).

Table 3-2. *Foreign and Domestic Premiums, Property-Liability and Life and Health, by State, 2006*
Units as indicated

	Property-liability			Life and health			Total industry	
State	*Direct foreign premiums written ($000)*	*Direct domestic premiums written ($000)*	*Domestic market share (%)*	*Direct foreign premiums written ($000)*	*Direct domestic premiums written ($000)*	*Domestic market share (%)*	*2006 domestic market share (%)*	*1995 domestic market share (%)*
Alabama	5,633,369	960,141	14.56	5,233,207	298,066	5.39	10.38	14.65
Alaska	1,326,310	199,073	13.05	834,761	...	0.00	8.43	8.70
Arizona	7,684,470	784,508	9.26	7,818,979	117,100	1.48	5.50	13.94
Arkansas	3,687,606	225,407	5.76	2,779,417	88,050	3.07	4.62	14.99
California	41,325,401	18,476,141	30.90	51,420,394	76,601	0.15	16.67	26.20
Colorado	7,414,151	318,006	4.11	8,353,160	328,631	3.79	3.94	8.34
Connecticut	5,892,576	1,159,682	16.44	6,870,055	8,968,009	56.62	44.24	36.86
Delaware	2,069,795	293,659	12.42	19,148,124	2,041,821	9.64	9.92	15.93
District of Columbia	1,499,298	34,574	2.25	1,824,004	2,917	0.16	1.12	2.06
Florida	28,341,802	10,703,313	27.41	29,349,453	117,188	0.40	15.79	14.71
Georgia	12,380,640	1,525,419	10.97	10,892,022	94,097	0.86	6.51	8.50
Hawaii	1,597,695	727,497	31.29	2,329,903	32,535	1.38	16.21	19.23
Idaho	1,567,678	286,125	15.43	1,804,369	11,343	0.62	8.11	13.11
Illinois	11,874,181	9,279,732	43.87	9,126,798	1,503,516	7.29	25.81	36.72
Indiana	7,150,200	1,363,405	16.01	8,315,297	1,463,280	14.96	15.45	24.98

Iowa	3,425,251	1,146,817	25.08	3,709,343	3,588,079	49.17	39.89	37.95
Kansas	4,052,270	488,023	10.75	6,762,640	271,152	3.85	6.56	20.94
Kentucky	4,821,563	984,111	16.95	4,095,719	40,643	0.98	10.31	11.89
Louisiana	7,090,656	1,661,061	18.98	6,346,595	189,099	2.89	12.10	12.77
Maine	1,515,482	457,457	23.19	1,819,433	20,841	1.13	12.54	15.72
Maryland	7,719,661	1,236,942	13.81	13,559,718	82,954	0.61	5.84	8.46
Massachusetts	6,639,900	5,243,219	44.12	11,917,922	1,256,083	9.53	25.94	31.02
Michigan	8,114,813	7,205,704	47.03	13,784,729	2,227,780	13.91	30.11	25.38
Minnesota	7,745,520	924,741	10.67	8,873,038	1,855,674	17.30	14.33	18.31
Mississippi	3,670,694	502,048	12.03	2,521,008	86,937	3.33	8.69	13.96
Missouri	7,956,991	1,097,600	12.12	8,715,275	274,014	3.05	7.60	13.90
Montana	1,530,070	27,744	1.78	941,543	5	0.00	1.11	1.42
Nebraska	2,789,080	382,762	12.07	3,146,838	482,480	13.29	12.72	26.28
Nevada	4,351,301	243,629	5.30	2,711,937	...	0.00	3.33	1.49
New Hampshire	1,877,017	278,221	12.91	2,138,006	3,896	0.18	6.57	8.90
New Jersey	12,339,874	5,017,773	28.91	23,774,434	3,997,113	14.39	19.98	23.90
New Mexico	2,410,956	154,322	6.02	1,822,503	150	0.01	3.52	3.91
New York	26,104,575	8,613,369	24.81	18,763,362	28,191,295	60.04	45.06	36.41
North Carolina	9,977,225	1,836,158	15.54	13,120,640	230,361	1.73	8.21	11.06
North Dakota	1,142,870	163,328	12.50	917,750	10,877	1.17	7.80	11.27
Ohio	8,265,065	5,049,116	37.92	16,121,765	2,078,124	11.42	22.62	28.53
Oklahoma	4,499,132	751,287	14.31	3,803,658	67,781	1.75	8.98	11.12
Oregon	4,052,243	1,380,963	25.42	4,195,542	319,697	7.08	17.09	17.50
Pennsylvania	15,013,048	4,953,342	24.81	21,565,944	451,255	2.05	12.87	15.90
Rhode Island	1,581,235	361,172	18.59	1,707,491	28,845	1.66	10.60	13.97

(continued)

Table 3-2. *Foreign and Domestic Premiums, Property-Liability and Life and Health, by State, 2006 (continued)*
Units as indicated

	Property-liability			Life and health			Total industry	
State	*Direct foreign premiums written ($000)*	*Direct domestic premiums written ($000)*	*Domestic market share (%)*	*Direct foreign premiums written ($000)*	*Direct domestic premiums written ($000)*	*Domestic market share (%)*	*2006 domestic market share (%)*	*1995 domestic market share (%)*
South Carolina	6,218,784	370,493	5.62	4,969,510	110,068	2.17	4.12	14.87
South Dakota	1,381,122	75,347	5.17	1,105,132	1,131	0.10	2.98	5.10
Tennessee	7,216,199	1,174,449	14.00	8,215,415	319,837	3.75	8.83	10.45
Texas	19,960,335	14,760,142	42.51	25,560,976	3,685,963	12.60	28.84	34.15
Utah	2,846,912	430,184	13.13	3,048,829	228,461	6.97	10.05	16.06
Vermont	988,760	122,421	11.02	953,128	19,632	2.02	6.82	10.50
Virginia	10,287,050	333,919	3.14	10,743,862	2,451,603	18.58	11.70	15.84
Washington	7,198,468	1,629,454	18.46	7,992,753	198,818	2.43	10.74	20.06
West Virginia	2,189,954	892,214	28.95	1,875,780	635	0.03	18.01	1.86
Wisconsin	4,343,890	3,673,437	45.82	8,523,553	789,986	8.48	25.75	31.95
Wyoming	775,488	60,704	7.26	695,591	...	0.00	3.96	3.32
Addendum								
Minimum			1.78			0.00	1.11	1.42
Mean			18.13			7.52	13.31	16.57
Weighted mean			24.92			13.33	18.93	22.78
Median			14.31			2.43	10.31	14.71
Maximum			47.03			60.04	45.06	37.95

Source: National Association of Insurance Commissioners (2006); market share calculations by author.

Second, the life insurance business is more interstate than the property-liability business: the average domestic market share is 7.52 percent for life-health insurers and 18.13 percent for property-liability insurers. The same is true for the median state: life-health insurers have much smaller domestic market shares than domestic property-liability companies. Even the overall average (weighted average, or the sum of the domestic markets' premiums in each state over total U.S. premiums written) shows that life-health insurance has a smaller domestic presence relative to property-liability insurance (domestic firms providing only 13.33 percent of life-health insurance).

Determining all of the factors causing this difference is beyond the scope of this chapter, but three factors come to mind. One, life insurance products and risks are more standardized, and thus there is less ability for local firms to have a comparative advantage in the provision of contracts. Two, property-liability policies are more likely to be subject to local restrictions and legal interpretations, which provide local providers with a comparative advantage over national companies. However, even property-liability insurance provided by domestic firms is small, with a weighted mean of 24.92 percent in 2006. Three, between 1995 and 2006 the total industry became more interstate, in the sense that indicators of domestic market share declined over the eleven-year period. Thus life insurance is more interstate than nonlife insurance, and the entire industry has become more interstate over time.

Martin Grace and Richard Phillips, in an effort to assess the cost efficiency aspects of regulatory aggregation, find evidence supporting an increase in efficiency with an increase in the level of regulation.[20] First, they find that the typical state has increasing returns to scale in regulation. The presence of economies of scale means that the average state could undertake the oversight of more producers or firms at lower average costs. This is consistent with the notion that the typical state is too small to regulate efficiently. Surprisingly, the authors also find that the biggest states have decreasing returns to scale. However, upon further investigation they find that the externalities operating among the states varied and that these externalities imposed costs on larger states. Specifically, it appears that larger states were doing the regulatory work of smaller states, as smaller states indirectly imposed their regulatory costs on larger states by relying on them to perform some of the functions belonging to the smaller states. The presence of this externality provides further evidence

---

20. Grace and Phillips (2007).

that the states are not the proper level of political jurisdictional control over the insurance industry.

Uniformity, Innovation, and Speed to Market

Another problem resulting from state regulation is the effect on product innovation, product approvals (speed to market), and interstate uniformity. If products are approved quickly, then firms can compete more efficiently on product innovation and design. However, if products are approved slowly, the incentive for insurers to develop and market new ideas is reduced. The problem is exacerbated if a product is approved in one state with a certain set of conditions and in another state with a different set of conditions. This differential approval also increases innovation costs. While federal pressure can produce more uniformity, this is not always the case.

Table 3-3 shows five model laws chosen to make specific points. One model law not included on the list is that based on the Risk-Based Capital Model Act.[21] We use it for comparison purposes, as it was adopted by every state within two years of its promulgation—and in almost identical form. This success may have stemmed from federal pressure, such as the criticism of state regulators by the House Commerce Committee for the insurance company failures of the late 1980s and early 1990s. However, federal pressure does not always generate quick adoption and uniformity. For example, the Gramm-Leach-Bliley Act (GLBA) required states to adopt reciprocal agent licensing provisions. The NAIC subsequently proposed a model law regarding producer licensing that would streamline licensing for agents. Table 3-3 shows the states that have adopted a producer licensing law.

---

21. National Association of Insurance Commissioners (2008). Note that, while the Risk-Based Capital Model Act has been uniformly adopted across the states, it says nothing about minimum initial (or continuing) capitalization requirements. In fact, each state separately sets these initial and continuing capitalization requirements, and they are not uniform. Risk-based capital is the capital requirement adjusted for the risk the company undertakes. It is different from initial or continuing capital requirements, which are unadjusted amounts of capital a company needs to start up or to continue in business. Compare, for example, Florida's initial minimum capital requirement of $5 million with Georgia's initial capital requirement of $1.5 million. In contrast, New York has separate requirements for minimum capital and surplus based on a company's line of business; the range is from $50,000 for glass coverage to $6 million for life insurance. The state would need to look at the risk-based capital law as well as its initial (or continuing) capital requirement statute to determine whether the company can continue to operate. See National Association of Insurance Commissioners (2007).

Table 3-3. *State Adoption of Model Law, Summary Data*[a]

State	Producer licensing		Life insurance disclosure model regulation		Unfair trade practices		Military sales		PC actuarial opinion	
	Law	*Related legislation*	*Law*	*Related legislation*	*Law*	*Related legislation*	*Law*	*Related legislation*	*Law*	*Related legislation*
Alabama	x		x			x				x
Alaska	x	x			x	x				x
Arizona	x		x		x		x			
Arkansas	x	x		x	x	x				
California		x	x		x	x				x
Colorado	x	x			x		x			
Connecticut	x	x	x		x	x				x
Delaware	x		x		x					
D.C.	x				x		x			
Florida	x	x	x		x	x	x			x
Georgia		x	x		x		x			x
Hawaii	x				x					
Idaho	x				x	x	x		x	
Illinois	x		x			x				
Indiana	x	x	x	x	x					x
Iowa	x	x			x		x			x
Kansas	x	x		x	x		x			
Kentucky	x	x		x	x	x				x
Louisiana	x	x		x	x		x			x
Maine	x	x	x		x					x

(continued)

Table 3-3. *State Adoption of Model Law, Summary Data (continued)*

State	Producer licensing		Life insurance disclosure model regulation		Unfair trade practices		Military sales		PC actuarial opinion	
	Law	Related legislation	Law	Related legislation	Law	Related legislation	Law	Related legislation	Law	Related legislation
Maryland		x	x		x				x	x
Massachusetts	x	x	x		x					
Michigan	x	x		x	x	x				
Minnesota	x				x					
Mississippi	x				x					
Missouri		x	x	x	x	x				
Montana		x	x		x					
Nebraska	x	x	x		x				x	
Nevada	x	x	x		x					
New Hampshire	x	x	x		x					
New Jersey	x	x	x		x					x
New Mexico		x	x		x		x			
New York		x	x		x		x			
North Carolina	x	x	x		x					
North Dakota	x	x	x		x					

	(1)	(2)	(3)	(4)	(5)	(6)	(7)
Ohio	x	x	x				
Oklahoma	x	x	x			x	
Oregon	x	x	x				x
Pennsylvania	x	x	x	x			
Rhode Island	x	x	x	x			
South Carolina	x		x	x			
South Dakota	x	x	x	x			x
Tennessee	x	x	x	x			
Texas		x	x			x	x
Utah	x	x	x	x			x
Vermont	x	x	x	x			x
Virginia		x				x	x
Washington	x	x	x	x		x	x
West Virginia	x		x	x			
Wisconsin		x	x		x		
Wyoming	x		x		x	x	x

Source: National Association of Insurance Commissioners (2008).

a. States identified in the column labeled "Law" have adopted the law in a "uniform and substantially similar manner." "Related legislation" means that the states have not adopted the law in a "uniform or substantially similar manner." These states may have an older version of the law or a law derived from other sources.

Although the GLBA was passed in 2000, nine years later not all of the states have adopted the law. In addition, states have adopted other measures or other rules that reduce the effect of uniformity among the states. In addition, state judges, in interpreting the law consistent with how the states' legal systems have evolved, can make conflicting interpretations of the same statute. Finally, certain large and important insurance states such as Texas and New York have not yet passed the model law. The Government Accountability Office (GAO) asserted in congressional testimony that the holdout states may believe that their standards are superior and do not desire to lower them.[22] However, no cost-benefit analysis supports this assertion. And even if such an analysis did support it, it would not likely account for the costs imposed on others outside the state. Thus by holding out, these states impose compliance costs on owners and policyholders of companies operating nationwide.

The life insurance disclosure model provides "rules for life insurance policy illustrations that will protect consumers and foster consumer education."[23] Policy illustrations are part of the marketing process for life insurance, as they provide information about expected investment returns or credited interest rates on policies. For example, if the previous twenty-year return credited to policies was 5 percent, a policy illustration might have a projected 8 percent return rather than the historic 5 percent return. This model law was proposed in 1976 in light of a wave of creative illustrations that promised high returns on investment performance. As of 2008 only thirty-two states had adopted it. Nonuniform disclosure regulations are costly. In contrast, all but five states have adopted the NAIC's unfair trade practices rule. This model act was proposed in 1947.

The table also shows the military sales model, proposed in 2007 as a result of a law enacted by Congress.[24] This regulation is designed to protect young soldiers, sailors, marines, and airmen from aggressive sales tactics directed at military personnel. To date only eighteen states have adopted it. Presumably, this was an important issue for Congress, yet it had not been adopted by a majority of states in its first two years.

The PC actuarial opinion model law, adopted in 2005, is designed to require an actuary to issue an opinion regarding the financial state of an insurance company and provides that the opinion must be based on the actuary's best estimate

22. U.S. Government Accountability Office (2002).
23. National Association of Insurance Commissioners (2008).
24. Military Personnel Financial Services Protection Act, P.L. 109-290 (2006). See also "NAIC Adopts Model Regulation on Military Sales" (www.naic.org/Releases/2007_docs/Military_sales.htm [May 2008]).

or a range of acceptable estimates. The law also requires certain documentation to be part of the opinion. This law was designed to increase the underlying analysis and accuracy of the annual reports of property-liability companies. The law has been adopted by eight states, while another nineteen have adopted other related (and possibly different) rules.

In addition to concerns about a lack of uniformity (which increases costs), a typical complaint about the current state system concerns delays between product development and approval. This is also an issue of uniformity, as each state must approve a product before it can be sold in a state. The NAIC has attempted to respond to insurers' concerns about product approval delays. The costs of getting products to market nationally are allegedly high; hence the NAIC's apparent desire to deal with the issue. The GAO testified that the initial attempt to streamline product approval was not, in fact, streamlined enough for insurers to obtain value. In fact, there were too many additional individual state requirements.[25] The NAIC has again tried to improve the process by the formation of the Interstate Insurance Product Regulation Commission (IIPRC) for life insurance, an interstate compact.[26]

Horizontal Equity with Other Financial Services Industries

Permanent or cash value life insurance and many types of annuities have significant savings components. If these products are generally viewed as savings vehicles, then a number of potential banking or financial institution substitutes exist, ranging from bank accounts to individual stock portfolios. Federally regulated banks have a potentially significant advantage compared to insurance companies and nonbank annuity providers. Financial institutions can ask their regulators for nationwide approval of a product and receive an answer within a relatively short period of time, compared to the time it takes for insurers to obtain state approval. This provides a financial institution with a significant advantage over insurers for the marketing of similar products.[27]

Further, the states have rules regulating insurers' investments that may put them at a further disadvantage vis-à-vis federally regulated financial institutions. According to Grace and Klein, federally regulated financial institutions are

---

25. U.S. Government Accountability Office (2002).

26. According to information on the IIPRC, thirty-three states and related jurisdictions were members as of December 2008. However, five large insurance states are missing from the compact: New York, California, Illinois, Florida, and Connecticut. New York, Illinois, and California have proposed legislation (www.insurancecompact.org [November 2008]).

27. Kelly Greene, "Mutual Funds Pitch Alternative to Annuities," *Wall Street Journal,* June 9, 2008, p. D8.

permitted to use relatively aggressive hedging strategies, whereas insurers typically are not.[28] The market is quickly and dramatically changing, yet states typically resist allowing insurers to use the strategies commonly applied by other financial institutions. It may be that state regulators are apprehensive because they lack the resources to monitor and evaluate these strategies. A federal regulator with better analytical resources could permit life insurers to engage in investment and hedging strategies that would be more appropriate, more efficient, and more consistent with the rules governing other financial institutions.

The Costs and Benefits of an OFC

Consider the costs of an OFC. First, there are the costs of regulation at two levels of government. Even if there were significant change to a federal charter by many insurers, there still would be many insurers left to be regulated by the states. It would be ideal if there were a reduction in state expenditures exactly offset by the increase in federal expenditures, but this is not likely to occur, as bureaucracies are difficult to eliminate even if their mission changes significantly. Thus federal insurance regulatory expenses are likely to go up more than any reduction in state regulatory expenses.

A second source of costs is the imperfection of the federal-state charter competition. While there is the potential for competition, there is the problem of stickiness. Once a national insurer obtains a federal charter, returning it to a state charter would be costly. Depending on how substantial these costs are, insurers could be "held up," in the sense that it would be so costly to quit the federal charter that the federal government could extract concessions on tangential issues. Congress could also significantly expand its authority over the industry. In fact, this has historically been one of the reasons trotted out as a critique of past federal regulatory proposals.[29] It is also important to understand that, even with a holdup problem, overall efficiency could still be improved by the regulatory competition that would be induced by an OFC.

A third potential cost is less consumer protection. There is a concern that consumers would find it more difficult to have their complaints resolved at the federal level. This can be dealt with by adequate federal resources and consumer education. Most consumer complaints are resolved over the telephone and not in

---

28. Grace and Klein (2007).

29. Hanson (1977); Sara Hansard, "Will Optional Federal Charter Lead to More Regulation?" *Investment News,* May 26, 2008, p. 3.

person. It just as easy to call the toll-free number of a federal regulator as it is to call the number of a state regulator. It is possible, however, that state regulators may be more responsive to local complaints due to the political consequences of not doing so.

A fourth cost issue arises from the difficulties of maintaining state guaranty funds and federal regulation.[30] As discussed at more length below (under the general subject of guaranty funds), this cost suggests that the OFC should include a federal guaranty fund and allow insurers to opt out of state guaranty funds.

These costs can be compared to a number of benefits that would arise from an OFC. These include cost reductions resulting from regulatory streamlining. In a competitive environment, these reductions are passed on in terms of lower prices for consumers. Grace and Klein suggest that there are also benefits to competition by increasing the size of the market. To the extent that state licensing is costly, it acts as a barrier to competitive entry. Removal of such barriers would increase competition. In addition, increased competition would increase efficiency-inducing mergers and acquisitions, which would be a gain in an industry with relatively low average efficiency levels.[31] Increased competition would also bring about product innovation and economic growth.[32] Finally, an OFC would reduce the negative externalities imposed on out-of-state customers and insurers resulting from the current state regulatory system.

Competitive Federalism

Henry Butler and Larry Ribstein argue for a framework that would allow an insurer to choose one state to be its regulator; the insurer would then be able to operate nationwide under the laws of its home state.[33] This model of single-state regulation is akin to how state corporate law is employed in an interstate market. Butler and Ribstein try to counter potential "race to the bottom" critiques to their proposal. They argue that with perfect information consumers presumably would shun insurers from states with known lax regulation. Given, however, that there would likely be some residual consumer uncertainty over the insurer's home state's consumer protection law, Butler and Ribstein suggest that the home state's laws require the insurer to disclose which level of consumer protection would be

---

30. National Association of Mutual Insurance Companies (2008).
31. Yuengert (1993); Cummins and Weiss (1993).
32. Jayaratne and Strahan (1996).
33. Butler and Ribstein (2008).

granted: that of the insurer's home state or that of the consumer's state. This information disclosure would help the consumer shop for appropriate coverage from a company warranting a given level of consumer protection.

This is not convincing. As we have explained, a key reason for insurance regulation is consumers' asymmetric and imperfect information. A disclosure document (which many consumers may not read or comprehend) is not a credible solution. A key feature of the current system is strong insurance regulation by most states. Those states (and Congress) will not accept the possibility of their consumers being exposed to lax regulation by another state. There is also the issue of enforcement. Indeed, for an OFC to have any political traction it will have to assure Congress that it will not lessen current state consumer protection.

The status quo is costly and will never realistically result in a reduction in compliance costs. This is because the states have no real incentive to work together. Even though states occasionally work together, as with their quick and universal adoption of risk-based capital requirements, this is not a likely scenario in other areas. State adoption of risk-based capital requirements was likely prompted by regulators' fear of federal intervention if they did not strengthen solvency standards. However, the agency licensing requirements of the GLBA have not been accomplished. If the states were going to work together, they would have done so by now. Further, there is evidence that even a congressional mandate requiring a certain level of market conduct regulation for military personnel has not been adopted quickly.

The insurance industry has become more of an interstate business over its entire history, and this trend is still continuing. In addition, as the industry becomes more interstate in nature, the ability of the states to impose externalities on consumers in other states is increasing. Because of this, the industry needs a new style of regulation. The banking industry, the mutual fund industry, and parts of the insurance industry compete for the savings dollars of consumers. New products become approved quickly in the noninsurance arena, but innovations in the insurance industry require a long and ponderous review. This puts the insurance industry at a competitive disadvantage.

While there is evidence of interstate externalities in regulation, there are also those caused by differing state polices. A model of competitive federalism could bring about a reduction in compliance costs and may have the ability to increase efficiency by internalizing costs and benefits to its virtual jurisdiction; we think that an OFC approach also has merit. An OFC law would internalize the costs and benefits of insurance regulation. In addition, a model, which has existed since the 1860s in the banking industry, shows how the system would work. However, while an OFC presents some potential advantages in the sense that it can internalize costs and benefits of regulation, the current law has some problems that need clarification.

The External Structure

With these considerations in mind, we now turn to options for how to design a federal insurance regulator to fit within the federal regulatory structure. Certain key issues must be considered: independence from the president, characteristics of the chief official, legislative jurisdiction, ad hoc oversight, funding, and lessons from state insurance regulation.

Independence

Some regulatory agencies, such as the Federal Reserve Board, are independent of the president. Others, such as the OCC, are instead housed within a cabinet department (Treasury, in the OCC's case, albeit with significant insulation from the secretary of the Treasury). The more independence, the less exposure there is to political pressure, but there is also the greater difficulty of coordinating policy among regulators, short of regulatory consolidation in an independent agency.

The federal insurance regulator could be part of a broader supervising agency. For example, the United Kingdom's Financial Services Authority (FSA) is an independent, consolidated agency encompassing the regulation of accounting, asset management, banking, securities, insurance, and other segments of the financial services industry, with separate "sector leaders" for each.[34] It operates as a company limited by guaranty and financed by the financial services industry, with a board selected by the United Kingdom's Treasury.[35]

There is also a difference between being exposed to political pressure and being political. For example, the five commissioners of the Securities and Exchange Commission (SEC) are split three to two along party lines, with the party in power having the majority. In practice, the commissioners from each party, while independent, have a natural tendency to coordinate their positions with their political benefactors (those who nominated them).

34. See www.fsa.gov.uk/Pages/About/Who/Management/Leaders/index.shtml.
35. See www.fsa.gov.uk/Pages/About/Who/index.shtml.

Chief Official

What should be the characteristics of the insurance regulator's chief official? Chief officials (and by implication agencies themselves) may operate with different degrees of insulation from the president. The most insulated model would involve a multimember chief official body, with characteristics such as staggered terms, bipartisan composition, and for-cause removal. The SEC and the Federal Reserve Board offer examples of this approach. Next, the agency might have one chief official with some sort of for-cause removal. An example is the Social Security Administration. Finally, the agency might have one chief official who serves at the pleasure of the president. An example here is the director of the Federal Bureau of Investigation. Often, agencies that are independent (as described above) also have chief officials who are more insulated. However, this is not always the case: although the Environmental Protection Agency is independent of any cabinet agency, the administrator serves at the pleasure of the president.

Legislative Jurisdiction

Every federal regulator is overseen by a particular congressional committee. For instance, the OCC and SEC report to the Senate Committee on Banking, Housing, and Urban Affairs, whereas the Federal Trade Commission reports to the Senate Committee on Commerce, Science, and Transportation. Which congressional committee should have jurisdiction over a federal insurance regulator? The banking committees seem appropriate to ensure parity of treatment with the treatment of financial institutions and to address the concerns raised above.

Ad Hoc Oversight

Quite separate from questions of oversight resulting from congressional committee jurisdiction, the formal organizational relationship with the president, appointment and removal of chief officials, and consolidation with other agencies, a federal insurance regulator may also be overseen by ad hoc institutions composed of various executive officials. Perhaps the most relevant group for an insurance regulator is the President's Working Group on Financial Markets, which currently includes the secretary of the Treasury, the chairman of the Federal Reserve, the chairman of the SEC, and the chairman of the Commodity Futures Trading Commission (CFTC). The new insurance regulator would be added to the mix.

Funding

Some regulators, such as the SEC, receive substantial amounts of their funding from congressional appropriations. Others, such as the FDIC and the OCC, receive no appropriations and are entirely funded by premiums, assessments, other fees, and earnings on investments. Reliance upon appropriations increases accountability to Congress but at the cost of independence from Congress.

Lessons from State Insurance Regulation

In considering what a federal regulator might look like, it is useful consider how state insurance regulators are organized and funded. The typical state insurance regulator is constituted as an autonomous agency, formally part of the executive branch, with one chief official appointed by the governor. An example of this paradigm is the New York State Insurance Department. It is headed by a superintendent, who is appointed by the governor. No state insurance regulator appears to operate through a multimember commission. Within state legislatures, insurance regulation is often through committee, the most common three being a committee on banking and financial regulation (twenty-one states), a committee on commerce or consumer protection (twelve states), and a committee on insurance specifically (eleven states). A minority of states has an elected chief official for insurance; these states often grant this official more formal independence from the executive than that granted to a committee. Delaware has an elected insurance commissioner, who is subject to removal only for "reasonable cause."[36] This structure cannot be constitutionally replicated within the federal administrative structure. In and of itself, this means that a federal regulator may be more responsive to popular political pressure.

Another minority of states brings insurance regulation within another executive department, which is usually devoted either to commerce and consumer affairs or to banking and other financial services. Most of these states go further by consolidating regulation within this department, such that the insurance regulator merely is a division of a larger regulator, akin to the U.K.'s FSA.[37] Michigan uses this option. Its insurance regulation is one of the functions of the Office of Financial and Insurance Services, which also oversees banking and securities. This office is itself a part of the Department of Labor and Economic Growth.

Oversight by an ad hoc authority is highly uncommon. The only significant example might be Florida, where the commissioner of the Office of Insurance

36. 18 Del. C. secs. 301, 303.
37. Sixteen states have consolidated financial supervision for insurance, banking, and securities; twelve states have consolidated supervision for banking and securities; one state (New Jersey) has consolidated supervision for banking and insurance; one state (Tennessee) has consolidated supervision for insurance and securities; and twenty-two states have separate supervision for all three sectors. Brown (2005).

Regulation is appointed and overseen by the Financial Services Commission. The Financial Services Commission is itself composed of the governor and the cabinet. This commission also appoints and oversees the head of the Office of Financial Regulation, which oversees banking and securities. Both the Office of Insurance Regulation and the Office of Financial Regulation are within the larger Department of Financial Services, which is headed by a constitutional officer and also has regulatory jurisdiction over Florida's state accounting and auditing, state funds, and workers' compensation system.

State insurance departments may take their operating revenue from a variety of sources, including premium taxes, fees and assessments, appropriations, and penalties.[38] There is considerable diversity among the states. In California, the Department of Insurance collects fees for licensing and examination of insurance companies and agents and deposits them into a dedicated fund; fines and penalties are deposited into the state's general fund. In Maine the Bureau of Insurance gathers operating revenue by making an annual assessment against all licensed insurers in proportion to each company's direct gross premium. In Nevada the legislature appropriates monies for the Department of Insurance from the general fund. Nevertheless, the most common approach gives the state insurance department considerable freedom to collect fees for service, allowing for a degree of independence and self-funding.

Summary

Some characteristics of state regulation are so prevalent that they may seem to be presumptively worthy of replication at the federal level, for a couple of reasons. First, multimember insurance commissions are entirely absent among the states, which suggests that a Federal Reserve or an SEC approach would not be appropriate at the federal level. However, state insurance regulators are not independent from the political process, perhaps because some of the consumer issues they deal with are so highly political. Multimember setups may be more appropriate for independent regulators, to ensure that the independent agency has political balance and is a substitute for more active political control. Second, the latitude given to state insurance departments in the setting and collecting of fees suggests that a national insurance regulator should be self-funding, at least in part. Self-funding would allow the regulator a degree of independence from the political process, akin to that enjoyed by the Federal Reserve system. However, the creation

38. NAIC (2007).

of another independent federal agency with its own source of funds may not be a desirable result.

The Treasury blueprint contemplates the creation, in the medium term, of an Office of National Insurance (ONI) within the Treasury to license and oversee federally chartered insurance companies. The office would be headed by a commissioner and would be self-funded by assessments on federally chartered firms. In the longer term, the blueprint contemplates splitting the function of this office, like the functions of other existing regulatory agencies, among a market stability regulator (the Federal Reserve), a prudential financial regulator (within the Treasury), and a business conduct regulator (apparently an independent agency). These three regulators would join the existing FDIC, together with a new independent corporate finance regulator, to form a federal regulatory structure with five peaks.

In our view, it would be preferable to create an OFC now and not wait for the medium term. Further, we believe that it would be a mistake to create an independent agency to regulate insurance. Such an agency would further fragment federal regulation, a step in the wrong direction. However, it would also not be wise to merge insurance and banking regulators, because banking considerations are likely to be dominant, given history and the public concern with systemic risk. Insurance would be a poor stepchild.[39] The best approach would be to create a separate insurance regulator but use that occasion to strengthen the powers and resources of the President's Working Group on Financial Markets. The Treasury blueprint contemplates strengthening these powers, and it is expected that an executive order to this effect will be issued. Such an arrangement might replicate the benefits of oversight provided by Florida's Financial Services Commission.

As an overall matter, in the medium term (not the long term, as contemplated by the Treasury) the federal government should pursue a more integrated regulatory structure. Rather than the Treasury's five-peak plan, it should create a structure similar to the U.K.'s twin peaks: a central bank (the Bank of England) and one overall financial regulator and supervisor (the FSA).[40] While the Bank of England has no supervisory authority, one could well envision giving the Federal Reserve such power, either exclusively or concurrently with authority of a U.S. version of the FSA. These twin peaks would supervise and regulate federally

39. Chesson (2000, p. 74), remarks of the NAIC: "The bank regulators would not be suitable . . . as we know from the savings and loan experience, the regulators had no trouble subordinating regulation and disclosure to their primary function of protecting the banks."

40. Hal Scott, statement in response to the blueprint (www.capmktsreg.org/pdfs/4-4-08_hal_s_scott_press_release.pdf).

chartered insurance firms, along with the other financial institutions. While some, like Elizabeth Brown, argue that we should no longer regulate by labels and that it is hard to identify exactly what "insurance" is, it should be noted that the U.K.'s FSA organizes its regulatory efforts across nine sectors, including insurance.[41] Indeed, given the unique aspects of insurance, there should be a division of insurance within a U.S. FSA. This FSA would be an independent body, so that all supervision of financial institutions, including insurance, would be outside of the Treasury.

As the failure of Northern Rock in the United Kingdom demonstrates, even twin peaks can have coordination problems. A memorandum of understanding currently governs the relationship of the Bank of England, the FSA, and the U.K.'s Treasury in dealing with financial system issues. Going forward, the United Kingdom envisions the need for stronger coordination.[42] Any revamping of U.S. regulation should include a similar memorandum among U.S. regulators.

Consolidated regulation could increase efficiency and allow coordination between insurance regulators and financial regulators. This coordination is important for ensuring fair competition between insurance institutions and those financial institutions that offer similar products. Such coordination is also important in dealing with foreign states, as it ensures a unified voice for U.S. regulation and allows for a more rapid response to changing international events. According to Brown, other virtues of consolidated regulation may include better handling of issues unique to financial conglomerates (such as conflicts of interest), greater resistance to capture by a particular sector in financial services, and reduced confusion for consumers seeking information or to file a complaint.[43] And as the subprime crisis has taught us, coordination may prevent issues from falling through the jurisdictional cracks. On the other hand, a consolidated regulator might become large and unwieldy and unresponsive to the needs of small firms.

The Internal Structure

The design of the federal chartering agency's internal structure raises a number of issues. As demonstrated below, there is considerable harmony across lines in terms of solvency regulation. This is not surprising, given the fact that solvency is a firm-based, rather than a product-based, phenomenon—and given as well the trend toward convergence across product lines. Further, the major differences among

41. Brown (2005).
42. See for example Bank of England (2008).
43. Brown (2005).

lines arise in the area of consumer protection regulation. Since commercial insurance for sophisticated purchasers does not require market conduct regulation or examination and since it is a competitive business, the arguments for its regulation are lessened compared to personal lines or life insurance. The ultimate questions, then, are whether and how the whole or partial integration of auto (and other retail property-casualty) insurance may be effected.

The following three sections consider the internal structure of the federal chartering agency for three categories of insurance: life insurance, private passenger automobile insurance, and commercial general liability insurance.[44] No state has a distinct set of rules for each area, nor would such regulatory tailoring be sensible given the existence of common issues and the fact that many insurers offer multiple lines of insurance.

Currently, insurance companies are organized and chartered as life-health companies, as property-liability companies, or as specialty companies such as title insurers. Legally, a life-health insurer can offer various lines or products within its general area, such as term life policies, whole life policies, and annuities. Similarly, a property-casualty insurer may offer personal auto and homeowners as well as commercial lines like commercial multiperil and workers' compensation. It is common for a number of affiliated insurance companies to belong to a group owned by a parent or holding company. The companies within a group are divided along various dimensions, such as lines of insurance or products, geography, and underwriting standards. To some extent, the creation and focus of specific insurance companies within a group may be influenced by regulation. However, the formation of companies within a group also often reflects how a group wishes to organize its operations from a business perspective. The structure of insurance companies affects the way they might be regulated under an OFC.

The principal rationale for states to retain solvency regulation is their concern for consumer protection (such as for life insurance policyholders or for the maintenance of guaranty funds). However, maximum cost savings are achievable only if all these functions are regulated at the federal level. Further, any split of functions between the states and the federal government will be difficult to design and administer.

---

44. The insurance industry is essentially divided among three principal sectors: life insurance and annuities, accident and health insurance, and property-casualty insurance. Within each of these sectors, there are a number of lines of insurance, which constitute specific markets in which particular products or types of coverage are offered. For example, in the property-casualty sector, there are many lines of insurance, including private passenger auto, homeowners, workers' compensation, medical malpractice, and commercial general liability, among others.

Nonetheless, the Treasury blueprint apparently contemplates that there would be federal chartering by sector. Health insurance is explicitly excluded from the OFC. Thus for a given insurance holding company or parent firm, some of its companies and products could be regulated at the federal level and others at the state level. Another approach might be the licensing of types of regulation. Thus it would be possible but not optimal for firms to have the choice of being regulated at the federal level for aspects of regulation that do not vary by sector, with the states regulating areas that do vary.[45] However, the cleanest and most efficient solution would be to license firms, rather than sectors, lines, or functions. Indeed, we have no historic experience with federal licensing of financial products: the entire national bank experience is based on the chartering of firms.

Each insurance product may be sold in a more or less competitive market, face different noninsurance competitors, and give rise to more or less concern for consumer protection. As a result, state regulators have taken different approaches to the regulation of life, individual auto, and commercial insurance.

Life Insurance

Life insurance companies offer life insurance contracts and other financial products (such as annuities) to retail customers, businesses, and groups. The market for life insurance products is highly competitive, a situation enhanced by increasing competition from banking and securities products. As industry executives and observers note, this is not simply a matter of banks offering life insurance in the wake of the Gramm-Leach-Bliley Act but of a more fundamental convergence taking place in the financial services industry. Life insurance companies have been among those most interested in an OFC.[46]

45. Minimum capitalization requirements vary by line and by state. During the 1990s the National Association of Insurance Commissioners (NAIC) sought to harmonize state regulation by adopting model minimum risk-based capitalization (RBC) requirements for most lines (including life and property-casualty). See for example N.Y. Ins. L. sec. 4103; see also Ettlinger, Hamilton, and Krohm (1995). A multistate, multiline insurer generally must meet the greater of its minimum RBC requirements or the minimum capital requirements of each state in which it is licensed to do business. There is no reason that a federal regulator could not promulgate solvency regulations that would be not only equally sensitive to the different risks posed by different product lines but also more uniform.

46. See Grace and Klein (2007) for a discussion of competition in life insurance markets; also see chapter 7, this volume, for a more detailed discussion of the implications of the convergence of financial services markets.

Solvency Regulation

Life insurers are subject to solvency regulation in each of the states and territories in which they do business. Solvency regulation encompasses chartering and licensing and involves periodic financial reporting and examination requirements. An insurer chartered as either a life-health insurance company or a property-casualty company will be licensed to issue one or more lines within these broad categories.[47] In order to be chartered and licensed, insurers must meet minimum capital and surplus requirements, which vary by sector and line. Considerable uniformity already has been imposed upon states' capital and surplus by their adoption of the Risk-Based Capital Model Act promulgated by the NAIC. However, almost every state has retained its own fixed minimum capital and surplus requirements. A multistate, multiline insurer generally must meet the greater of NAIC's minimum risk-based capital requirements or the minimum capital requirements of each state in which it is licensed to do business.[48] In addition to minimum capital requirements, states regulate market entry through seasoning and other requirements. After becoming licensed, both life-health and property-casualty insurers must file annual and quarterly financial reports and submit to periodic full-scope, and occasional targeted, financial examinations.

Because the underwriting risks faced by life insurers are distinct (for example, the long time frame of life insurance contracts), state regulators have subjected these companies to chartering and licensing requirements and accounting standards that differ from those applied either to property-casualty insurers or to banks. Life insurers are subject to investment restrictions that differ from those imposed upon property-casualty insurers and are required to account differently for their policy reserves. Moreover, both life and property-casualty insurers must comply with accounting principles that are more conservative than those applied to banks. Insurers are required to file financial reports in keeping with statutory accounting principles (SAP) rather than generally accepted accounting principles (GAAP). SAP differs from GAAP in terms of the valuation, realization, and continuity issues imposed on reporting companies (SAP generally takes a liquidation rather than going-concern perspective). Otherwise,

47. The separation between life and property-casualty insurers seems to be the historical legacy of "monoline" insurance regulation, which began with the New York legislature's 1849 decision to require each insurance company to issue only a single line. Insurers began offering multiple lines during the early twentieth century; however, legislation providing for the licensing of multiline insurers was not adopted by the states until after 1945.

48. Capital requirements for insurance companies are explained in greater detail by Klein (2005).

the financial reporting and examination requirements imposed upon the life insurance industry by state regulators are similar to those imposed upon the banking industry by the OCC.

Many states already base their financial reporting requirements upon universal standards prescribed by the NAIC and accept zone examinations of multistate insurers; therefore, insurers and the federal regulator will reap limited (though welcome) cost savings from a single federal reporting and examination system.[49] However, federal regulatory oversight of insurer solvency could further enhance the efficiency of the insurance industry. A federal regulator could abolish the traditional division of solvency regulation between life and property-casualty insurance. While these types of insurance face distinct risks, so do the different individual sublines of property-casualty insurance, which nevertheless may be offered by a single insurer.[50] Following state regulators' shift to a risk-based capital model, the federal regulator may contemplate chartering consolidated federal insurance companies authorized to do business in any sector or line of insurance, provided they have adequate risk-adjusted capital and surplus.[51]

In addition, a federal regulator could consider either the elimination of capital or surplus requirements for life insurance companies or a convergence with banking capital requirements and accounting standards. To the extent that the capital requirements of life insurers are more conservative than those of banks and securities firms offering similar products, insurers will be at a competitive disadvantage. The reconciliation of SAP and GAAP would eliminate those inconsistencies that may give either insurers or their competitors an advantage in the market for financial services and would provide regulatory efficiencies (consistency and comparability) as financial services converge. Finally, a federal regulator should ensure relative ease of entry and exit.

Rates, Policy Forms, and Consumer Protection

Life insurance rates generally are lightly regulated or unregulated by the states. However, this light touch is significantly offset by requirements in most states that

49. The federal regulator may reduce costs by conducting financial examination on an as-needed or prioritized basis (that is, in response to a complaint or lawbreaking) rather than on a strictly periodic basis. The current proposal would require the commissioner to conduct an on-site examination of each federally chartered insurance company at least once every three years; however, insurance agencies would be subject to examination only in response to a complaint or lawbreaking. See NIA sec. 1125.

50. See for example N.Y. Ins. L. secs. 4101–02.

51. The current proposal would not allow a national insurer to hold licenses for both life and property-casualty insurance. See NIA sec. 1203.

policy forms be subject to prior approval by the state insurance department. Thus in order to introduce a new product a life insurer must seek the approval of the insurance regulator in each state in which it does business. Life insurers also are subject to state market conduct regulation and examination (such as advertising restrictions).

Life insurers report significant direct and indirect costs arising from this contradictory and fragmented mélange of state regulation.[52] For example, life insurers may have to create different versions of products, tailored to the regulations of particular states, and may employ multiple state-based compliance staffs. This puts life insurers at a competitive disadvantage vis-à-vis banks and securities firms.

Unification of the regulation of rates and policy forms in a single federal regulator obviously would reduce compliance costs to life insurers; elimination of prior approval of rates and policy forms would be a further boon, enabling life insurers to compete with banks and securities firms on a more even playing field.[53] Because the market for life insurance products is highly competitive, the main consumer protection issue facing the federal regulator will be that of retail consumers' informational inadequacy. This consumer protection should take the form of simple regulations regarding market conduct, along with efforts to inform retail consumers.

Commercial Insurance

Property-casualty companies offer commercial general liability insurance to businesses, often along with other lines like commercial auto and workers' compensation insurance. The market for commercial insurance is highly competitive. The buyers of commercial insurance vary greatly in size and in terms of their needs for insurance coverage. Small businesses tend to purchase standardized insurance policies, while larger firms are more likely to arrange customized insurance contracts to meet their specific needs. The sophistication of commercial insurance buyers also varies directly with their size; large firms are relatively sophisticated and benefit little if at all from regulatory protections.

Solvency Regulation

Like life insurers, commercial property-casualty insurers are subject to minimum capital and surplus requirements for chartering and licensing as well as to periodic

52. See ACLI (2005) for the industry's view of this problem.

53. As noted above, the NIA would establish a file-and-use system for life insurance policy forms and allow the commissioner to exempt particular categories from the filing requirement. Life insurers would be allowed to classify policyholders and set rates freely. NIA sec. 1213.

financial reporting and examination by state insurance regulators. The rationale for these requirements obviously is to ensure the solvency of insurers, who have promised to deliver future contingent benefits to policyholders or their beneficiaries. A federal insurance regulator could lower regulatory costs through more uniform and consistent chartering, licensing, and financial reporting requirements. And competition may be enhanced by a consolidated federal insurance company option.

Insofar as these products are sold in competitive markets to presumptively sophisticated buyers, a federal insurance regulator may decide to eliminate capital and surplus requirements altogether for commercial insurers. Commercial insurers face increased competition from the growing market in alternative risk-transfer mechanisms, such as credit derivatives. To the extent that suppliers of alternative risk-transfer products are subject to lower (or no) capital requirements, prices and consumer choice may be distorted in the market for commercial lines. Minimum capital and surplus requirements also hamper the entry of new commercial insurers, whose products might find willing, sophisticated buyers. Financial reporting and examination may be justified insofar as it cost-effectively reduces the risk of insolvency, in part by eliminating duplicative diligence costs undertaken by customers.

Rates, Policy Forms, and Consumer Protection

Like life insurance, commercial insurance enjoys de facto rate deregulation but (rather surprisingly) remains subject to considerable policy form regulation.[54] Over time, many states have deregulated commercial insurance for larger buyers, but the pattern of deregulation is inconsistent and subject to state-specific criteria.[55] Prior approval of policy forms increases commercial insurers' time to market, disadvantaging them vis-à-vis securities firms offering alternative risk-transfer products. As with life insurance, it is not clear what purpose prior approval of policy forms serves when rates are deregulated.[56] Other than fraud investigation, consumer protection issues are not implicated by commercial general liability insurance.

---

54. See Butler (2002).

55. For example, the states employ different criteria for determining how "large" or "sophisticated" a firm must be in order for it to purchase insurance that is not subject to the rate and form regulation that applies to insurance purchased by smaller firms.

56. As noted above, the NIA would establish a use-and-file system for property-casualty insurers and would prohibit the commissioner from requiring property-casualty insurers to use "any particular rate, rating element, price, or form." NIA sec. 1214.

Automobile Insurance

Property-casualty insurers also offer voluntary auto insurance to retail consumers in strictly regulated markets. Universal coverage often is mandated or encouraged by regulators, and residual market mechanisms have been created to provide insurance to individuals who cannot obtain coverage from a private carrier. Consumer groups have objected to the extension of federal chartering to auto insurance and other retail property-casualty insurance on the grounds that the federal regulator would be unable or unwilling to provide adequate consumer protection.

Solvency Regulation

Retail auto insurance, like other lines, is subject to minimum capital and surplus requirements for chartering and licensing and to periodic financial reporting and examination by state insurance regulators. The rationale for such supervision is strong in the case of auto insurance, where it may be necessary to protect consumers with limited information and monitoring capacity from unscrupulous insurers. The basic contours of federal solvency regulation and its benefits are substantially the same as those discussed above. The need for clear communication between financial supervision and consumer affairs bureaus is greatest for proper solvency regulation of auto insurers.

Rates, Policy Forms, and Consumer Protection

Auto insurance regulation touches all aspects of consumer protection, including rates, policy forms, market conduct, consumer education, and consumer complaints. Some states strictly regulate rates and policy forms. For example, until 2008 Massachusetts set uniform rates and rating classes for insurance companies. It still requires prior approval of rates. However, rate and policy form regulation differs greatly among states. Two prior approval states may even impose different burdens upon insurers, depending upon the stringency and speed of review as well as the use of such regulation to suppress rates.[57] Moreover, rate and policy form regulation is intimately tied to state policies favoring universal coverage. State regulators are strict in enforcing market conduct regulation and swift in responding to consumer complaints.

The variety of rate and policy form regulations among states imposes considerable direct and indirect costs upon auto insurers and results in various cross-subsidies among consumers with different risk profiles. Even if a federal regulator

---

57. See Harrington (2000).

required prior approval of rates and policy forms, regulatory costs would be low-ered. However, because the market for voluntary auto insurance in most states is highly competitive, a federal regulator may choose to deregulate rates or policy forms. Illinois completely deregulated rates for voluntary auto insurance in 1971 (it still regulates insolvency, market conduct, and other areas). Observers report that in Illinois auto insurance is widely available and rates are competitive; more-over, deregulation seems to have had no adverse effect upon loss ratios, the size of the uninsured and residual market, or insurer solvency. Competition in a dereg-ulated rate environment may be buttressed by modification of the federal antitrust exemption for national insurers, although it is not clear that this would have any material effect on markets that are already highly competitive.[58]

Even in a competitive, rate-deregulated national auto insurance market, the federal insurance regulator may desire to regulate market conduct for the protec-tion of consumers. Such an initiative may require a distinct division of market conduct and consumer protection dedicated to retail policyholders and benefici-aries. The more lines that can be regulated at the federal level that raise such con-sumer concerns, the more justification there would be for a separate division.

Residual Market Mechanisms

To guarantee the availability of auto insurance, every state has a residual market facility (for example, an assigned risk pool) for drivers unable to secure voluntary auto insurance. Like state guaranty plans (discussed below), auto insurers doing business in a state participate in its residual market mechanism on a pro rata basis. State workers' compensation insurance generally has a similar mechanism. The NIA would not create a national residual market mechanism. Instead, federally chartered insurers would remain subject to applicable state law relating to partic-ipation in a residual market mechanism. The Treasury blueprint seems to take the same approach.

If auto insurance were offered an OFC, the internal structure of the federal reg-ulator would be affected greatly by the legislative decision regarding the creation of a national residual market mechanism. If national insurers were required to par-ticipate in state residual market facilities, regulatory supervision would be divided between the federal government (solvency and consumer protection) and state governments (residual market compliance), which may raise not only direct com-

---

58. California's Proposition 103 did this at a state level. In chapter 5 Martin Grace and Robert Klein argue that the industry's current limited antitrust exemption has not promoted anticompeti-tive behavior.

pliance costs to insurers but also indirect costs related to increased time to market for new products.

There are two other alternatives: the creation of a national residual market mechanism and the preemption of state residual market mechanisms without the creation of a new one. Obviously, a national residual market mechanism would require national administration of a regulatory function unique to this kind of insurance. More important, national pooling would alter the spread of the costs of underwriting losses among insurers. If broader spreading of risks were to result in cost savings to national insurers, presumably they (and their policyholders) would benefit, to the detriment of state-chartered insurers. On the other hand, those insurance companies that predominantly insure policies in states with safer drivers might believe that wider risk spreading would raise costs. Abolishing all residual risk insurance would not be a practical alternative.

Guaranty Funds

The state guaranty fund system, an important facet of insurance regulation, has been a cause of concern for federal chartering. These funds are in place to compensate for the losses suffered by third parties and policyholders due to insurance company insolvency. Since insurance regulators are responsible for preventing this insolvency, guaranty funds may be framed as a sort of product warranty for the quality of regulation.[59] The general perception is that the administration of state guaranty funds has been one of the most effective components of state insurance regulation. The proposed federal legislation and the Treasury blueprint would keep the state guaranty system intact and require federally chartered insurance firms to participate in the system.

States began to create these funds in 1969, at the behest of insurance companies and perhaps in response to pressure for federal regulation. The first wave of funds provided protection for life-health insurers, with subsequent waves spreading coverage to property-casualty insurers. These product divisions remain today and often include subdivisions, or accounts, for particular lines of insurance. Assessments for policyholders' claims against insolvent insurers are made against the appropriate account. The funds typically are organized as compulsory membership, nonprofit associations of all insurance companies licensed in the state. They are administered by a board composed of representatives from insurance companies and the state insurance regulator, with some states including representatives of the

59. Ely (2000).

public as well. Most state guaranty assessments are not risk sensitive, which has been a source of criticism. Also, some states allow insurers, especially life-health insurers, to offset the taxes they pay on premiums by the amount of guaranty fund assessments paid. As a result, some of the cost of insolvency losses is passed along to taxpayers, who must make up for any shortfall in taxation created by these offsets.

The two most often praised features of the state guaranty fund system are its basis for assessments and its level of coverage. With the exception of New York, every state administers its guaranty fund on a postassessment basis. That means that member insurance companies do not pay into a fund until around the end of the year—and only to the extent necessary to compensate for losses. This may be contrasted with funding on a preassessment basis, wherein companies would pay into the fund before losses are known, as is the case with the FDIC fund for banks. In 2007 the New York state legislature took advantage of its state's preassessment fund by siphoning off the fund's resources for general spending. This suggests that any prefunding mechanism needs to be highly insulated from the political process.

Additionally, state guaranty funds generally have low coverage limits. Commentators hail these limits as promoting efficient behavior by insurance companies. Due to the low limits, companies have incentives to self-insure by controlling their risk of insolvency. These incentives tend to minimize losses. Were coverage limits to be higher, insurance companies would be more likely to engage in risky behavior, such as writing more high-risk policies, due to moral hazard. These are the same issues encountered in setting the level of FDIC insurance for banks.

Owing to this positive appraisal of state guaranty funds, many commentators have adopted an approach along the lines of, If it ain't broke, don't fix it. Indeed, postassessment funding and low coverage limits suggest that state guaranty funds do not suffer from the same weaknesses of overregulation and inefficiency that might justify more general reform of insurance regulation. Of course, postassessment funding and low coverage could also be implemented at the federal level.

If it is assumed that state guaranty funds operate well and should continue in operation, then the question is whether an OFC might impair the effectiveness of the state guaranty system. There are a few reasons to think that such impairment might occur. First, federal regulators might worry about relying upon state funds in the case of insolvency. If a large national insurance company were to fail, then some state funds might have insufficient assessment resources to compensate for the losses of third parties and policyholders within that state's jurisdiction. Second, state funds do not exhibit a uniform level of protection, which means that different federally chartered insurers would have different insolvency protection, depending upon where they operate.[60] Federal regulators might insist upon uniform minimum standards for the operation of state guaranty funds. Unsurprisingly, the insurance industry and state regulators have generally supported the state guaranty approach.[61]

However, federal regulation with state guarantees necessitates severing the link between regulation and guaranty that is the backbone of the idea of guaranty as product warranty. This idea is premised upon the notion that regulators will act more effectively if they must bear the cost of poor regulation. This efficacy will not obtain if state funds bear the costs of poor federal regulation. It was precisely this concern that led to federal involvement in safety and soundness regulation for state-chartered banks using federal deposit insurance.[62]

Concerns about the potentially adverse impact of federal regulation upon the state guaranty system might be grounds for installing a federal guaranty fund for federally chartered insurers. Such a fund would successfully tie federal regulation to a federal guaranty, thereby satisfying the product warranty rationale. There might also be some subsidiary benefits of a federal fund. It would imply uniformity of protection for federally chartered insurers. If a diverse group of insurers choose to operate under federal charter, then there might be better pooling of risk as compared with state funds, which have a more limited geographic base from which to draw members.

Additionally, there would be no passing off of externalities from one state to another.[63] Currently, state regulators have less incentive to regulate multistate insurers because other states' funds share the costs of insolvency. A federal fund would eliminate this practice for federally chartered insurers, because the federal fund would not be able to pass the buck of insolvency on to other funds. On the other hand, some argue that the possibility of externalities to insolvency actually improves state regulation because it gives state regulators an incentive to monitor the quality of regulation in domiciliary states.[64]

Were legislators to opt for establishing a federal guaranty fund, then there are a number of structural concerns they would need to address. As discussed earlier, most state funds have divisions and subdivisions keyed to different insurance products. The presence and extent of such divisions in a federal fund would be

60. "Coverage limits vary from state to state, up to $500,000, by type of insurance product and by type of liability (prepaid premiums versus actual loss, cash values versus life insurance death benefits, and so forth)." Ely (2000, p. 142).

61. See Harrington (2000).

62. Ely (2000).

63. See, for example, Grace and Phillips (2007).

64. Macey and Miller (2003).

something to be decided. Further, legislators would have to consider whether state-chartered insurers would be eligible for the fund, just as state-chartered banks are eligible for federal deposit insurance. Another question is how premiums would be assessed. Risk-based premiums seem ideal, even though they are difficult to implement. If the federal guaranty fund is structured like federal deposit insurance, then it might even make sense for the FDIC to administer the fund. Regardless, the relationship between the fund and federal regulators, possibly including a federal insurance regulator, should be clarified. Additionally, a number of unique concerns would arise during the transition by insurers from membership in state funds to membership in a federal fund.[65]

If, as contemplated by the blueprint, lines and not firms were federally chartered, the administration of the guaranty funds would become even more complicated. The same firm could be engaged in state-chartered and federally chartered activities, and the states would obviously have an interest in the solvency of state activities. Under this scenario, state guaranty funds could guarantee state lines, while the federal guaranty fund would guaranty federal lines.

Conclusions

Several important issues need to be considered in designing a regulatory structure for an OFC. First and foremost, the objectives of insurance regulation and the rationale for an OFC must guide regulatory design. Second, lessons learned from existing federal and state financial services regulators regarding the external structure of such an agency must be borne in mind. Chief among these lessons is the disjunction between the accelerating convergence of financial services and the current fragmentation of our regulatory system. Third, it would be preferable to charter firms, rather than lines or regulatory functions, at the federal level. The extent of federal chartering of lines would be a major factor in designing the internal structure of the federal agency. Fourth, the participation of national insurers in state residual market mechanisms and guaranty funds must be determined, with reference to both consumer protection and efficiency goals. Finally, in the medium term, insurance supervision and regulation should be part of a new twin-peak regulatory function, consisting of the Federal Reserve and a new U.S. FSA.

In the shorter term, while the federal government should have primacy in the regulation of insurance, it would be a mistake to establish an independent Office

---

65. Examples include need for exit fees to prevent exodus from state to federal regulation in lieu of an assessment due to failure of a large company and for a mechanism for dealing with insolvency of newly chartered federal companies (Broome, 2002).

of National Insurance (as contemplated by the NIA), which would further fragment federal regulation of financial services. Neither would it be wise to consolidate federal regulation of banking and insurance under a single agency (a point
upon which both the NAIC and multistate insurance companies agree). In our
view, the optimal external structure would involve the establishment of a distinct
insurance regulator subject to oversight by the President's Working Group on
Financial Markets. This approach is most likely to provide the greatest benefits arising from an OFC—cost savings from uniformity, economies of scale, and appropriate deregulation, along with the benefits of coordinated financial services
regulation—at the lowest cost. It also would combine regulatory expertise and
independence with strong political oversight and accountability. Finally, it might
serve as a first step toward consolidated federal financial services regulation, beginning with the reconciliation of capital requirements and accounting standards for
all financial services firms.

The federal regulator of insurance should provide a true federal option:
national insurers should be subject only to federal regulation of their solvency and
product offerings and should be able to offer many lines of insurance. A federal
regulator would be well situated to set and enforce appropriate risk-based capital
requirements for national insurers, based upon their product lines and other relevant risk factors. Indeed, a federal regulator could consider removing the traditional barrier between life and property-casualty insurers. The benefits of an OFC
would be maximized—and the potential for duplicative and conflicting regulation reduced—by allowing national insurers to offer as many lines of insurance as
possible. Retaining state policy form regulation for national auto and workers'
compensation insurance (as contemplated by the NIA) would reduce greatly the
benefits of rate deregulation for these lines, as we have seen from states' "deregulation" of commercial insurance. Alternatively, limiting national property-casualty
insurers to commercial insurance would require them to charter separate workers'
compensation companies in each state in order to provide "full service."

Clearly, licensing national insurers to offer certain lines, such as auto insurance,
would implicate important consumer protection issues. Generally speaking, the
regulation of insurers, like that of banks, should be prudential in approach and
effected through examination. However, the more "retail" lines offered by a
national insurer, the more a federal regulator would be required to promulgate
market conduct regulation, investigate consumer complaints, enforce penalties for
violations, and provide for consumer education. If such lines are offered, the federal regulator should create a distinct division of market conduct and consumer
protection dedicated to retail policyholders and beneficiaries.

Furthermore, the relationship of national insurers to state residual market mechanisms and guaranty funds must be determined. The creation of a national residual market mechanism and a national guaranty fund would require federal administration of regulatory functions unique to insurance—and historically the province of the states. However, federal administration of these functions would enable national pooling of residual and insolvency risks and would allow for regulatory innovations (for example, risk-based premiums for the national guaranty fund). Indeed, either or both pools could be open to the participation of state-chartered insurers, allowing them to enjoy any economies of scale provided by federal administration. An important issue to consider is that allowing national insurers to participate in state residual market mechanisms and guaranty funds, however well administered, might lead to different or even contradictory regulation of federally chartered insurers. In contrast, a national guaranty fund would allow the federal government to consolidate solvency regulation from "cradle to grave," albeit at some cost and risk.

To sum up, the design of a regulatory structure for an OFC for insurance should provide for strong and efficient federal regulation of what is a national and international financial service activity. Insofar as is possible, the federal option should give insurers the choice to be subject only to federal, rather than state, regulation and law enforcement. And insofar as the convergence of financial services is accelerating, the creation of a federal option should be a first step toward more complete consolidation of federal financial services regulation. Such a system would level the playing field both nationally and internationally and provide consumers with the most efficient and transparent options.

The discussion here assumes that federal chartering would be optional. However, it may well be that federal regulation, if not chartering, will become mandatory for the systemically important insurance companies, given the Federal Reserve's $85 billion loan to AIG in September 2008 (accompanied by a 79.9 percent equity interest), later supplemented by an additional loan of $37.8 billion in October, and still a third round of net additional funding by the Treasury of $25 billion in November (Treasury bought $40 billion of preferred stock, while the Federal Reserve reduced its September loan by $15 billion). On top of this actual funding, two new credit facilities established in November, totaling $52.5 billion, further increased the Federal Reserve's potential exposure. One should also note that insurance companies are generally eligible for Treasury assistance under the Troubled Asset Relief Program (TARP).[66] As the AIG case

---

66. Emergency Economic Stabilization Act of 2008, H.R. 1424, sec. 3(5) specifically includes a state regulated insurance company as a "financial institution" eligible for assistance under sec. 101.

shows, there are large insurers that have a potential for imposing systemic risk to the economy. If such firms are to be rescued by the federal government, it seems reasonable to insist that the federal government have supervisory and regulatory powers over such firms. This issue is outside the scope of this chapter but is illustrative of the continuing evolution of regulatory issues facing the financial services industries.

References

Bank of England. 2008. H.M. Treasury and Financial Services Authority. CM 7308. *Financial Stability and Depositor Protection: Strengthening the Framework.*

Broome, Lissa. 2002. "A Federal Charter Option for Insurance Companies: Lessons from the Bank Experience." Abstract. University of North Carolina School of Law (http://ssrn.com/abstract=334440).

Brown, Elizabeth F. 2005. "E Pluribus Unum—Out of Many, One: Why the United States Needs a Single Financial Services Agency." *University of Miami Business Law Review* 14, no. 1: 10–19.

Butler, Henry N., and Larry E. Ribstein. 2008. "A Single-License Approach to Regulating Insurance." Northwestern Law and Economics Research Paper 08-10. Northwestern University.

Butler, Richard J. 2002. "Form Regulation in Commercial Insurance." In *Deregulating Property-Liability Insurance: Restoring Competition and Increasing Market Efficiency,* edited by J. David Cummins, pp. 321–60. Washington: AEI-Brookings Joint Center for Regulatory Studies.

Chesson, Jack. 2000. "The Views of the National Association of Insurance Commissioners." In *Optional Federal Chartering and Regulation of Insurance Companies,* edited by Peter J. Wallison, pp. 73–75. Washington: American Enterprise Institute.

Cummins, J. David, and Mary Weiss. 1993. "Measuring Cost Efficiency in the Property-Liability Insurance Industry." *Journal of Banking and Finance* 17 nos. 2–3: 463–81.

Day, John. 1970. *Economic Regulation of Insurance.* Government Printing Office.

Ely, Bert. 2000. "The Fate of the State Guaranty Funds after the Advent of Federal Insurance Chartering." In *Optional Federal Chartering and Regulation of Insurance Companies,* edited by Peter J. Wallison, pp. 135–52. Washington: American Enterprise Institute.

Ettlinger, Kathleen, Karen Hamilton, and Gregory Krohm. 1995. *State Insurance Regulation.* Malvern, Pa.: Insurance Institute of America.

Grace, Martin F., and Robert W. Klein. 2000. "Efficiency Implications of Alternative Regulatory Insurance Structures." In *Optional Federal Chartering and Regulation of Insurance Companies,* edited by Peter J. Wallison, pp. 89–131. Washington: American Enterprise Institute.

———. 2007. "The Effects of an Optional Federal Charter on Competition in the U.S. Insurance Industry." Washington: American Council of Life Insurers.

Grace, Martin F., Robert W. Klein, and Richard D. Phillips. 2007. "Insurance Company Failures: Why Do They Cost So Much?" Washington: American Council of Life Insurers.

Grace, Martin F., and Richard D. Phillips. 2007. "The Allocation of Government Regulatory Supervision within a Federal System of Government: Fiscal Federalism and the Case of Insurance Regulatory Oversight." *Journal of Risk and Insurance* 74, no. 1: 207–38.

Hanson, Jon S. 1977. "The Disadvantages of Federal Insurance Regulation as Highlighted by the Brooke Bill." *Forum* 13: 605–22.

Harrington, Scott. 2000. *Insurance Deregulation and the Public Interest.* Washington: AEI-Brookings Joint Center for Regulatory Studies.

————. 2006. *Federal Chartering of Insurance Companies: Options and Alternatives for Transforming Insurance Regulation.* Policy Brief 2006-PB-02. Indianapolis: Networks Financial Institute.

Inman, Robert, and Daniel Rubenfeld. 1997. "Rethinking Federalism." *Journal of Economic Perspectives* 11, no. 4: 43–64.

Jayaratne, Jith, and Philip E. Strahan. 1996. "The Finance-Growth Nexus: Evidence from Bank Branch Deregulation." *Quarterly Journal of Economics* 111, no. 3: 639–70.

Klein, Robert W. 2005. *A Regulator's Introduction to the Insurance Industry.* Kansas City, Mo.: National Association of Insurance Commissioners.

National Association of Insurance Commissioners. 2006. *Annual Statement.* Kansas City, Mo.

————. 2007. *Compendium of State Laws on Insurance Topics.* Kansas City, Mo.

————. 2008. *Model Laws, Regulations, and Guidelines.* Kansas City, Mo.

National Association of Mutual Insurance Companies. 2008. *Insurance Regulation.* Washington (www.namic.org/fedkey/08regulation.asp).

Oates, Wallace E. 1972. *Fiscal Federalism.* New York: Harcourt Brace Jovanovich.

Pottier, Steven W. 2007. "State Insurance Regulation of Life Insurers: Implications for Economic Efficiency and Financial Strength." Report to the American Council of Life Insurers. University of Georgia.

Randall, Susan. 1999. "Insurance Regulation in the United States: Regulatory Federalism and the National Association of Insurance Commissioners." *Florida State Law Review* 26, no. 3: 625–99.

Regan, Laureen. 2007. "The Option Federal Charter: Implications for Life Insurance Producers." Report to the American Council of Life Insurers. Temple University.

U.S. Department of the Treasury. 2008. *Blueprint for a Modernized Financial Regulatory Structure.*

U.S. Government Accountability Office. 2002. "State Insurance Regulation." Testimony before the Subcommittee on Capital Markets, Insurance, and Government-Sponsored Enterprises, Committee on Financial Services, U.S. House of Representatives.

Yuengert, Andrew. 1993. "The Measurement of Efficiency in Life Insurance: Estimates of a Mixed Normal-Gamma Error Model." *Journal of Banking and Finance* 17, nos. 2–3: 483–96.

4

Dual Insurance Chartering: Potential Consequences

Robert Detlefsen

The release in March 2008 of the U.S. Treasury Department's *Blueprint for a Modernized Financial Regulatory Structure* added fuel to a long-simmering debate over the relative merits of state and federal insurance regulation.[1] The blueprint was developed in response to concerns expressed by some policymakers and capital market participants that the current financial services regulatory structure is ill suited to the globalization of capital markets and the increasing complexity of new products. Examining the history and current status of U.S. financial regulation, the blueprint focuses on four sectors: depository institutions, futures, securities, and insurance. The blueprint's verdict on insurance is foreshadowed by its observation that "having the functional regulation of a major national financial services industry such as insurance rest in a fragmented and non-uniform state-by-state regulatory system is unique to the United States. Other developed countries have consolidated insurance regulatory regimes, and some have moved to a single consolidated regulator for all financial institutions."[2] To the blueprint's authors, it could hardly be more obvious that this country's multijurisdictional approach to insurance regulation is a quaint anachronism that is ripe for overhaul.

1. U.S. Department of the Treasury (2008), p. 127.
2. U.S. Department of the Treasury (2008), p. 127.

The solution the blueprint proposes is an optional federal charter (OFC) for insurance companies that would allow insurers to choose federal rather than state regulation. As it happens, a nearly identical proposal, the National Insurance Act of 2007 (NIA), has been introduced in both houses of Congress.[3] For ease of exposition, the following discussion focuses on the OFC proposal described in the Treasury blueprint.

To explain how an insurance OFC would work, proponents typically draw analogies to the dual-chartering structure under which banks operate.[4] The competition between state and federal bank regulators said to be promoted by the dual-banking system "keeps both sets of regulators alert to changes in the economy and financial system that alter the competitive environment for banks."[5] Such regulatory competition is fostered by the ability of banks to readily switch their charters from state to federal and from federal to state. According to its proponents, an insurance OFC "will set up a similar competitive environment in the insurance industry, improving conditions for all insurers, even those that remain state-chartered and regulated."[6]

While the concept of an OFC seems simple enough, the National Insurance Act in which it is embodied is a testament to the extraordinary complexity surrounding its implementation. The bill weighs in at 330 pages, nearly a third of which describe the powers of the Office of National Insurance (ONI), a new regulatory agency that would take its place within the sprawling federal bureaucracy. In their assessments of the OFC proposal, advocates and scholars alike focus on the structural and jurisdictional features of an OFC regime, assuming that salutary policy outcomes will result if the implementation of an OFC is handled correctly.[7]

---

3. S. 40, 110 Cong. 1 sess., May 24, 2007; H.R. 3200, 110 Cong. 1 sess., July 26, 2007. The blueprint notes in a footnote that "there are currently pending bills in both the House (H.R. 3200) and Senate (S. 40) entitled 'The National Insurance Act of 2007' that would create an OFC and establish an ONI. It is not Treasury's intent at this time to opine on the details or merits of the pending legislation, but rather to set forth general guidelines as to the basics that it believes any ultimate legislation should contain in establishing an ONI and creating an OFC. That said, there are many positive attributes to these bills as they address many of the concepts raised in this report." U.S. Department of the Treasury (2008), p. 128, n. 110.

4. The blueprint, for example, states that the OFC it proposes is "similar to the current dual chartering system for banking." U.S. Department of the Treasury (2008), p. 126.

5. Wallison (2006), p. 4.

6. Wallison (2006), p. 4.

7. England (2005).

Critics, however, identify several structural pitfalls, including the likelihood that a dual system of regulation would create inequities among firms competing within the same markets; confusion among consumers as to who is responsible for regulating their insurer and the rules that apply to that insurer; and a new federal bureaucracy. Moreover, the presumption that federal regulators would be more competent than state regulators seems dubious in light of the performance of federal regulators responsible for overseeing financial institutions and markets that are currently mired in crisis. By contrast, the insurance solvency regulatory system, which is already uniform and highly coordinated among the states, has performed remarkably well under conditions that have threatened and in some cases destroyed the solvency of federally regulated banks and financial holding companies. In this chapter I examine several additional problems associated with the OFC proposal that have generally been overlooked.

Any discussion of insurance regulation must begin by acknowledging the remarkable heterogeneity of the insurance enterprise. The functional and operational differences among the three basic types of insurance—life, health, and property-casualty—are substantial enough that they are best understood, at least for regulatory purposes, as distinct industries. Thus structural regulatory reform that leads to generally positive outcomes in life insurance may have negative consequences for property-casualty insurance, and vice versa.[8] This stark reality is not easily reconciled with the current enthusiasm in some quarters (and nowhere more evident than in the Treasury blueprint) for new approaches to financial services regulation designed to streamline or consolidate existing regulatory structures, agencies, and jurisdictions.

Furthermore, while overall dissatisfaction with the current state of insurance regulation in the United States is probably as widespread among property-casualty insurers as it is among life and health insurers, the particular sources of discontent vary considerably across the three insurance sectors. For example, while both life insurance and property-casualty insurance sectors are harmed by cumbersome and time-consuming multijurisdictional licensing requirements and speed-to-market impediments, property-casualty insurance markets are particularly distorted by rate regulation and restrictions on underwriting freedom. This type of regulation leads to adverse selection, moral hazard, cross-subsidization of risk among insureds, and reduced availability of insurance, particularly for personal automobile and

8. Indeed, the most persuasive arguments for an OFC focus primarily if not exclusively on life insurance. See for example Grace and Klein (2007); Bair and others (2004).

homeowners coverage. Such regulation exists to varying degrees in nearly every state, especially in those with large markets.

The specific question addressed in this chapter is whether an OFC will significantly reduce the extent of harmful, politically opportunistic regulation of rates and underwriting practices in property-casualty insurance. I argue that there is ample reason to doubt that an OFC will have this effect. Put differently, there is little reason to believe that, over time, an OFC would not replicate many of the same market-distorting inefficiencies currently found in the most dysfunctional state regulatory regimes. If we cannot be reasonably confident that an OFC will produce efficiency-enhancing reforms, the case for its enactment is weak. If, at the same time, there are valid reasons to fear that an OFC could worsen the state of insurance regulation, the case against its adoption would seem compelling.

A Dual Bank-Chartering System as a Model for Competitive Insurance Regulation

Because the current dual-chartering system for banks is the model for the proposed optional chartering system for insurance, some attention must be paid to that system. Henry Butler and Jonathan Macey argue convincingly that the United States never intended to have a dual-chartering system for banks, nor was the system intended to engender competition between state and federal regulators, if by competition one means an environment in which each regulator attempts to increase its share of the "market" for regulation by attracting additional chartered entities.[9] Rather, the dual-banking system is a residue of a deliberate effort by the federal government to usurp state authority over banking regulation and extract rents from banks. That effort has largely succeeded, according to Butler and Macey.

The first banks in the United States were established under state charters, and while Congress eventually chartered several banks, state-chartered banking remained the norm throughout the first half of the nineteenth century. That changed with the onset of the Civil War, an event that greatly expanded the size of the federal government and the scope of its authority. Thus in 1863 Congress passed the National Bank Act not so much to improve the quality of bank regulation as to raise funds to finance the Union war effort. It would do this by creating a uniform currency of national banknotes and selling these notes to the public. To maximize revenue, the act also imposed a 2 percent tax on state banknotes. Congress

9. Butler and Macey (1988), p. 678.

expected that state banks would switch to a national charter and issue national banknotes to avoid paying the tax.[10] The resulting federal bank monopoly would generate even more revenue for the federal government. When the 2 percent tax turned out to be an insufficient inducement to state banks to switch their charters, Congress in 1865 increased the tax on state banknotes to 10 percent. The clear intention of Congress was not to offer banks a federal charter as an *option* to state charters but rather to have federal regulation of banks supplant state regulation of banks.[11] The strategy failed only because of the advent of checking accounts, which banks were able to offer as inexpensive substitutes for banknotes.[12]

Today, competition between state bank regulators and federal bank regulators is largely illusory. In reality, the dual-bank regulatory system is one in which "Congress delegates the authority to regulate banks not only to federal regulators such as the FDIC and the Comptroller of the Currency, but also to individual states and state banking authorities."[13] Butler and Macey attribute the dominance of federal authority in bank regulation to several factors that are unique to banking, such as the necessity of obtaining federal deposit insurance, but also to at least one factor that is relevant to insurance regulation, the supremacy clause of the U.S. Constitution, which Congress uses "to force the states to accept their limited role in the regulation of banks."[14]

Indeed, the threat of federal preemption would loom large under an OFC not least because state-based insurance regulation would continue to operate under the provisions of the McCarran-Ferguson Act.[15] Far from constituting a form of "reverse preemption," as some commentators aver, McCarran-Ferguson provides for a limited delegation of federal authority to the states that is fully consistent with Congress's preemption authority under the supremacy clause.[16] The act permits state insurance law to override federal law but only to the extent that states actively regulate insurance. Moreover, the act preserves Congress's ability to trump state insurance regulation at any time; Congress need only enact statutes that pertain specifically to the business of insurance. Indeed, in 2008 Congress considered several bills that would profoundly affect the business practices of insurers.

10. Broome (2002), pp. 13–14.
11. Broome (2002), pp. 13–14.
12. Butler and Macey (1988), p. 681.
13. Butler and Macey (1988), p. 679.
14. Butler and Macey (1988), p. 679.
15. P.L. 15, March 9, 1945 (codified at 15 U.S.C. secs. 1101–15).
16. See for example Scott (2008), p. 1; U.S. Department of the Treasury (2008), pp. 62–63.

It is important to remember that the federal system established by the Constitution assigns primacy to Congress in the exercise of its enumerated powers. That Congress's authority to regulate interstate commerce permits it to regulate the business of insurance has not been in doubt since 1944, when the U.S. Supreme Court decided the case of *United States* v. *South-Eastern Underwriters Association*.[17] Any attempt to create a regulatory system that assigns a formal role to both the federal government and the states must take account of the intrinsic preeminence of federal authority.

Prospects for Regulatory Competition under an OFC

In theory, regulatory competition between the states on the one hand and the federal government on the other would create a powerful incentive for state-based reforms and at the same time deter federal regulators from launching their own politically opportunistic market interventions. The result of such competition, according to the competitive regulation theory advanced by some OFC proponents, would be a more efficient regulatory regime at both the federal and state levels, increasing insurance availability and reducing or eliminating the pathologies associated with rate regulation and underwriting restrictions. From the perspective of property-casualty insurers, the prospect that an OFC would foster genuine jurisdictional competition between federal and state regulators holds considerable appeal. It must be noted, however, that while some scholars and insurance industry proponents of an OFC tout its purported ability to facilitate regulatory competition, the Treasury blueprint is silent on this subject. Nor is it mentioned in the speeches and writings of the congressional sponsors of the NIA, which leads one to suspect that jurisdictional competition with the states is not what pro-OFC federal government officials have in mind.

In any event, true regulatory competition will occur only if most insurers can switch charters at a relatively low cost. Unfortunately, the administrative cost to an insurer of adopting a federal charter and adapting to the new federal regulatory compliance regime is likely to be quite high, and switching back to a state charter could be still more expensive. While it is true that charter switching occurs with some frequency among banks, this can be attributed in large measure to the fact that a multistate bank that decides to switch from federal regulation to state regulation need obtain a charter in only one state, thanks to the widespread acceptance among state regulators of branch banking across state lines. Because there is

17. 322 U.S. 533 (1944).

no insurance equivalent of branching, a multistate insurer that wished to jettison its federal charter would have to apply for charters in each of the states in which it does business. This process could prove daunting even for large, highly capitalized companies.

As a practical matter, then, many insurers that opted for a federal charter would find themselves permanently trapped in the federal regulatory regime. This alone would undermine the goal of regulatory competition. But the other dynamic—the prospect of federal preemption of state insurance regulation—would further preclude any semblance of regulatory competition. That is, even if federally regulated insurers could bear the expense of returning to state regulation to escape an unexpectedly onerous federal regime, they would have no incentive to do so if the federal government were to use its preemption authority to impose federal rules and standards on the states. Indeed, the mere threat of federal preemption would likely cause the states to enact their own versions of whatever underwriting restrictions or rate regulation that Congress or the ONI might impose on insurers. This scenario has become institutionalized in bank regulation through state "wild card" statutes, which provide for the automatic adoption at the state level of new federal banking regulations, thereby "discourag[ing] the provision of diverse legal rules and lead[ing] to federally-imposed uniform regulations."[18]

Insurance Regulation as a Tool of Social Welfare Policy

Even if the optional federal charter turned out not to be optional in practice, what is the basis for doubting that a federal regime will not be superior to the state-based regime it replaces? The answer becomes apparent when one considers a fundamental difference between property-casualty insurance and other financial service products. Property-casualty insurance operates as a mechanism for distributing risk, and risk distribution is closely aligned with wealth distribution. Hence to the extent that regulation can redistribute risk, it can also redistribute wealth, which is one of several ways that insurance regulation serves as an instrument of social welfare policy. The likelihood that property-casualty insurance regulation will become politicized is thus very great, regardless of the source of regulatory authority.

Far more than in the regulation of other financial service sectors, insurance regulation is the product of normative conceptions of social welfare and economic

18. Butler and Macey (1988), pp. 678–79.

fairness. The Treasury blueprint, for example, posits "two broad categories" of insurance regulation:[19]

—Solvency or financial regulation, which focuses on preventing insurer insolvencies and mitigating consumer losses upon insolvencies.

—Consumer protection or market regulation, which focuses on such anti-consumer practices as deceptive advertising, unfair policy terms, and discriminatory or unfair treatment of policyholders.

The first category is technical and straightforward, but the second is, in practice, quite complicated and susceptible to a variety of competing interpretations. State insurance regulators and legislators are forever confronting questions about whether particular underwriting, marketing, and pricing practices are "fair" to policyholders and consumers. Below is a partial list of such questions that are currently salient:

—Should insurers be allowed to use credit-based insurance scores to set premiums and to determine whether to offer coverage for automobile and homeowners insurance, even if doing so has a disproportionate adverse impact on particular racial, ethnic, or income groups?

—Should the risk-spreading function of insurance be understood to mean that the property insurance costs of people who live in regions especially prone to natural catastrophes such as hurricanes and earthquakes must be subsidized by property owners who reside in less risky areas?

—Should insurers be allowed to insert anticoncurrent causation clauses in property insurance contracts to avoid paying claims on losses for which they did not agree to provide coverage?

—Should insurers be required to offer all-perils homeowners policies as a condition of being allowed to sell homeowners insurance?

—Should inner-city drivers and homeowners pay more for insurance than their suburban and rural counterparts because they live in areas with higher accident rates, greater litigation and medical costs, and higher rates of theft, vandalism, and fire?

—Do legislators and regulators have a responsibility to ensure that automobile and homeowners insurance remains affordable for all consumers, regardless of the risk they present? What does *affordable* mean in the context of insurance pricing?

19. U.S. Department of the Treasury (2008), pp. 63–64.

Insurance regulation raises such questions because of the risk-distributing nature of the insurance enterprise and the different purposes that people think insurance should serve. Phrases such as "unfair policy terms" and "discriminatory or unfair treatment of policyholders" mean vastly different things to different people. Whereas solvency regulation is technical and formulaic, regulation intended to protect and advance the welfare of insurance consumers is the stuff of politics.[20] When the Treasury blueprint declares that "legislation authorizing a federal regulatory structure and an OFC should address anti-consumer practices such as deceptive advertising, unfair policy terms, and discriminatory or unfair treatment of policyholders," it is simply inviting members of Congress and the ONI to involve themselves in the same kinds of political questions that have provoked controversy and conflict at the state level.

The sources and resolutions of these conflicts can be explained in part by interest group theory, which in simplified form holds that legislators and regulators use regulation to strategically distribute economic benefits and costs among competing interest groups in a manner calculated to maximize the political benefit (or utility) that legislators and regulators derive through the exercise of their regulatory authority. But ideas, beliefs, and values are also powerful determinants of regulatory outcomes. An idea that permeates much of the debate over insurance regulation, particularly where issues of fairness are concerned, is what might be termed the *egalitarian standard of insurance fairness*.[21]

In its purest form, an egalitarian standard of fair risk distribution in insurance would lead to regulation that encouraged universal risk spreading, with the result that all policyholders would pay the same rate for identical coverage, without regard to variations in the risk presented by individual policyholders. A less extreme version of egalitarian insurance would prohibit insurers from charging different rates for insurance coverage based on risk factors that are thought to be beyond the insured's control. In personal auto and homeowners insurance, such factors might include where a person lives or the fact that he has a low consumer credit score.

An egalitarian insurance regulatory regime would regard many of the personal attributes and circumstances that lead to disparities in risk as the product of a natural lottery over which people have little control and for which they should not

20. The political scientist Harold Laswell famously defined politics as the process of determining "who gets what, when, and how," a description that aptly describes the politics of insurance regulation. Laswell (1935).
21. The discussion that follows is derived principally from Abraham (1986), pp. 26–29.

be held accountable. If an insured has no means of controlling a risk he poses, it would violate egalitarian principles to charge him more for insurance coverage than those who are fortunate enough to be free of that risk. Thus egalitarian insurance would at the very least prohibit such immutable characteristics as race, ethnicity, and sex from being considered in setting insurance premiums, even if these characteristics were strongly associated with risk. But an egalitarian view of insurance could also entail the prohibition of risk variables that are oblivious to these characteristics but that have a disproportionate adverse impact on particular demographic groups.

Other characteristics that may appear to be beyond the insured's control would likewise be prohibited. For example, it could be argued that an individual cannot control the risk associated with the physical environment in which he resides, whether the risk stems from natural factors such as earthquakes, windstorms, and floods or social factors such as crime and traffic congestion. Under an egalitarian risk-distribution standard, these characteristics could be precluded from consideration in the issuance and pricing of insurance coverage, notwithstanding their association with risk.

Of course, insurance regulators and politicians do not typically express their conception of insurance in such rarefied terms. But anyone who has spent much time in their company knows that even those who may not consciously subscribe to egalitarian principles of insurance are often influenced by this way of thinking. It usually manifests itself in the rhetoric of consumer protection, a catchall term that comprises not just matters such as fraudulent claim handling and deceptive marketing practices but issues of insurance affordability and availability as well.

Egalitarian notions of fairness applied to insurance risk classification and pricing provide a normative framework that rationalizes support for laws and regulations that serve nakedly political ends. It is a familiar truism that the public policies most likely to be enacted and sustained over time are those that concentrate benefits and disperse costs. "Because the benefits are concentrated," explains the political scientist James Q. Wilson, "the group that is to receive those benefits has an incentive to organize and work to get them. But because the costs are widely distributed . . . those who pay the costs may be either unaware of any costs or indifferent to them."[22] Insurance regulation that suppresses rates and impedes risk-based underwriting concentrates benefits among a relatively small cohort of high-risk individuals and disperses costs among a relatively large cohort of low-

22. Wilson (1992), p. 435.

risk individuals in precisely the manner described by Wilson. Thus insurance regulation, regardless of its source, is likely to be influenced by two complementary forces: the pursuit of fairness, defined according to egalitarian principles, and the desire of regulators and politicians to placate one constituency at the expense of another.

A key question is whether a federal system of insurance regulation would lean more toward an egalitarian approach or a competitive-market approach in dealing with fairness issues. The state-based system's fragmented structure and lack of uniformity regarding fairness issues have created a laboratory for experimenting with alternative approaches while at the same time giving expression to local norms and values that may vary from state to state. Proposals for federal regulation not only promise greater uniformity but also assume that national regulators will provide a regulatory regime that is rooted more firmly and reliably in free market principles compared to the regimes of most states. The Treasury blueprint is adamant that "insurers should neither be subject to rate regulation nor be required to use any particular rate, element, or price."[23]

However, in addition to directly regulating prices, imposing constraints on underwriting selection is another way in which government officials may attempt to override market forces in order to socialize insurance costs. And on this subject, both the blueprint and the National Insurance Act are silent. Given Treasury's stated goal of eliminating "inefficiencies and undue regulatory burdens," this is a remarkable omission. Regulation that limits or impairs the ability of insurers to engage in risk assessment and classification has far-reaching implications for the entire insurance system. Government restrictions on underwriting freedom ostensibly guard against unfair business practices and ensure that insurance will be available to meet market demand. In many instances, however, these regulatory interventions only create market conditions that are dysfunctional and therefore detrimental to insurance consumers. Among the more harmful distortions to the competitive insurance system caused by underwriting restriction are adverse selection, moral hazard, and cross-subsidies:

—Adverse selection: Adverse selection occurs when low-risk insureds purchase less coverage, and high-risk insureds purchase more coverage, than they would if the price of insurance more closely reflected the expected loss for each group. When an insurer is unable to distinguish among individuals according to the level of risk they present—either because it lacks the ability to accurately assess and

---

23. U.S. Department of the Treasury (2008), p. 130.

classify risk or because it is prevented from doing so by regulation—adverse selection is the likely result.

—Moral hazard: Underwriting restrictions that prevent insurers from accurately assessing risk can create incentives for policyholders to conduct their affairs in a manner that is less risk averse than if they had no insurance. The most effective method of addressing moral hazard is to accurately assess and classify risk, varying the price of coverage according to the expected loss of each class of insureds. By making it more difficult for insurers to address the problem of moral hazard, restrictions on underwriting freedom increase overall claim costs, thereby driving up the price of coverage for all insureds.

—Cross-subsidies: Underwriting restrictions weaken the link between expected loss costs and premiums, creating cross-subsidies that flow from low-risk insureds to high-risk insureds. In addition to the injustice entailed by such compulsory wealth transfers, cross-subsidization of insurance rates has a number of adverse consequences. When high-risk individuals do not pay the full marginal costs they impose on the insurance system, they lack incentive to take precautions to avoid loss. The net effect of misguided attempts to lower premiums for high-risk individuals through cross-subsidies is likely to be an increase in accident rates and insurance loss costs, adding to the inflationary pressures on insurance premiums.

As with rate regulation, state governments have developed divergent regulatory responses to various underwriting practices. To take one example, some form of legislation pertaining to credit-based insurance scoring has been enacted in forty-seven states. The laws range from narrow restrictions that apply only in limited circumstances to absolute prohibitions on the use of insurance scoring. It is impossible to predict what kind of legislation Congress would enact to address credit-based insurance scoring and other underwriting practices that some interest groups may not like or that may seem unfair to individual members of Congress. What we do know is that whatever Congress and federal insurance regulators decide will apply to the entire country. That alone is reason to fear the prospect of unitary federal regulation. Not only would the resulting inefficiencies and incentive distortions affect the entire national insurance enterprise, but compared to the states, reversing such policies would inevitably be more difficult at the federal level, where policy mistakes have a tendency to get locked in even when they are widely recognized as mistakes. A case in point is the Sarbanes-Oxley Act, which saddled publicly traded companies with a huge new regulatory burden in exchange for few if any benefits to investors or the economy. Yet there has been no serious effort to reform the legislation.

Federal Regulation Confronts Property Insurance:
A Cautionary Tale

There is, to be sure, considerable uncertainty as to what would actually happen if an OFC proposal were enacted, although for the reasons cited earlier, it is safe to assume that no meaningful competition between federal and state regulators will occur. Moreover, federal regulation will almost certainly predominate either by supplanting state regulation altogether or by dictating the content of state regulation through the threat (or actual use) of federal preemption. Speculating about the nature of particular rules that might emerge—and their likely effect on property-casualty insurance markets—necessarily involves some guesswork. That said, there are clues as to how a federal insurance regulatory agency might behave.

Consider, for example, the Department of Housing and Urban Development (HUD). In 1994 HUD announced that it was forming a special task force to investigate allegations of redlining—that is, practicing unfair discrimination against a particular geographic area—in the sale of homeowners insurance, citing its responsibility for implementing the Fair Housing Act of 1968. The act makes it unlawful "to discriminate against any person in the terms, conditions, or privileges of sale or rental of a dwelling, or in the provision of services or facilities in connection therewith, because of race, color, religion, sex, familial status, or national origin."[24] Shortly before HUD announced its investigation, Assistant Secretary Roberta Achtenberg sent a memorandum advising the agency's regional directors that "cases which have been brought [against insurers] under the Fair Housing Act should now be analyzed using a disparate impact analysis. . . . Under a disparate impact analysis, a policy, standard, practice or procedure which, in operation, disproportionately adversely affects persons protected by the Fair Housing Act coverages may violate the Act."[25] The memorandum goes on to note that "a respondent may rebut a *prima facie* case by evidence that the policy is justified by a business necessity which is sufficiently compelling to overcome the discriminatory effect" but urges HUD investigators to regard claims of "business necessity" with a high degree of skepticism:

> Each [respondent] should be investigated to determine if there are genuine business reasons for the policy. The respondent should also be queried as to whether or not the respondent considered any alternatives to the particular policy, and what the reasons for rejecting the alternatives, if any, were. . . .

24. 42 U.S.C. sec. 3604.
25. U.S. Department of Housing and Urban Development (1993), p. 1.

The investigation should consider whether there are any less discriminatory ways in which the respondent's business justifications may be addressed. These steps are important because if there is a less discriminatory way by which genuine business necessities may be addressed, it may be argued that the respondent should have adopted a less discriminatory alternative.[26]

HUD swiftly moved to apply this strategy in cases involving property insurers that considered the age, market value, and location of a home to determine the type of policy they would offer and the premium they would charge. The agency's use of disparate-impact analysis allowed it to accuse insurers of unlawful, race-based, discrimination merely because their application of these risk-based underwriting criteria happened to yield statistical disparities among racial and ethnic groups. It was not necessary for HUD to show that the insurers intended to unfairly discriminate nor that they had treated policyholders or applicants for homeowners insurance "differently *because of* race, color, religion, sex, handicap, familial status, or national origin." The result was a series of consent decrees, settlements, and negotiations with HUD and the Department of Justice that essentially forced property insurers to abandon the use of these "unfairly discriminatory" risk factors in underwriting and pricing.[27]

HUD's aggressive use of disparate-impact analysis in the 1990s to effectively prohibit the use of risk-based underwriting criteria in homeowners insurance markets should not be viewed as an aberration. Indeed, HUD's actions during that time foreshadowed current federal efforts to apply disparate-impact analysis to the use of property insurers' use of consumer credit information to underwrite and price automobile and homeowners insurance coverage. The Federal Trade Commission is currently conducting a congressionally mandated study analyzing whether insurers' use of credit-based insurance scores affects the affordability and availability of insurance and other financial services products, including the degree to which it may have a disparate impact on various demographic groups. Meanwhile, two bills were introduced in the 110th Congress that would effectively impose a nationwide ban on the use of credit information for insurance underwriting purposes.[28]

26. U.S. Department of Housing and Urban Development (1993), p. 2.

27. See Consent Decree, *U.S.* v. *American Family Mutual Insurance Co.* (E.D. Wis. 1995) 9-C-0759; "State Farm Unit Seeks Bias Settlement with HUD," *Washington Post,* April 8, 1995, p. E10; "Allstate Relaxes Standards on Selling Homeowners' Policies in Poor Areas," *Wall Street Journal,* August 14, 1996, p. A3.

28. See H.R. 5633, "Nondiscriminatory Use of Consumer Reports and Consumer Information Act of 2008"; H.R. 6062, "Personal Lines of Insurance Fairness Act of 2008."

Prospects for Market-Oriented Regulatory Reform under an OFC

Three questions about the OFC proposal seem paramount. First, will the proposal's promise of rate deregulation for federally chartered insurers be realized over time? It is tempting to imagine that the federal government that abolished price controls in the trucking, railroad, and airline industries during the 1970s would do the same for insurance today if given the chance. But it seems unlikely that the same political dynamic that makes it so difficult to achieve price competition in the states will not also manifest itself at the federal level. Just as political opportunism and an egalitarian view of insurance regularly lead some state officeholders and regulators to call for insurance price controls and rate rollbacks, so too will there inevitably be occasions when their federal counterparts do the same. If the dual-chartering scheme fails to promote robust regulatory competition between the state and federal governments—as it almost certainly will—the political and ideological appeal of rate regulation at the federal level will go unchecked. Sooner or later, whatever measure of pricing freedom insurers are afforded under the current versions of the National Insurance Act is likely to disappear.

The second question that must be addressed is whether Congress and the Office of National Insurance will recognize that unfettered risk discrimination is essential to accurate underwriting and competitive pricing. The examples reviewed in this chapter of the federal government's regulatory encounters with property-casualty insurance provide ample reason to suspect that the eventual erosion of pricing freedom under federal regulation will be accompanied by measures that will restrict insurers' ability to use risk-based underwriting variables that are deemed unfair by federal regulators and members of Congress.

Many politicians—especially those whose constituents include large concentrations of high-risk insureds—find it easy to ignore compelling evidence that restrictions on risk-based underwriting discourage risk mitigation, force low-risk consumers to subsidize the insurance costs of high-risk consumers, and decrease the availability of insurance. As noted above, the House and Senate OFC bills do nothing to protect underwriting freedom. The bills' promise of rate deregulation for federally chartered insurers will mean little if federal regulators are allowed to impose underwriting restrictions that impair the ability of insurers to charge premiums based on risk.

Finally, one should reflect on the human element that inevitably drives the behavior of all federal bureaucracies. This means asking about the kind of person that will self-select into a career as a federal insurance regulator. As the familiar themes of "protecting consumers" and "making insurance available and affordable" inexorably make their way into presidential and congressional election campaigns, what promises will candidates make to voters on issues related to property insurance? What assurance do we have that the men and women appointed by future administrations to lead the Office of National Insurance will be knowledgeable, principled devotees of free markets and regulatory forbearance?

If Not an OFC, Then What?

Discussion of an alternative means of federal insurance regulatory reform is beyond the scope of this chapter. However, in light of the foregoing discussion, it would appear that the most prudent course is to continue the pursuit of market-oriented reforms at the state level, state by state. States have not been oblivious to the criticisms leveled against them. They have made significant progress in addressing antiquated rules such as those involving price controls and company licensing restrictions. Regarding price regulation:

—Nine states have adopted flex-band rating systems for property-casualty products to replace the rigid system of price controls.

—Fourteen states have adopted the more flexible use-and-file system.

—Twenty-four states have established no filing requirements, mostly for large commercial risks.

—Only sixteen states still require statutory prior approval. Several of these states, however, are among the largest in the country, accounting for 40.8 percent of the total auto insurance market and 41.4 percent of the total homeowners insurance market nationwide.

There have been other reforms:

—With respect to insurer licensing, the Uniform Certificate of Authority Application is now used in all insurance jurisdictions.

—A system of electronic filing has been implemented by most states and has streamlined the process by which rates and forms are filed by companies.

—Thirty-three states have now adopted the Interstate Insurance Product Regulation Commission, which serves as a single point of filing for life insurance products.

—The National Conference of Insurance Legislators (NCOIL), the National Conference of State Legislatures, and the American Legislative Exchange Council have all endorsed competition as the best regulator of rates. NCOIL has adopted a significant model law that would create a use-and-file system for personal lines and an informational filing system for commercial lines.

—NCOIL has also adopted a market conduct model law that would bring significant reform to that area of state regulation.

While these results are encouraging, much more needs to be done. One possible federal approach that warrants serious consideration is the primary state regulator (or single-license) concept, which was recently illuminated in an important paper by Henry Butler and Larry Ribstein.[29] The authors explain that "an alternative to the federal domination that is likely to occur under OFC or the other federalization of insurance proposals . . . is to model federal insurance regulation after corporate chartering" rather than bank chartering.[30] Their proposal "would allow an insurer to be chartered in a primary state of its choice, and then would be licensed to sell in any state provided the insurer met minimum federal standards."[31] Significantly, the Butler-Ribstein proposal would create genuine regulatory competition among fifty-six state and territorial insurance regulators.

Conclusion

History teaches that, once established, federal agencies tend to mushroom in size and to expand their authority, often at the expense of state and local governments. When the U.S. Department of Education was created in 1980, critics warned that it would eventually usurp authority that historically belonged to the states. One of those critics was Ronald Reagan, who promised during his presidential election campaign to abolish the department. Today, after nearly three decades, it is larger and more intrusive than ever, embraced and further aggrandized by recent administrations.

There is every reason to believe that a federal insurance regulator would follow a similar path. Viewed superficially, the optional federal charter proposal precludes a federal takeover of insurance regulation by allowing insurers to eschew federal regulation in favor of state regulation. This notion is belied, however, by the experience of the dual-banking regulatory system on which the OFC proposal is based. Likewise, the notion that an OFC would foster competition between state and federal insurance regulators, which in turn would lead to salutary regulatory reform, is also contradicted by the experience of the dual-banking system.

29. Butler and Ribstein (2008).
30. Butler and Ribstein (2008), p. 14.
31. Butler and Ribstein (2008), p. 14; also see Harrington (2006).

Federal regulatory encounters with the business of property-casualty insurance during the past twenty years suggest that rate regulation and underwriting restrictions that exist to varying extents in the states today would not disappear under a federal regulatory regime. To the contrary, there is ample reason to suspect, and little reason to doubt, that federal regulation of property-casualty insurance markets would lead more often than not to regulatory zealotry rather than regulatory forbearance.

References

Abraham, Kenneth S. 1986. *Distributing Risk: Insurance, Legal Theory, and Public Policy.* Yale University Press.

Bair, Sheila, and others. 2004. "Consumer Ramifications of an Optional Federal Charter for Life Insurers." University of Massachusetts.

Broome, Lissa Lamkin. 2002. "A Federal Charter Option for Insurance Companies: Lessons from the Bank Experience." Working Paper. University of North Carolina.

Butler, Henry N., and Jonathan R. Macey. 1988. "The Myth of Competition in the Dual Banking System." *Cornell Law Review* 73: 677–718.

Butler, Henry N., and Larry E. Ribstein. 2008. "A Single-License Approach to Regulating Insurance." Northwestern Law and Economics Research Paper 08-10. Northwestern University.

England, Catherine. 2005. "Federal Insurance Chartering: The Devil's in the Details." Washington: Competitive Enterprise Institute.

Grace, Martin F., and Robert W. Klein. 2007. "The Effects of an Optional Federal Charter on Competition in the Life Insurance Industry." Report to the American Council of Life Insurers. Georgia State University.

Harrington, Scott E. 2006. "Federal Chartering of Insurance Companies: Options and Alternatives for Transforming Insurance Regulation." Policy Brief 2006-PB-02. Networks Financial Institute, Indiana State University.

Laswell, Harold. 1935. *Politics: Who Gets What, When, How.* New York: McGraw-Hill.

Scott, Hal. 2008. "Optional Federal Chartering of Insurance: Design of a Regulatory Structure." Paper prepared for the symposium "Insurance Markets and Regulation," Northwestern University School of Law, April 14–15.

U.S. Department of Housing and Urban Development. 1993. "Applicability of Disparate Impact Analysis to Fair Housing Cases." Memorandum to regional directors, Office of Fair Housing and Equal Opportunity, December 17.

U.S. Department of the Treasury. 2008. *Blueprint for a Modernized Financial Regulatory Structure.*

Wallison, Peter. 2006. "Competitive Equity: An Optional Federal Charter for Insurance Companies." Washington: American Enterprise Institute.

Wilson, James Q. 1992. *American Government: Institutions and Policies,* 5th ed. Lexington, Mass.: D. C. Heath.

PART TWO

Insurance Regulatory Policies

5

Insurance Regulation: The Need for Policy Reform

Martin F. Grace and Robert W. Klein

B eyond the push for increasing the federal role in insurance regulation, there is strong pressure for reforming insurance regulatory policies. Indeed, proponents of an optional federal charter (OFC) for insurance envision that federal officials would adopt policies that would significantly diverge from current state regulatory policies in a number of key areas. At the same time, the creation of an OFC would still leave an optional state framework in place, and the states would need to reconsider their regulatory policies in a new environment. Further, the constituency for improving insurance regulation extends beyond OFC proponents to segments of the industry that continue to support a state framework. Many economists also advocate significant changes in the way insurance is regulated. Hence the drumbeat for policy reform has been strong and growing for some time. Reform remains relevant regardless of how the institutional framework for insurance regulation evolves.

This chapter discusses needed reform in U.S. insurance regulatory policies in critical areas. An assessment of insurance regulatory policies is valuable to guide both federal and state authorities as institutions change. We identify and evaluate the most significant policies in the principal areas of financial oversight, market regulation, and antitrust. Our evaluation considers the principles that should guide how insurance is regulated as well as the issues associated with specific policy reforms and their implications. We also comment on the prospects for reform under several frameworks.

Solvency Regulation

The approach to overseeing the financial condition and risk of insurance companies should be foremost in any discussion of regulatory policies. This is an area of considerable concern, as the current U.S. system is outmoded and lagging behind the evolution of the industry and the systems employed or being developed in other jurisdictions, such as the European Union (EU).[1] As noted in chapter 2, the states have applied a prescriptive, or rules-based, approach to regulating insurers' financial condition, an approach that is heavily influenced by an accounting perspective. This approach is reflected in numerous laws, regulations, rules, and other measures that govern insurers' financial structure and activities. Regulators tend to focus on insurers' compliance with these rules rather than on how well they manage their financial risk.

An accounting approach to solvency regulation focuses on the valuation of insurers' assets and liabilities. It can be contrasted with a financial approach, which encompasses a comprehensive assessment of the risks that an insurer faces and looks forward in terms of its vulnerability to adverse developments that could cause it to encounter financial distress. This approach is typically associated with a dynamic financial analysis, which involves some form of scenario-based, or stochastic, modeling to evaluate an insurer's financial risk.

The emphasis on an accounting view rather than a financial risk view in U.S. regulation, as well as its prescriptive approach, affects insurers' incentives and ability to manage their financial risk. It places certain constraints on an insurer's financial structure that may or may not be warranted based on a more sophisticated assessment of its financial risk and how that risk is being managed. The U.S. approach also does not explicitly require or encourage insurers to manage their financial risk. There may be an assumption that if an insurer complies with all regulations that its risk is low, but there is no assurance that this is the case. Some U.S. insurers do perform internal risk modeling, but the regulatory system does not recognize or reward insurers for conducting this kind of analysis.

The U.S. approach also affects U.S. insurers' efficiency and their ability to compete in international insurance markets. It places constraints on insurers and com-

---

1. See for example Klein and Wang (2007) for an assessment and comparison of U.S. and EU insurance financial regulation.

Figure 5-1. *Company Impairments, Property-Casualty and Life-Health Insurers, 1969–2007*

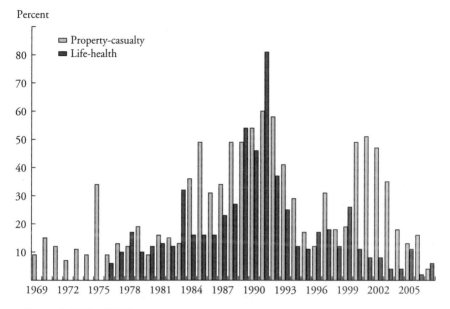

Source: A. M. Best (2008).

pels them to meet requirements that are not imposed on their foreign competitors. Further, over time, U.S. insurers may find it difficult to qualify for "regulatory equivalence" treatment in a foreign jurisdiction if the U.S. system is deemed inadequate or substandard relative to the system employed in that jurisdiction.[2]

There have been improvements in financial regulation in the United States (see chapter 2 and the following discussion). These changes have likely had some beneficial effects on the industry. However, the enhanced financial strength of U.S. insurers cannot be attributed solely to regulatory changes. Although the number of U.S. insurance company insolvencies has generally declined in the last thirty years (figure 5-1), only part of this trend is probably due to better regulation. Stricter rating agency standards and other industry developments have likely been significant contributing factors. This does not obviate the need for regulators to employ best practices, as not all insurers may be adequately disciplined by the market, and unnecessary or excessive regulatory constraints can undermine insurers' efficiency.

2. In chapter 8 John Cooke and Harold Skipper discuss cross-border regulatory issues in insurance in greater depth.

Unlike the United States, an increasing number of countries (for example, the United Kingdom and other EU members) have employed or are moving toward what might be labeled a principles-based approach within a prudential system for insurance regulation. In this system, emphasis is placed on insurers' maintaining an adequate solvency margin and management competence, with an insurer's financial risk being the ultimate point of focus for supervisors. Insurance companies are given greater flexibility in meeting regulatory standards if they act prudently in managing their financial risk according to the principles established by regulators. This philosophy is embodied in the EU's collective insurance solvency initiatives, which set common standards for all EU member countries.[3] It is also reflected in the development of international insurance regulatory standards.[4] These initiatives have been influenced by the Basel II accords for bank regulation but differ in several respects.[5]

EU regulators tend not to subject insurers to the kind of extensive and detailed rules used in the United States. Instead, they maintain closer scrutiny of how insurers are managed and exercise greater discretion in the actions or interventions they may employ to correct practices or problems as they deem necessary. In addition, many EU countries, compared to their U.S. counterparts, have more quickly embraced a financial-economic approach to insurer regulation. This approach, which includes an enterprise risk-management perspective, allows insurers greater freedom as long as they use that freedom judiciously, do not engage in excessively hazardous ventures or transactions, and ultimately keep their financial risk within reasonable bounds. This more progressive approach to the financial regulation of insurers is reflected in the EU's Solvency II initiative, which is scheduled for implementation in 2012–13.

Virtually every aspect of insurer financial regulation in the United States is driven by its prevailing philosophy and approach. Most of the standards that insurers are required to meet are stated in terms of accounting values. Hence insurers' compliance with these standards is assessed by examining the financial statements and other financial reports they are required to submit. Clearly, the filing of financial statements according to a set of accounting principles is an essential part of any financial regulatory system. The concern is that U.S. regulators place too much emphasis on these financial statements and the accounting values

3. Commission of the European Communities (2007). See also Eling, Schmeiser, and Schmit (2007) for a more a detailed review of EU solvency initiatives.

4. International Association of Insurance Supervisors (2007).

5. Klein and Wang (2007).

reported as well as on compliance with detailed rules. Accounting values may not provide a true picture of an insurer's financial condition and are inadequate for assessing an insurer's financial risk. Further, an insurer can comply (or at least appear to comply) with all regulatory rules yet still assume an excessive level of risk.

Capital Standards

One of the most important elements of the U.S. financial regulatory system—risk-based capital (RBC) requirements—has several limitations, which include but are not confined to their reliance on accounting values. RBC requirements are based on standard formulas (for property-casualty and life and health insurers) developed by the National Association of Insurance Commissioners (NAIC) that are both complex and flawed.[6] When these standards were adopted in the early 1990s, many may have viewed them as being relatively sophisticated, but they are now being eclipsed by more advanced methods. All of the "charges" used to calculate an insurer's RBC requirement involve the application of selected factors to various accounting values. All but a few companies greatly exceed their RBC requirements, which are considerably less stringent than the capital standards set by rating agencies.[7] The low bar set by regulators is reflected in figure 5-2, which compares NAIC capital requirements for property-casualty insurers with those set by A. M. Best (a prominent insurance company rating agency).[8] The imperfections in the U.S. approach have likely compelled regulators to set the bar fairly low to avoid being forced to take actions against insurers that are financially sound. Also, the term *risk-based* is arguably a misnomer, because the United States does not employ methods that many experts and the most progressive regulators believe are needed to assess an insurer's financial risk and the adequacy of its capital.[9]

The complexity of the RBC formulas gives a false sense of accuracy. Most important, these formulas take a static approach based on historic, reported

6. See Cummins, Harrington, and Klein (1995); Grace, Harrington, and Klein (1998); and Cummins, Grace, and Phillips (1999) for evaluations of the NAIC's risk-based capital standards and its financial monitoring systems.

7. Klein and Wang (2007).

8. The ratio between total adjusted capital (TAC) and risk-based capital (RBC) and the best capital adequacy ratio (BCAR) both measure an insurer's actual capital to its minimum capital requirement but do so using different systems. Most insurers have an RBC-BCAR ratio that considerably exceeds 200 percent, indicating that their BCARs are significantly lower than their RBC ratios. In the regulatory system, insurers with TAC-RBC ratios below 200 percent are subject to some form of regulatory action. Under the A. M. Best system, insurers with a BCAR of 100–200 percent are deemed to be adequately capitalized.

9. Eling and Holzmuller (2008).

Figure 5-2. *Capital Requirements, Property-Casualty Insurers, 2006*[a]

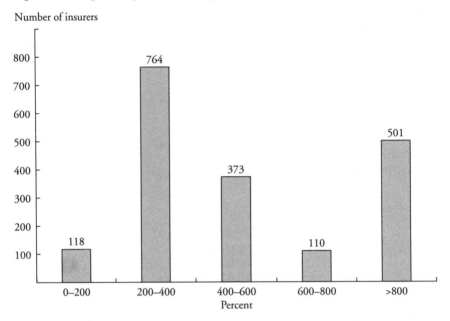

Number of insurers

Percent

Source: National Association of Insurance Commissioners (2008); A. M. Best (2008); authors' calculations.
a. Percentages determined by dividing the ratio between an insurer's total adjusted capital and its risk-based captial by the best capital adequacy ratio.

accounting values. Unlike systems that use dynamic financial analysis, these formulas do not look forward to consider how an insurer might fare under future scenarios. Proposals to incorporate dynamic financial analysis were rejected by regulators when the formulas were being developed. Also, accounting values can be either erroneous or manipulated to obtain more favorable regulatory assessments. For example, David Cummins, Scott Harrington, and Robert Klein observe that the current property-casualty formula encourages insurers to lower their loss reserves to reduce the associated RBC charge.[10]

Further, while not all risks can be quantified, the formulas omit some that can be (such as operational risks), using methodological tools now available. It is also important to note that the U.S. property-casualty RBC formula contains no explicit adjustment for the size of an insurer or its catastrophe exposure. Factors for both were proposed in the initial development of this formula but were

10. Cummins, Harrington, and Klein (1995).

rejected. The NAIC is currently considering adding a catastrophe component to the formula, but this initiative is bogged down in a debate that is unlikely to be resolved any time soon.

Risk-based capital formulas could employ better methods to model some of the risks that they attempt to measure, or the formulas could use more appropriate factors. While some elements of the formulas could be improved, the U.S. system is increasingly becoming antiquated, with inherent limits to what it can accomplish. Currently, U.S. insurers are not subject to any requirements to perform internal risk modeling, nor are they allowed to use such modeling as an optional approach to demonstrate the adequacy of their capital and financial risk management. U.S. regulatory standards also have not embraced enterprise risk management in requiring insurers to evaluate the full range of risks they face and their interaction. Of course, there are limits to what quantitative methods can reveal, which underlines the importance of qualitative assessments in the overall solvency monitoring process (see below).

U.S. regulators need to move more quickly and radically to revamp their capital standards in line with the development of international regulatory standards as well as the approach used in determining capital requirements for other U.S. financial institution, like banks. To date, the country's initiatives have been limited and tentative, such as the effort to adopt a catastrophe component to the property-casualty RBC formula. A more sophisticated approach to determining insurers' capital adequacy could be made more palatable to insurers if it were accompanied by the elimination, or easing, of those prescriptive regulatory requirements that no longer serve any purpose. If new capital standards are simply heaped on top of existing rules and requirements, insurers will not perceive a net gain in regulatory efficiency and will be more likely to strongly oppose such a move.

Financial Monitoring

The United States has a highly developed monitoring framework, which arguably is motivated in part by its relatively low capital requirements. However, this framework is based on static, ratio-based tools.[11] As with the country's RBC standards, it involves no dynamic testing or modeling—which admittedly is difficult

---

11. U.S. regulators effectively employ two early warning systems based on financial ratios. The Insurance Regulatory Information System was created in the early 1970s; its results are available to the public. The Financial Analysis Solvency Tools system was developed in the early 1990s; its results are not made public. See Klein (2005) for a more detailed explanation of both systems and how they are used.

to perform using a standard approach but is not impossible.[12] Financial examinations also primarily focus on verifying the accuracy of an insurer's financial statement and its compliance with regulations, although regulators have the authority to examine all aspects of an insurer's management and operations. Targeted examinations can focus on a certain aspect of an insurer's financial condition or operations, but such exams are generally triggered by a review of an insurer's financial statement and early warning systems subject to the limits noted above.

Capital standards, financial ratio analysis, and examinations should be augmented by other methods and information to gain greater insight into an insurer's true financial condition and risk. A broader analysis would include both quantitative and qualitative factors, such as management competence, corporate governance, and internal risk management. Some of these aspects of financial monitoring are discussed in the materials provided to regulators to guide their analysis activities.[13] However, the evidence does not indicate that this has become a significant component of the solvency monitoring process.[14]

The inadequacies of the U.S. system were revealed by the costly failure of the Reliance insurance group in 2001, which exhibited high-risk behavior several years before regulators took corrective action. By the time regulators seized the company, it was at least $2 billion in the red and far beyond rehabilitation. The fact that Reliance was able to dig a $2 billion hole before it was stopped demonstrates the inadequacy of not only the country's RBC standards but also its financial monitoring process. The failure of five Florida insurers (following the 2004–05 hurricanes) that were allowed to underwrite excessive concentrations of coastal exposures offers another example of the deficiencies in U.S. financial regulation.[15]

A more comprehensive and hands-on approach to financial monitoring would naturally be melded with a shift toward the use of dynamic financial analysis to determine the adequacy of an insurer's risk management and capital. Of course, in a prudential system, the quality of oversight is only as good as the regulators

---

12. Cummins, Grace, and Phillips (1999) demonstrate how this can be done.

13. The NAIC publishes financial analysis handbooks for property-casualty and life-health insurance companies to guide regulatory examiners and analysts.

14. For example, insurers are required to file a supplement ("Management's Discussion and Analysis") to their annual financial statement. Insurers use this document to explain trends and anomalies in their financial statements and are also expected to discuss material events that might affect their future financial condition. However, these reports are not used to outline an insurer's future business plans and their implications for its financial risk.

15. Klein (2007).

who perform it. This could prove to be a greater challenge within a state-based framework.[16]

Estimation of Loss Reserves

One troublesome area that has significant implications for a property-casualty insurer's financial condition is its estimates of reserves for unpaid losses. This is especially true for long-tail lines, in which some claims are not reported and fully paid until several years after the associated insurance policy is in effect. The evidence indicates that many insurers substantially underestimate their loss reserves during soft markets and when claim costs are rising. This causes insurers' reported income and surplus to be overstated and is a significant contributor to insurance company insolvencies. A study by A. M. Best finds that inadequate loss reserves have been the primary cause of 38 percent of property-casualty insurer failures.[17]

This is a difficult problem to solve but one that clearly warrants attention. Under the current system, insurers are required to file an actuarial opinion that its loss reserves are adequate. However, this actuarial opinion can be issued by a company actuary, and regulatory evaluations of these opinions do not appear to be rigorous. Strong consideration should be given to more rigorous external reviews of the adequacy of insurers' reserves or other measures that strengthen this critical aspect of solvency oversight.

Reinsurance

Another problem lies with the U.S. approach toward foreign reinsurers. For a U.S. insurer to claim accounting credit for reinsurance recoverables, its reinsurers must be licensed in the United States or must post collateral equal to its obligations to U.S. insurers. This increases the cost of reinsurance for U.S. insurers and creates a disincentive to purchase optimal amounts of reinsurance.[18] It also places U.S. insurers at a competitive disadvantage relative to non-U.S. insurers. In contrast, the EU's Solvency II initiative would eliminate collateral requirements for foreign reinsurers.

The NAIC has adopted (but not yet implemented) a new framework for determining reinsurers' collateral requirements. Under this new framework, U.S.

16. In the early 1990s the states and the NAIC adopted an accreditation program to certify the adequacy of each state's financial regulation. While there is evidence that the program helped to improve states' financial regulation, evaluating a state's performance in applying a prudential regulatory approach could prove to be a more daunting task.

17. A. M. Best (2008).

18. Cummins (2007).

insurers may qualify as "national reinsurers" regulated by their home states. Non-U.S. reinsurers may qualify as port-of-entry reinsurers by using an eligible state as a port of entry. A port-of-entry reinsurer will be subject to oversight by its port-of-entry supervisor. Both national reinsurers and port-of-entry reinsurers will be subject to collateral requirements that will be scaled according to something resembling a financial strength rating. U.S. and non-U.S. reinsurers that do not become qualified as national or port-of-entry reinsurers will remain subject to current state laws and regulations governing credit for reinsurance. An NAIC Reinsurance Review Supervision Division will be established to implement the new framework, including determining those states that will qualify as the supervisors for national and port-of-entry reinsurers. While this new system could be viewed as an improvement, it could also prove to be quite cumbersome. Under an OFC, regulatory treatment of reinsurance would likely be much more efficient; and even without an OFC, federal legislation may be enacted that would preempt current state regulatory requirements.

Intervention and Managing Insolvencies

Another aspect of U.S. solvency regulation that should be reformed is its system for intervention against financially distressed insurers and managing their insolvencies (termed *receiverships*). Martin Grace, Robert Klein, and Richard Phillips identify a number of problems with the U.S. receivership system and also find evidence that regulators exercise excessive forbearance in dealing with troubled insurers.[19] Under the current system, each state manages the receiverships of its domiciliary insurers that become insolvent. Receivership management is highly inefficient and largely opaque to anyone other than the receivers. Grace, Klein, and Phillips estimate the average cost of property-casualty insurer insolvencies (over the period 1986–99) to be $1.10 per $1.00 of preinsolvency assets, which is considerably higher than the estimated costs of bank insolvencies.[20] They find evidence of three major factors contributing to higher insurer insolvency costs: the financial condition of an insurer before insolvency and the moral hazard incentives of its managers; regulatory forbearance; and regulatory management of insurer receiverships. The moral hazard that can arise from insolvency guarantees increases the importance of effective regulatory oversight.

19. Grace, Klein, and Phillips (2002a).
20. Hall (2000) estimates this cost at $1.22 for each $1.00 of preinsolvency assets, using the shorter time period of 1986–94. These costs are substantially higher than those for U.S. bank insolvencies, with estimates ranging between $0.20 and $0.30 per $1.00 of preinsolvency assets. See James (1991); Kaufmann (2001).

State guaranty associations (discussed in chapter 2) play a principal role in this system. As with any system that provides insolvency guarantees, there is a moral hazard concern. This problem is most commonly addressed through adopting financial standards for institutions backed by government guarantees, such as those enforced by the Federal Deposit Insurance Corporation (FDIC) for banks. However, there is not a comparable arrangement for insurance guaranty associations. Further, there is evidence that insolvency guarantees reduce state regulators' incentives to act quickly in dealing with distressed insurers, managing receiverships, and minimizing insolvency costs.[21] This is a persistent problem and requires attention in any institutional framework for insurance regulation.

After the issuance of the Grace, Klein, and Phillips report and other critiques, the NAIC embarked on a tortuous process to reform some aspects of the system. Unfortunately, this effort has been bogged down by a fierce battle between groups with strong vested interests in the current system and other stakeholders who advocate significant reforms. It is unclear when and how this battle will be resolved, but the outcome is likely to fall short of what many external experts and stakeholders believe is needed. We should note that the proposed OFC legislation retains reliance on state guaranty associations, subject to federal standards.[22] However, the proposed OFC system could create a greater disconnection between insolvency guarantees and the locus of financial oversight of insurance companies.

Moving toward a Better System

There is a strong need to upgrade U.S. solvency regulation to what experts would consider to be best practices. The EU's Solvency II could be used as a template, but U.S. regulators need not mimic any particular system to create the best possible system. It is fairly clear that the United States needs to move to a more comprehensive approach to financial regulation that employs some form of dynamic modeling and relies on more than financial statements (and other standard reports) to assess insurers' risk. Dynamic modeling is best performed by each insurer, using an internal model subject to regulatory review. This is a reasonable requirement for larger insurers but may be problematic for smaller insurers, as the EU has found. Smaller insurers could be required to use a standard dynamic model (the EU is developing such a model), which will be less informative than a

---

21. Willenborg (2000); Grace, Klein, and Phillips (2002a).
22. The main reason for this is the concern that a separate guaranty system for federally regulated insurers would substantially diminish the financial capacity of state guaranty associations. However, when the authority for solvency oversight and the management of insolvency guarantees are not integrated, issues and problems can arise.

customized, internal model but better than the current static solvency testing employed by U.S. regulators.

U.S. regulators have talked about employing a principles-based approach to solvency oversight, but the current system falls far short of this vision. The NAIC's creation of a working group to look at the adoption of this approach is commendable, but its activities have been confined to developing a principles-based system for life insurers' policy reserves; how far the states are willing to go beyond this remains to be seen. Admittedly, this will be a huge task and challenge, as it would involve replacing the rules currently in place with new principles and standards that regulators would need to understand, apply, and enforce. Such a shift in the current regulatory paradigm may not occur within the foreseeable future without a regime change or substantial economic pressure.

We should note that the industry has not been pushing for a major overhaul of the U.S. financial regulatory system, although it has advocated some specific reforms that would make the system more efficient. Some (possibly many) U.S. insurers might view an EU-type of system as superior, but they are likely skeptical that U.S. regulators would substitute their extensive rules and reporting requirements with a more efficient and effective system. Ultimately, international pressure may be the primary catalyst for substantive reform of the U.S. system. A federal regulator might embrace a new paradigm, and a regime change presents an opportunity for significant reform, but there is no guarantee that reform would occur.

Market Regulation

The industry push for policy reform is aimed primarily at market regulation. Insurers probably view the broad array of market regulations and the variation in state policies as the most significant drain on their efficiency, especially in terms of their interstate operations. Even OFC opponents see a need for significant improvement in market regulation. Hence many advocates of market reform continue to press their case at the state level, while OFC proponents also pray for a federal solution.

Price Regulation

The most prominent and criticized policy is rate regulation. The extent and the stringency of rate regulation vary significantly by line and by state. The lines subject to the greatest rate regulation are personal auto, homeowners, and workers' compensation insurance. Table 5-1 summarizes the type of rate regulatory system

Table 5-1. *Rate Filing Requirements, Property-Liability Insurance, by State*[a]

State	Private passenger auto	Homeowners	Workers' compensation
Alabama	Prior approval	Prior approval	Prior approval
Alaska	Flex rating	Flex rating	Flex rating
Arizona	Use and file	Use and file	File and use
Arkansas	File and use	File and use	Prior approval
California	Prior approval	Prior approval	Prior approval
Colorado	File and use	File and use	File and use
Connecticut	File and use	File and use	File and use
Delaware	Prior approval	Prior approval	Prior approval
District of Columbia	File and use	File and use	Prior approval
Florida	File and use	File and use	Prior approval
Georgia	File and use	File and use	File and use
Hawaii	Prior approval	Prior approval	Prior approval
Idaho	Use and file	Use and file	Prior approval
Illinois	Use and file	Use and file	Use and file
Indiana	File and use	File and use	File and use
Iowa	File and use	File and use	Prior approval
Kansas	File and use	File and use	Prior approval
Kentucky	Flex rating	Flex rating	Flex rating
Louisiana	Prior approval	Prior approval	File and use
Maine	File and use	File and use	Prior approval
Maryland	File and use	File and use	File and use
Massachusetts	Prior approval	Prior approval	Prior approval
Michigan	File and use	File and use	File and use
Minnesota	File and use	File and use	Prior approval
Mississippi	Prior approval	Prior approval	Prior approval
Missouri	Use and file	Use and file	Use and file
Montana	File and use	File and use	File and use
Nebraska	File and use	File and use	Prior approval
Nevada	Prior approval	Prior approval	Prior approval
New Hampshire	File and use	File and use	Use and file
New Jersey	Flex rating	Flex rating	Prior approval
New Mexico	File and use	File and use	Prior approval
New York	Prior approval	File and use	Prior approval
North Carolina	Prior approval	Prior approval	File and use
North Dakota	Prior approval	Prior approval	Prior approval
Ohio	File and use	File and use	File and use
Oklahoma	Use and file	Use and file	Use and file
Oregon	File and use	File and use	Prior approval
Pennsylvania	Prior approval	Prior approval	Prior approval
Rhode Island	File and use	File and use	Prior approval
South Carolina	Flex rating	Flex rating	Prior approval
South Dakota	File and use	File and use	Prior approval

(continued)

Table 5-1. *Rate Filing Requirements, Property-Liability Insurance,*
by State[a]*(continued)*

State	Private passenger auto	Homeowners	Workers' compensation
Tennessee	Prior approval	Prior approval	Prior approval
Texas	File and use	File and use	File and use
Utah	Use and file	Use and file	File and use
Vermont	Use and file	Use and file	File and use
Virginia	File and use	File and use	Prior approval
Washington	Prior approval	Prior approval	Prior approval
West Virginia	Prior approval	Prior approval	Prior approval
Wisconsin	Use and file	Use and file	Prior approval
Wyoming[b]	No file	No file	No file

Source: National Association of Insurance Commissioners (2008); Insurance Information Institute (2008).

a. Under a prior approval system, insurers must receive regulatory approval of rates before they are implemented. Under a modified prior approval system, insurers are required to obtain regulatory approval of rate changes due to changes in their expense or profit loadings or modifications of the rate relativities for different risk classes. Under a file-and-use system, insurers may implement rates after they are filed. Under a use-and-file system, insurers must files rates within a certain time after they have been implemented. Under a flex-rating system, only rate changes that exceed certain bounds are subject to prior approval. Prior approval is generally categorized as a noncompetitive rating system, while the other systems are considered to be competitive rating systems.

b. Insurers in Wyoming are not required to file their rates.

employed by each state for these principal lines. The various systems can be divided into two basic categories: noncompetitive rating systems and competitive rating systems.[23] In noncompetitive rating systems, regulators can easily constrain rates below levels that insurers would otherwise charge, although they may choose not to do so. In competitive rating systems, in theory, regulators essentially rely on the market to set prices and do not attempt to constrain rates. However, even states with so-called competitive rating systems may still seek to impose binding price constraints.

The reality is that, in most states and markets at a given point in time, regulators do not attempt to impose severe price constraints. The problem arises when strong cost pressure compels insurers to raise their prices and regulators resist market forces in an ill-fated attempt to ease the impact on consumers. Regulators may seek to suppress overall rate levels or to compress rate structures (for example, the rate differentials between low- and high-risk insureds). Inevitably, severe market

23. National Association of Insurance Commissioners (2008).

distortions occur. Ultimately, insurance markets can be sucked into a downward spiral, as the supply of private insurance evaporates and state mechanisms are forced to cover the gap. Rate suppression or compression also can decrease incentives to reduce risk, which can lead to rising claim costs, which further increases pricing and market pressure. Together, these developments can create major crises in the cost and supply of insurance. Florida's property insurance crisis offers the most current example of regulation gone awry.[24] Other adverse effects of rate regulation may be less apparent but are nonetheless corrosive: among these effects are price rigidity, insurer exits, diminished quality of service, and reduced commitments of insurer capital.[25]

The argument for rate deregulation is fairly straightforward. One would expect that prices in competitive insurance markets would be actuarially fair and not excessive. Also, competition should drive insurers to be efficient, and prices should gravitate to the lowest possible level. If insurers would charge competitive prices in the absence of government intervention, then the need for regulation would evaporate. The empirical research overwhelmingly confirms both the competitive nature of insurance markets and the lack of benefits from rate regulation.[26] Requiring or authorizing regulators to regulate rates invites political pressure and interference, which can lead to the dismal scenario described above. Several states have recently deregulated auto insurance rates (for example, Georgia and New Jersey), but deregulation needs to be extended to all states for all lines of insurance: fifteen states still have prior approval requirements for personal auto insurance rates, fourteen require prior approval for homeowners insurance rates, and thirty require prior approval for workers' compensation rates.[27] Unfortunately, some states, like Florida, that had competitive rating systems have moved back to noncompetitive rating systems. Hence reregulation remains a constant threat and warrants vigilance and informed discourse.

24. Klein (2007).

25. Insurers will be less inclined to lower rates when claim costs fall if they anticipate that regulators will constrain their ability to raise rates when costs rise.

26. For analyses of competition in insurance markets, see Cummins and Weiss (1991); Klein (2005); and Grace and Klein (2007).

27. See Cummins (2002) for a collection of case studies of good and bad regulatory policies in selected states. An econometric analysis by Harrington (2002) further affirms the findings of earlier studies, that rate regulation produces no appreciable benefits to consumers but can create significant market distortions. Richard A. Derrig and Sharon L. Tennyson, in a 2008 assessment of auto insurance regulation in Massachusetts, illustrate the problems caused when regulators significantly constrain the rates paid by high-risk drivers. See "The Impact of Rate Regulation on Claims: Evidence from Massachusetts Automobile Insurance" (ssrn.com/abstract=1115377).

Residual Market Mechanisms

A more obscure aspect of insurance, except when major problems develop, is the management of residual market mechanisms (RMMs). These mechanisms take on different forms, but their stated intention is to provide a source of insurance coverage for buyers who cannot obtain coverage from an insurer in what is called the voluntary market. RMMs are commonly found in personal auto insurance and workers' compensation and (in the majority of states) in homeowners insurance. It could be argued that these mechanisms serve a legitimate purpose and may be unavoidable in the presence of compulsory insurance requirements. Further, these mechanisms generally remain small in states in which insurers are allowed to charge risk-based prices and in which the RMM is managed as a true market of last resort, with adequate rates and stringent eligibility requirements.

However, significant problems can arise when the voluntary market is subject to severe regulatory constraints and the residual market mechanism is mismanaged. Poor RMM administration can encompass inadequate rates, lax eligibility requirements, and excessive coverage. When these regulatory policies converge, RMMs can grow rapidly and incur substantial deficits, which are assessed back to voluntary market insureds. This can lead to the infamous downward spiral (described above), in which the voluntary market begins to implode as the RMM explodes.

Figure 5-3 illustrates the trends in auto insurance residual markets in several states. It also shows how these mechanisms shrank in some states as regulatory conditions improved (for example, South Carolina).[28] Unfortunately, North Carolina has not joined their ranks, as its residual market accounts for approximately 25 percent of all vehicles insured in the state. Fixing this kind of problem can be politically challenging, as it entails raising premiums, at least in the short term, for high-risk drivers. Over the long term, high-risk drivers can obtain lower rates if they decrease their risk.

The circumstance facing residual property insurance markets is somewhat different. The principal dilemma here lies with property owners in coastal areas that are vulnerable to hurricanes. Insurers are reluctant to write large numbers of policies in these areas that subject them to excessive catastrophe losses. The growth of RMMs in these areas can be exacerbated by the regulation of voluntary market rates and the underpricing of insurance in the residual market. The financing of these mechanisms is also fragile, as they can incur substantial deficits in the event of a hurricane, which must be repaid through voluntary market assessments.

---

28. Grace, Klein, and Phillips (2002b) analyze the turnaround in South Carolina when it reformed its regulation of auto insurance.

Figure 5-3. *Auto Insurance, Residual Market, Selected States, 1996–2005*

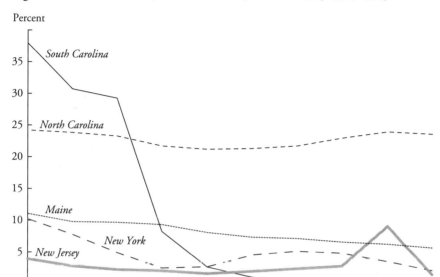

Percent

Source: Automobile Insurance Plan Services Office (2008); Insurance Information Institute (2008).

Florida illustrates how excessive regulation and residual market mismanagement can converge to create severe problems: its residual market facility for property insurance has grown substantially and accounted for 20 percent of its homeowners insurance market in 2007 (figure 5-4). Residual market mechanisms in other coastal states are relatively smaller but still can incur substantial financial deficits. Fixing these problems in coastal states can be a daunting political challenge because it entails much higher rates for coastal property owners.[29]

Hence good rate regulatory policies—preferably price deregulation—should be accompanied by the proper design and administration of residual market mechanisms. This requires that RMMs charge risk-based rates, enforce strict eligibility requirements, and avoid funding shortfalls. These policies facilitate the movement of insureds from state mechanisms to the private market. They also mitigate the moral hazard problems created by cross-subsidies and can lead to decreased risk and lower insurance costs.

29. It is probably easier or less costly for high-risk drivers than for coastal property owners to reduce their risk and qualify for lower rates.

Figure 5-4. *Florida Property Insurance, Residual Market, 1993–2007*

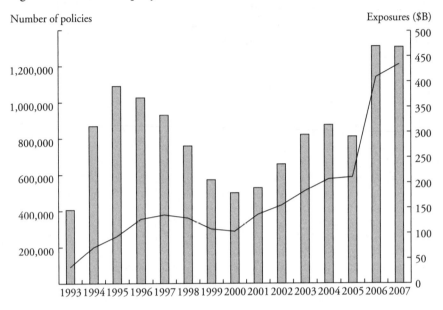

Source: Citizens Property Insurance Corporation (2008).

Product Regulation

A third aspect of market regulation that receives considerable scrutiny is that of policy forms and insurers' products. In a competitive market most insurers would develop and offer legitimate insurance products that serve consumers' needs and preferences according to the kinds and extent of coverage consumers are willing to pay for. At the same time, because of consumers' difficulty in understanding insurance policy provisions, some insurers might seek to exploit consumer ignorance by selling them products that contain substantial coverage gaps or unfavorable terms that are not transparent. This problem should be largely confined to individual consumers and possibly small business owners but would not be expected to extend to larger, more sophisticated commercial buyers.

Hence reforming product regulation is a more complicated proposition than deregulating prices. There are two elements of product regulation that require particular attention. The first is mandated coverages or prohibitions on the exclusions that may be offered in a policy.[30] The second element is the arduous review process

---

30. Harrington (2006).

that insurers must undergo to get products approved and introduced in the market. While the industry might support broad deregulation of insurance products, regulatory experts might understandably differ on how far such deregulation should go.

State-mandated coverages and benefits are a significant problem, especially in health insurance. State health insurance mandates vary greatly and cover a broad range of benefits and other policy provisions.[31] They can include mandated benefits or covered services such as cancer screening, infertility treatments, mental illness, and substance abuse. While mandating such benefits may seem well intended, such benefits can significantly increase the cost of health insurance and limit its availability to all consumers. It would be preferable to allow employers or employees and other consumers to choose the benefits they are willing to pay for.

The lengthy and sometimes tortuous review and approval of insurance products can create significant inefficiencies and hamper market competition. The concern does not lie with ensuring that certain kinds of policies, such as homeowners insurance, provide standard coverages and that coverage terms and exclusions be relatively transparent. The biggest problem lies with life insurance and annuity products, where variation and innovation are integral to market competition and efficiency.[32] As indicated in table 5-2, most states subject life insurance policy forms to prior approval, and only thirty-three states participate in an interstate commission intended to ease the filing and approval process. The high costs and delays in introducing new life insurance products are substantial competitive impediments in life insurance.

In our opinion, some degree of regulatory oversight of personal insurance products is warranted. However, the regulatory requirements for personal insurance products should be rationalized and standardized. Mandated coverages or benefits need to be greatly curtailed. Further, the review process should be greatly streamlined and expedited. Finally, insurance products purchased by commercial insurance buyers should be fully deregulated. These reforms may be the most difficult to achieve under the current system of state regulation.

Underwriting and Other Market Practices

Another complex area is the scope of activities encompassed within the underwriting function. These include risk assessment, risk classification, acceptance or

31. See National Association of Insurance Commissioners (2008).
32. Grace and Klein (2007).

Table 5-2. *Rate Filing Requirements, Life Insurance, by State*

State	Filing requirement	Interstate compact member	State	Filing requirement	Interstate compact member
Alabama	No provision	No	Montana	Prior approval	No
Alaska	Prior approval	Yes	Nebraska	Prior approval	Yes
Arizona	Prior approval	No	Nevada	Prior approval	No
Arkansas	Prior approval	No	New Hampshire	File and use	Yes
California	File and use	No	New Jersey	Prior approval	No
Colorado	No provision	Yes	New Mexico	Prior approval	No
Connecticut	Prior approval	No	New York	Prior approval	No
Delaware	Prior approval	No	North Carolina	Prior approval	Yes
District of Columbia	File and use	No	North Dakota	Prior approval	No
Florida	Prior approval	No	Ohio	Prior approval	Yes
Georgia	Prior approval	Yes	Oklahoma	Prior approval	Yes
Hawaii	Prior approval	Yes	Oregon	Prior approval	No
Idaho	File and use	Yes	Pennsylvania	Prior approval	Yes
Illinois	Prior approval	No	Puerto Rico	Prior approval	Yes
Indiana	Prior approval	Yes	Rhode Island	Prior approval	Yes
Iowa	Prior approval	Yes	South Carolina	Prior approval	No
Kansas	Prior approval	Yes	South Dakota	Prior approval	No
Kentucky	Prior approval	Yes	Tennessee	Prior approval	Yes
Louisiana	Prior approval	No	Texas	File and use	Yes
Maine	Prior approval	Yes	Utah	File and use	Yes
Maryland	Prior approval	Yes	Vermont	Prior approval	Yes
Massachusetts	File and use	Yes	Virginia	Prior approval	Yes
Michigan	Prior approval	Yes	Washington	Prior approval	Yes
Minnesota	Prior approval	Yes	West Virginia	Prior approval	Yes
Mississippi	Prior approval	No	Wisconsin	Prior approval	Yes
Missouri	Prior approval	No	Wyoming	Prior approval	Yes

Source: National Association of Insurance Commissioners (2008).

rejection of insurance applications, nonrenewal or cancellation of existing policies, determination of the premium, product assignment, and special terms and
conditions. Underwriting restrictions and price regulation are closely linked, as
they represent important elements of an integrated process. Regulatory rules and
interference with underwriting activities vary by state and line. For the most part,
regulators generally give insurers fairly wide discretion in underwriting risks, but
some notable exceptions warrant attention. They include mandatory offer requirements, restrictions on the use of certain factors in underwriting and pricing, and
interference with an insurer's efforts to restructure its portfolio of exposures.

Some states impose mandatory offer requirements, also called take-all-comers laws, which compel insurers to accept all applicants who meet minimal insurability requirements. These requirements are often imposed in auto and home insurance, which are viewed as essential insurance coverages. These requirements undermine an insurer's efforts to achieve a balanced portfolio of risks and to avoid adverse selection. They are especially problematic when regulators constrain insurers' rate structures, and the coupling of a mandatory offer requirement and price regulation is not a sheer coincidence.

A related problem is created by prohibitions of or limitations on the underwriting and pricing factors used by insurers. Clearly, characteristics such as race are inappropriate. The problem lies with constraining insurers' use of factors that are statistically correlated with the risk of loss and do not violate societal norms. One example is the use of credit scores in auto and home insurance. There is considerable statistical evidence that credit scores are strongly correlated with risk, but their use has been highly controversial.[33] Critics contend that there is not a causal link between a credit score and the risk of filing a claim—and that credit scores give false indications for some insureds. Correspondingly, an increasing number of states are limiting the use of credit scoring in underwriting and pricing.

However, one could make similar observations about many of the underwriting and pricing factors that insurers use in auto and home insurance. The fundamental issue is whether insurers should be allowed to use factors that improve the overall accuracy of their underwriting and pricing or whether they should be allowed to only use factors that are likely to give a correct indication of a given insured's risk level. Risk classification is inherently imperfect, and competition should drive insurers to use the best factors, because their failure to do so will expose them to adverse selection and cherry-picking by their competitors. This issue is also likely to be contentious in any effort to reform regulatory policies; it would be desirable to develop a set of principles that would guide regulation in this area.

There is also the problem of regulatory attempts to prevent or hamper insurers in restructuring their portfolios of exposures. The best and most current example of this policy is Florida's attempt to constrain insurers' retrenchment from high-risk coastal areas. Florida officials are seeking to preserve the availability of insurance, but retrenching insurers want to reduce excessive concentrations of exposures that greatly increase their financial vulnerability to hurricane losses and that are unsustainable from a business perspective. Ultimately, these kinds of

33. Brockett and Golden (2007).

government constraints are doomed to fail and will only impede the readjustment of insurance markets to new, sustainable equilibriums. As insurers with excessive concentrations of coastal exposures retrench, opportunities are created for insurers that are well positioned to fill the gap if they are allowed to charge adequate rates and take other prudent steps to manage their financial risk.[34] This may be a difficult pill to swallow for politicians, but it is the only viable solution without a federal bailout through, for example, a federal catastrophe insurance-reinsurance program. It appears that coastal politicians are counting heavily on such a bailout, but they may be disappointed.

Additionally, the general system for regulating insurers' market conduct needs to be dramatically revamped. Currently, the states subject insurers to extensive, duplicative, and costly examinations that focus too much on minor errors and too little on major patterns of abuse. In other words, regulators miss the forest for the trees. Regulators also fail to recognize and encourage insurer self-compliance efforts. Robert Klein and James Schacht discuss the problems with the current system and suggest a more effective and efficient approach to market conduct monitoring that would maximize reliance on self-regulatory mechanisms and target regulatory investigation and enforcement to significant problems.[35] The NAIC has been working on "improving" the system for market conduct regulation. Some elements of this initiative may increase efficiency, such as greater uniformity in market conduct standards. However, other elements of the NAIC's plans, like market conduct data reporting, may create new burdens for insurers.

Prospects for Market Regulatory Reforms

It is likely that progress in market regulatory reforms at the state level will continue. There is strong industry pressure for policy changes, and many regulators recognize the need to improve the efficiency of market regulation. That said, state regulators' views vary greatly as to what reforms are appropriate. It is reasonable to expect that some states will strongly resist rate deregulation and other policy changes discussed above. Further, some states and the NAIC favor extending or strengthening market regulation in certain areas despite industry opposition to these measures. While the industry should not be the sole authority on what polices should be adopted, the wide divergence of opinions and the heated debates suggest that reform at the state level will be piecemeal at best and will fall far short of what many experts believe is warranted.

34. Grace, Klein, and Liu (2006).
35. Klein and Schacht (2001).

How insurance markets would be regulated under an OFC is uncertain. It is clear in the OFC legislation that has been proposed (and in the views of its advocates) that insurance rates would be deregulated. However, the legislation is essentially silent on other aspects of market regulation. It is conceivable that any legislation that is enacted will be more explicit on some areas of regulation, while other areas may be left to the discretion of federal regulators or addressed in subsequent legislation. Reform advocates might hope that a federal system will adopt rational and efficient policies, but there is no assurance that this will occur.

Insurance and Antitrust Policy

The McCarran-Ferguson Act (MFA) provides a commerce clause exemption to the insurance industry to allow it to operate under the regulatory authority of the states and not the federal antitrust laws.[36] Hence insurers are given a limited antitrust exemption that is coordinated with compensating regulation by the states. The principal objective of the exemption was to allow insurers to use uniform price structures developed by industry rating organizations and approved by state regulators. However, industry conditions and practices have changed substantially since the MFA was enacted, and its antitrust exemption warrants reconsideration. Indeed, the proposal for an insurance OFC would scale back this exemption to the protection of the sharing of loss data and common policy forms.

The industry has grown dramatically in a number of dimensions since the 1940s and has many more ties to the national and international insurance markets. Insurance rating or advisory organizations no longer issue uniform rate structures that insurers are required to follow. Insurers have a better understanding of how to price insurance products, and markets are more competitive and dynamic. The pertinent questions are whether some form of insurance antitrust exemption should be preserved and, if so, what practices should be protected.

The most relevant discussions of the antitrust exemption concern insurers' ability to share data and the use of advisory organizations to analyze these data to develop and file indicated loss costs for certain lines of insurance.[37] The data shared are loss

---

36. Grace and Klein (2008) discuss insurance antitrust issues in greater detail.

37. Almost universally, any discussion of the repeal of the MFA includes a safe harbor provision for the sharing of data. See American Bar Association, *Comments to the Antitrust Modernization Commission,* section on antitrust law (www.abanet.org/antitrust/at-comments/2006/04-06/com-amc-mccarranferguson.pdf). "Indicated loss costs" refer to the expected losses (such as claims costs) for certain lines of business in each state. This information is provided in manuals or circulars that include factors that can be used to calculate the expected loss cost for a given exposure according to its characteristics.

related and are provided to insurers to assist them in developing accurate rates.[38] Pooled industry data can be more reliable and actuarially credible than individual company data, especially for small insurers. The larger the volume of business an insurer writes, the more it can rely on its own data for pricing. Medium-sized insurers may use a combination of both their own and industry data, and the largest insurers may rely solely on their own data. Ultimately, the compilation and dissemination of industry loss data can facilitate competition and more efficient markets. Information is the most important resource in the insurance industry: data pooling not only reduces entry barriers but also offers other operational efficiencies.[39]

Such data sharing has been facilitated by private entities known collectively as advisory or statistical agents. Statistical agents only collect and disseminate data and generally perform minimal processing and analysis of the data they collect. Advisory organizations not only collect data but also perform more extensive analysis and develop indicated loss costs. The two largest advisory organizations are the Insurance Services Office (ISO) and the National Council on Compensation Insurance (NCCI). ISO collects data on members' premiums, exposures, and losses; aggregates this information; and provides indicated loss costs for various property-casualty insurance lines. The NCCI provides the same services for workers' compensation insurance companies. Both organizations file indicated loss costs with regulators in most states that do not include provisions for expenses and profits. When these filings are approved by regulators, individual insurers may use these loss costs, with or without modification, in filing their specific rates (which include provisions for expenses and profits).[40]

Arguably, the historical interpretation of the antitrust exemption under the MFA is quite narrow. Permitted activities are those that have a potential benefi-

---

38. The most sophisticated and useful compilations include premium, loss, and exposure information organized by various rating characteristics that are essential to determining the expected loss cost for a given exposure (for example, a house or auto insured for one year). For example, in homeowners insurance, these rating characteristics include the location of a home and its type of construction, among many others.

39. Coincidentally, regulators also access and use this information in performing their functions. Hence it has been more often the case that regulators and not insurers have advocated more extensive data reporting.

40. In the early 1990s the ISO voluntarily decided to no longer provide advisory rates to its subscribers. Instead it provides indicated loss costs; these do not include expense and profit information, which a subscriber could then use in developing its own rates. The ISO undertook this change to avoid falling outside the limited antitrust exemption under the MFA. The U.S. Department of Justice has summarized its understanding of what the ISO purported to do: it decided that it

cial effect on competition. These include data sharing, joint development of products and policy forms, and other joint ventures to expand insurance markets, lower costs, and increase competition. These same activities are likely to be viewed as legal without the MFA antitrust exemption. Because the interpretation is narrow and seems to match the types of behavior subject to the rule-of-reason test, it could be argued that the repeal of the MFA exemption would not have a material effect on the industry. At the margin, however, the repeal of the MFA antitrust exemption would create uncertainty surrounding these arrangements, which can be resolved only though litigation. This litigation could be costly and also could have a chilling effect on activities that enhance the efficiency of insurance markets. Hence it would be beneficial to reaffirm, in any federal legislation that would alter its antitrust exemption, the legality of limited joint industry activities.

Summary and Conclusions

In sum, the economic and political context surrounding proposals for insurance regulatory reforms is complex. Proponents of federal regulation believe they have a strong case, and there are a number of arguments that can be made in support of a federal framework. However, the real world is messy, and advocates of federal regulation face formidable political opposition that has so far stymied OFC legislation. Both practical considerations and politics will encumber efforts to rationalize insurance regulation. Hence a major revamping of the current system is unlikely to occur in the near future.

What we are likely to see are small and incremental changes at both the state and federal level, which have been the industry's legacy. These changes will not achieve the objectives of the reformists, but they may set the stage for more substantive reforms under more favorable political conditions. Regardless of how the institutional framework for insurance regulation evolves, it clear that many policies should be reformed to promote market efficiency. This is a prescription that both state and federal regulators should follow, as their authorities and roles are considered and possibly changed by Congress.

---

would offer no challenges to its activities but reserved the right to do so in the future if circumstances warranted. See letter, January 25, 1994, from Assistant U.S. Attorney General Anne Bingaman to Mr. Joel Cohen, acting on behalf of ISO (www.usdoj.gov/atr/public/busreview/211724.htm). The NCCI came to a similar decision shortly thereafter.

References

A. M. Best. 2008. *Best's Impairment Rate and Rating Transition Study—1977–2007.* Oldwick, N.J.

Automobile Insurance Plan Services Office. 2008. *AIPSO Facts: 2006.* Johnston, R.I.

Brockett, Patrick L., and Linda L. Golden. 2007. "Biological and Psychobehavioral Correlates of Credit Scores and Automobile Insurance Losses: Toward an Explication of Why Credit Scoring Works." *Journal of Risk and Insurance* 74, no. 1: 23–63.

Citizens Property Insurance Corporation. 2008. *Citizens Combined Summary Report.* Jacksonville, Fla.

Commission of the European Communities. 2007. "Proposal for a Directive of the European Parliament of the Council on the Taking-Up and Pursuit of the Business of Insurance and Reinsurance: Solvency II." Brussels.

Cummins, J. David. 2007. "Reinsurance for Natural and Man-Made Catastrophes in the United States: Current State of the Market and Regulatory Reforms." *Risk Management and Insurance Review* 10, no. 2: 179–220.

———, ed. 2002. *Deregulating Property-Liability Insurance: Restoring Competition and Increasing Market Efficiency.* Washington: AEI-Brookings Joint Center for Regulatory Studies.

Cummins, J. David, Martin F. Grace, and Richard D. Phillips. 1999. "Regulatory Solvency Prediction in Property-Liability Insurance: Risk-Based Capital, Audit Ratios, and Cash Flow Simulation." *Journal of Risk and Insurance* 66, no. 3: 417–58.

Cummins, J. David, Scott E. Harrington, and Robert W. Klein. 1995. "Insolvency Experience, Risk-Based Capital, and Prompt Corrective Action in Property-Liability Insurance." *Journal of Banking and Finance* 19, nos. 3–4: 511–27.

Cummins, J. David, and Mary A. Weiss. 1991. "The Structure, Conduct, and Regulation of the Property-Liability Insurance Industry." Federal Reserve Bank of Boston, *Conference Series,* 117–64.

Eling, Martin, and Ines Holzmuller. 2008. "An International Overview and Evaluation of Risk-Based Capital Standards." Working Paper. University of St. Gallen, Switzerland.

Eling, Martin, Hato Schmeiser, and Joan T. Schmit. 2007. "The Solvency II Process: Overview and Critical Analysis." *Risk Management and Insurance Review* 10, no. 1: 69–85.

Grace, Martin F., Scott E. Harrington, and Robert W. Klein. 1998. "Risk-Based Capital and Solvency Screening in Property-Liability Insurance." *Journal of Risk and Insurance* 65, no. 2: 213–43.

Grace, Martin F., and Robert W. Klein. 2007. "The Effects of an Optional Federal Charter on Competition in the Life Insurance Industry." Report to the American Council of Life Insurers. Georgia State University.

———. 2008. "The Past and Future of Insurance Regulation: The McCarran-Ferguson Act and Beyond." Working Paper. Georgia State University.

Grace, Martin F., Robert W. Klein, and Zhiyong Liu. 2006. "Mother Nature on the Rampage: Implications for Insurance Markets." Working Paper. Georgia State University.

Grace, Martin F., Robert W. Klein, and Richard D. Phillips. 2002a. "Managing the Cost of Property-Casualty Insurer Insolvencies." Report to the National Association of Insurance Commissioners. Georgia State University.

———. 2002b. "Auto Insurance Reform: Salvation in South Carolina." In *Deregulating Property-Liability Insurance: Restoring Competition and Increasing Market Efficiency,* edited by J. David Cummins, pp. 148–94. Washington: AEI-Brookings Joint Center for Regulatory Studies.

Hall, Brian J. 2000. "Regulatory Free Cash Flow and the High Cost of Insurance Company Failures." *Journal of Risk and Insurance* 67, no. 3: 415–38.

Harrington, Scott E. 2002. "Effects of Prior Approval Rate Regulation of Auto Insurance." In *Deregulating Property-Liability Insurance: Restoring Competition and Increasing Market Efficiency,* edited by J. David Cummins, pp. 285–314. Washington: AEI-Brookings Joint Center for Regulatory Studies.

———. 2006. "Federal Chartering of Insurance Companies: Options and Alternatives for Transforming Insurance Regulation." Policy Brief 2006-PB-02. Networks Financial Institute, Indiana State University.

Insurance Information Institute. 2008. *The Fact Book 2008*. Washington.

International Association of Insurance Supervisors. 2007. *The IAIS Common Structure for the Assessment of Insurer Solvency*. Basel.

James, C. 1991. "The Losses Realized in Bank Failures." *Journal of Finance* 46, no. 4: 1223–42.

Kaufmann, G. 2001. Testimony of George G. Kaufmann, U.S. Senate Committee on Banking, Housing, and Urban Affairs, September 11, 2001.

Klein, Robert W. 2005. *A Regulator's Introduction to the Insurance Industry*. Kansas City, Mo.: National Association of Insurance Commissioners.

———. 2007. "Catastrophe Risk and the Regulation of Property Insurance: A Comparison of Five States." Working Paper. Georgia State University.

Klein, Robert W., and James Schacht. 2001. "An Assessment of Insurance Market Conduct Surveillance." *Journal of Insurance Regulation* 20, no. 1: 51–93.

Klein, Robert W., and Shaun Wang. 2007. "Catastrophe Risk Financing in the United States and the European Union: A Comparison of Alternative Regulatory Approaches." Working Paper. Georgia State University.

National Association of Insurance Commissioners. 2008. *Compendium of State Laws on Insurance Topics*. Kansas City, Mo.

Willenborg, Michael. 2000. "Regulatory Separation as a Mechanism to Curb Capture: A Study of the Decision to Act against Distressed Insurers." *Journal of Risk and Insurance* 67, no. 4: 593–616.

6

Consumer Benefits of an Optional Federal Charter: The Case of Auto Insurance

Robert E. Litan and Phil O'Connor

A key element of most legislative proposals to establish an optional federal charter (OFC) for insurers is that market competition rather than government regulation would set insurance rates. Insurers choosing the federal charter, therefore, would be free to set premiums based on their actuarial calculations of risk and other competitive considerations. The market would discipline insurers and, as in other sectors, would keep premiums in line with claims, other expenses, and a reasonable allowance for profit (taking account of the relative risks involved in underwriting particular kinds of insurance).

In fact this is how insurance rates are generally set today in certain lines of insurance that would be affected by OFC legislation, notably life insurance and most commercial lines. Although technically rates for these lines of insurance must be filed with state regulators, in practice regulators rarely challenge them, and insurers are free to charge the rates they file without prior regulatory approval.

A notable exception to this general pattern is personal auto insurance, in which many state insurance commissions play a major role in dictating the premiums that insurers charge, and a few state insurance commissions actively set rates.[1] The

---

1. We concentrate throughout this chapter on personal auto insurance, as distinct from commercial auto insurance, since much of the political concern about insurance rates is confined to the personal auto line.

fear that unregulated auto insurance rates would lead consumers in some states to pay more for this insurance than they do now is one of the reasons that some in Congress may be reluctant to include auto insurance, and perhaps personal lines more broadly, in any OFC legislation.

Is there really a basis for this concern? Economists who have studied auto insurance regulation consistently conclude that rate regulation distorts the market, rewarding higher-risk drivers, who would pay more without rate controls, at the expense of safer drivers, who would pay less. The *average* effects—that is, the impact of rate regulation on the average consumer or on all consumers in a given state—seem more ambiguous; while total insurance costs may be suppressed or reduced by rate regulation in the short run, they may be increased over the longer run. The presence of rate regulation can discourage insurers from lowering premiums when claims costs and expenses are falling. Further, the distortion in the rate structure due to regulation fails to discourage the imprudent driving behavior of higher-risk drivers. As a result, rate regulation can raise claims costs, and ultimately premiums, over the long run.

Given the strong interest in auto insurance markets and their seeming centrality to the coverage of any OFC legislation that may eventually pass Congress, we concentrate here on what the evidence suggests would be the most likely impact of enabling federally chartered auto insurers to charge rates for auto insurance determined by market competition; that is to say, the question is, What most likely would happen if Congress eventually approves OFC legislation that would extend to auto insurance? By implication, the conclusions reached here also should apply to homeowners insurance.[2]

The most statistically valid studies of the impact of rate regulation on average premiums are those that control for other relevant factors that may affect rates. The most recent studies of this kind, those reported in a 2002 volume edited by David Cummins and published by the AEI-Brookings Joint Center for Regulatory Studies, establish that the nature and degree of rate regulation has no statistically significant effect on rates over the long run, and indeed, to the extent that rate regulation fails to discourage higher-risk drivers from driving more carefully, may lead to *higher* rates.[3] We summarize the key findings of the Cummins study in the first part of this chapter.

2. In what follows, we concentrate solely on rate regulation or deregulation and do not address other forms of regulation, such as the solvency of insurers and perhaps some sort of regulation of insurance products or policy forms, that would continue to be appropriate for federally chartered insurers under an OFC system.

3. Cummins (2002).

A simpler, though admittedly less rigorous, way to assess the impact of rate regulation on average premiums is simply to compare average premiums, or proxy measures of average premiums, in the relatively few years before and after a change in the regulatory regime: either deregulation or regulation. By limiting the comparison to just a few years on either side of the change in regime, this before-after analysis can, to some extent, control for other factors (which are not likely to change significantly over such a relatively short period). In addition, before-after comparisons are likely to be better understood by policymakers and voters than more rigorous statistical tests would be.

We therefore report in the second part of this chapter the results from three before-after comparisons: two partial deregulatory episodes in South Carolina (1999) and New Jersey (2003) and one episode of the opposite nature, the adoption of a strict prior approval regulatory regime in California (Proposition 103, which became effective in 1989). In addition, we summarize some recent, more rigorous statistical analysis of the link between rate regulation and overall claims losses—and thus, indirectly, premiums—in Massachusetts, another state in which rates have been tightly regulated.

The main conclusions from the three before-after comparisons are consistent with the statistical conclusions from the Cummins study. The behavior of premiums after rates were partially deregulated in both South Carolina and New Jersey broadly indicates, at the very least, that average auto insurance consumers were not harmed by, and indeed could well have benefited from, the policy change. Conversely, despite popular perceptions to the contrary, some key data before and after California adopted Proposition 103 suggest that consumers have not benefited from that law—and indeed may have been harmed.

Finally, statistical analysis of rates in Massachusetts confirms what economic theory would predict: that by distorting the rate structure, rate regulation actually leads to higher loss costs, and thus higher premiums, on average, than would be the case under market competition. Massachusetts may be taking that lesson to heart in recent reforms that introduce somewhat greater flexibility in the setting of insurance rates by market forces. In addition, the substantial decline in the share of market accounted for by residual market plans in New Jersey and South Carolina after each state allowed more room for competition also indicates that partial deregulation in those states has dramatically reduced the distortions in the rate structures that had the effect of subsidizing higher-risk drivers.

The clear implication for federal policymakers who may be considering OFC legislation is that there is no basis for fearing that market competition in lieu of state rate regulation would harm consumers. This should not be surprising given the structure of the auto insurance market, and indeed other insurance markets, in which large numbers of insurers do business and the markets are not concentrated.

Rationale for and Impact of Auto Insurance Rate Regulation: Prior Studies

Most states play a major role in dictating the premiums that insurers charge for auto insurance. According to the most recent count we have been able to find, thirty-one states require rates to be approved before they can become effective.[4] Two states, California and Massachusetts, are widely considered to have the most tightly regulated insurance markets (New Jersey belonged to this group until 2003, as discussed in more detail below). In some other states, insurers do not need prior approval to charge what they believe the market will allow, although regulators can subsequently disapprove a rate. This rarely happens, in large part because insurers are hesitant in these states to implement rates that might trigger subsequent disapproval, and thus they negotiate rates with regulators or wait for them to approve the filed rates. As a result, even in many states that do not require prior approval of rates, market forces are not entirely free to operate.

Why would any state (or any other level of government) regulate the rate or price of any service, such as auto insurance? Economic theory suggests that price or rate regulation can improve consumer welfare if a market is subject to a natural monopoly (because the unique nature of the product or service exhibits large economies of scale such that the market can only support a single competitor), or if the market is highly concentrated with only a few sellers or producers, who, because of significant barriers to entry from others, can charge prices above competitive levels. In such circumstances, if rates or prices are set by regulation at or close to average costs, consumers are likely to pay less, and output of the product or service is likely to be greater, than in the absence of regulation.[5]

At the federal level, policymakers over the past several decades (beginning primarily in the Carter administration and continuing thereafter) have recognized

---

4. Cummins (2002), p. 3.

5. We say "likely" because it is always possible that regulators can make mistakes or succumb to political pressures so that any price or rate ceilings are suboptimal. Indeed, that is precisely what the evidence suggests has happened in the states that have most tightly regulated auto insurance rates (where, as the text demonstrates, there is no compelling economic rationale for rate regulation in the first place).

that neither of these conditions—natural monopoly or high seller concentration with entry barriers—held (if they ever did) in a number of services in which prices or rates historically had been regulated: airlines, trucking, railroads, telecommunications, and banking. Economists broadly agree that price deregulation in these areas clearly benefited consumers, saving them billions of dollars each year.[6]

Do the economic conditions warranting regulation of rates apply to personal auto insurance? As is true for all other lines of insurance, the auto insurance business is not a natural monopoly. To the contrary, more than a thousand insurers offer the service nationwide. Significant numbers of companies offer auto insurance in any single state. Still, the numbers of insurers doing business and thus the concentration levels in any specific state can depend on the presence and nature of rate regulation. For example, one year after South Carolina partially deregulated its auto insurance rates in 1999 (discussed in more detail below), the number of auto insurers doing business in the state tripled, from 55 the previous year to roughly 150.[7]

What, then, might account for the tight regulation of auto insurance rates in California and Massachusetts? To return to economic theory, is it possible that, despite the unconcentrated nature of the industry, auto insurers nonetheless take advantage of the antitrust exemption under the McCarran-Ferguson Act to implicitly or even explicitly collude? In that event, state rate regulation could be justified as a way of offsetting any anticonsumer impacts of joint rate setting by insurers.

That supposition is not supported by the facts. Since the 1970s rate setting by insurance rating bureaus has declined substantially in importance. There is no evidence of which we are aware that insurers today collude on premiums, explicitly or implicitly. Indeed, the prevailing academic opinion about McCarran-Ferguson is that it has little or no effect on insurance premiums.[8]

The best explanation for auto insurance rate regulation is that it is a political response to concerns about high and rising auto premiums. These concerns tend to be most pronounced in states where premiums in fact are high or rising rapidly or where there is significant variability in premiums across geographical regions and among classes of drivers. Under such circumstances, the highest-risk drivers facing the highest premiums are likely to have the most interest in supporting elected officials who promise lower rates, even though rate regulation tends to penalize lower-

6. See, for example, Winston (1993).
7. Grace, Klein, and Phillips (2002), p. 163.
8. Grace and Klein (2008).

risk drivers (who most likely are unaware that they end up subsidizing higher-risk groups under rate regulatory regimes).[9] It is no accident, therefore, that auto insurance rates have been most tightly regulated in California and Massachusetts, where auto claims costs have been and still are among the highest in the nation.[10]

The foregoing propositions are extensively documented in what is surely the most thorough study of auto insurance regulation to date. This study was conducted by a team of researchers organized by David Cummins of the University of Pennsylvania's Wharton School of Finance. Cummins, who is one of the most highly regarded academic scholars of insurance, convened a distinguished group of scholars to examine the effects of the regulation of auto insurance rates in a number of states: those where rates have been tightly regulated (California, Massachusetts, and at the time, New Jersey), one state where regulation as of that time had become less intrusive (South Carolina), and one state where rates had long been deregulated (Illinois). The results were published in 2002 by the AEI-Brookings Joint Center for Regulatory Studies.[11]

The researchers in the Cummins project focused primarily on personal auto insurance because, as indicated, these rates are more commonly tightly regulated than the rates for any other type of insurance (except for workers' compensation).[12] This focus made it possible to compare the performance of insurance markets in states where rates were more tightly regulated than in states where this was not the case. In addition, two of the researchers were able to conduct before-after comparisons for California, after it adopted Proposition 103 regulating rates much more tightly, and for South Carolina, which partially deregulated auto insurance rates in 1999. Because one state (South Carolina) had moved in a deregulatory direction, researchers could conduct a limited before-after comparison to determine the impact of that sort of change.

9. Grace, Klein, and Phillips (2002).

10. Interestingly, until Proposition 103 was enacted in 1989, California had long relied on market forces to determine auto insurance rates. Likewise, Massachusetts had adopted so-called "competitive rating" in the late 1970s but later abandoned that approach.

11. Robert Litan, along with Robert Hahn, was a founding director of the Joint Center for Regulatory Studies. He asked David Cummins to lead this project. In late 2007 the center was dissolved.

12. As Cummins (2002) notes in the introduction, a study issued several years before the AEI-Brookings Joint Center study found the perversities of rate regulation in the market for workers' compensation to be similar to those found where auto insurance rates were tightly regulated. See Danzon and Harrington (1997). Two chapters in the Cummins book address the property-liability insurance market more broadly, both in the United States and elsewhere around the world. However, most of the chapters focus on the automobile insurance market, which is also the focus here.

The Cummins study published several important findings. For purposes of brevity, we highlight the most pertinent ones here. First, the study contains two statistical analyses that come to the same conclusion. In his statistical cross-section analysis of auto insurance rates in fifty states over the 1972–98 period, Scott Harrington finds that, on average, prior approval regulation has little or no effect on average rate levels for any given level of claims costs.[13] Similarly, Stephen D'Arcy, using regressions estimated over the 1980–98 period, reports that the presence or type of regulation in different states for fourteen auto insurers has no statistically significant effect on the ratios of their incurred losses to total premiums (a proxy for premium levels).[14] In conjunction with the state case studies, the two statistical analyses imply that deregulation of rates should not raise average premiums for consumers in the long run.[15]

Second, notwithstanding the absence of long-run impacts on average rates, various authors on the Cummins team discuss how rate regulation distorts rate structures, causing low-risk drivers to pay more than is actuarially justified in order to subsidize higher-risk drivers. As we discuss in more detail below, this distortion reduces incentives for higher-risk drivers to behave more carefully, which should raise total claims losses. One author team (Dwight Jaffee and Thomas Russell) suggests that this adverse effect could be offset, at least partially, by rating plans that take account of drivers' experiences (violations and accidents).[16]

Third, the presence or absence of rate regulation clearly has an effect on the number and fraction of a state's drivers who can obtain insurance only from a state's residual market facility (an insurance pool of last resort for those high-risk drivers who cannot buy insurance in the open, voluntary market because insurers are not willing to sell them policies at the regulated rates). The findings of several of the case studies, together with Harrington's statistical analysis, confirm that regulation does indeed compel more drivers to obtain their insurance through residual market facilities.

---

13. Harrington (2002). Harrington did not examine the question, discussed next, as to whether regulation might increase total claims costs by failing to encourage more careful driving.

14. D'Arcy (2002).

15. It is possible, of course, that rate regulation may suppress rates in the short run, but insurers operating under some form of prior approval regulation appear to have been able to compensate for this effect by not fully passing along declining costs in lower premiums for fear that they would be unable to raise premiums when costs increased.

16. Jaffee and Russell (2002).

Finally, Harrington finds that, because of its short-run impacts on insurer pricing behavior, rate regulation increases volatility in both insurance premiums and insurer cash flow. This increase in cash flow volatility in turn raises the cost of capital for insurers, which is likely to translate into higher rates over the long run.

Additional Before-After Comparisons

Much of the analysis in the Cummins study rests on the application of standard statistical techniques: regression analysis to control for various factors that can determine insurance rates (or a proxy, such as the ratio of incurred losses to premiums), in order to isolate the effect, if any, of rate regulation on rates over time. A less rigorous, though more transparent, way to assess this impact is to compare rates (or proxy variables) before and after any change in a regulatory regime. By keeping the before-after period relatively short, and comparing rates in a particular state to some benchmark like the national average, it may be possible to generate results that are the functional equivalent of a regression analysis. In effect, this is what is done by researchers who conduct event studies, that is, looking at how certain events affect stock prices: they limit the time period before and after the event and compare the effect on the price of a particular stock to the changes in stock prices over the same periods for the market as a whole.

Here, we look more closely at several such "natural experiments" in auto insurance rate regulation. Two of them relate to deregulatory measures that allow greater (but not complete) pricing flexibility by insurers. In one case, the insurers did business in South Carolina after deregulation in 1999; in the second case, the insurers did business in New Jersey after deregulation in 2003, after a change in policy.[17] In each case, we look at what happened to average premiums before and after these events and compare the changes to those observed over the same time periods for the nation as a whole. We are aware, of course, that different consumers will have fared differently in each state after deregulation. Indeed, we believe we can safely assume that any moves toward deregulation benefited low-risk drivers in particular, since rate regulation historically requires them to subsidize high-risk drivers. Perhaps an equally important question for federal

17. Effective in March 1999 South Carolina introduced a flex rating system that dispensed with prior approval of rate changes plus or minus 7 percent and that permitted insurers much greater freedom to match rates with the risk profiles of drivers. In addition, the state began to phase out certain unusual features of its residual market facility, including subsidies, which had led to both rapid growth and cost escalation in the immediately preceding years.

policymakers considering OFC legislation, however, is whether consumers, considered as a group, have been harmed by rate deregulation in the states that have tried it. That is why we focus here on the impacts of regime change on average premiums (or proxies for that measure).

The simple comparisons of average premiums cannot control for changes in the average level or type of coverage bought by consumers. For example, a decline in insurance rates might prompt some consumers to purchase "more" insurance, such as policies with lower deductibles or higher policy limits. The opposite would be expected if rates were to increase. The average premium figures cannot capture such effects, but supposing they exist, they reinforce the conclusions reached simply by looking at the change in average premiums. Thus if the average coverage level increases after rates fall, then the effective price of insurance is even lower than the average premium may imply.

We also revisit some relevant data before and after California adopted Proposition 103, which ostensibly made California's regulatory regime one of the strictest in the country. This episode was studied extensively by Jaffee and Russell in the Cummins work, with the authors finding then that apparently none of the negative effects generally associated with rate regulation (that firms exit the market, that the state's assigned risk pool would expand, and that the regulated industry would earn lower profits) actually materialized. Indeed, it seems to be conventional wisdom that California's system of rate regulation, which froze premiums for five years, benefited California's auto insurance consumers. But to us the more relevant question, which cannot be answered by simply looking at premiums before and after Proposition 103 went into effect in 1989, is, What would have happened to California's consumers had rates not been regulated? That is, based on data prior to that event, what can one infer about the level of market-determined rates? Is it possible that California's consumers might have been better off had rates there never been frozen and then subject to strict prior approval thereafter? We also examine this question.

Experiments in Rate Deregulation

The first experiment we look at is South Carolina's partial deregulation in 1999. The authors of the chapter dealing with that state in the Cummins study (Martin Grace, Robert Klein, and Richard Phillips) identify some preliminary salutary effects of that change.[18] But can anything else be said?

18. Grace, Klein, and Phillips (2002).

Table 6-1. *Average Auto Insurance Premiums, South Carolina and United States, 1997–2001*
Units as indicated

Year	South Carolina	United States
	Dollars	
1997	629.10	705.30
1998	655.30	702.70
1999[a]	593.30	683.40
2000[a]	619.60	686.30
2001[a]	616.90	717.70
	Percent change	
1997–98	4.2	−0.4
1998–99[a]	−9.5	−2.8
1998–2001[a]	−5.9	2.1

Source: National Association of Insurance Commissioners (2003).
a. After partial deregulation.

Again, only in event studies that make before-after comparisons is it appropriate to limit the period on either side of the regulatory regime as a way of controlling for other factors that may influence rates. Accordingly, table 6-1 compares average premiums in South Carolina versus those for the nation as a whole in the two years preceding the change in policy, in 1999, and in the two subsequent years. Notably, average premiums in South Carolina in the year before the reform increased by 4.2 percent, compared to a decline nationwide of 0.4 percent. Following the reform of 1999, this pattern was reversed: South Carolina premiums declined by 5.9 percent versus a nationwide increase of 2.1 percent. Premiums declined most substantially in South Carolina in the year of the reform itself, 1999: by 9.5 percent, a much steeper decline than the 2.8 percentage point drop in nationwide premiums.

Table 6-2 reports similar data for New Jersey, after it partially deregulated auto insurance premiums in 2003. As in South Carolina, premiums increased at a faster pace in the year before deregulation, 2001–02, than nationwide. In contrast to the immediate relative decline in premiums after deregulation in South Carolina, in New Jersey premiums rose at a slightly faster pace than the national average after deregulation in the first two years, but by the third year, or 2005, this pattern apparently reversed. Indeed, one prominent media report indicates that by 2005 deregulation was having revolutionary impacts in the state: 75 percent of the

Table 6-2. *Average Auto Insurance Premiums, New Jersey and the United States, 2001–05*
Units as indicated

Year	New Jersey		United States
		Dollars	
2001	1,027.70		725.60[a]
2002	1,125.20		780.80
2003[b]	1,193.20		824.50
2004[b]	1,221.10		840.00
2005[b]	1,183.50		829.20
		Percent change	
2001–02	9.5		7.6
2002–03[b]	6.0		5.6
2002–04[b]	8.5		7.6
2002–05[b]	5.2		6.2

Source: National Association of Insurance Commissioners (2007).

a. The 2001 number for the national average differs from the 2001 figure reported in table 6-1 because the data in this table are from a subsequent NAIC publication.

b. After partial deregulation.

state's customers, including those with poor driving records, were paying less for auto insurance than when rates were regulated, and further reductions were expected. Savings of as much as 30–40 percent were common for many customers.[19] On the whole, we interpret the evidence from the South Carolina and New Jersey "natural experiments" as being inconsistent with the view that rate deregulation necessarily harms consumers, on average, while providing some evidence that it might actually benefit consumers.

It is also instructive to examine what happened to the percentage of the auto insurance market accounted for by residual market plans in each of the two states after the deregulatory measures. As noted, residual market plans are last-resort insurance facilities for individuals who cannot purchase insurance in the voluntary market. In a competitive market, insurers will charge rates that reflect the risks posed by different drivers. In regulated settings, rates for higher-risk drivers tend to be capped, which leaves them no choice but to purchase insurance in the resid-

19. Joseph Treaster, "Car Insurance Rates Drop in New Jersey," *New York Times,* August 24, 2006; Joe Donohue, "NJ Auto Insurance Profit Shows 4th Straight Annual Decline," *Star-Ledger,* February 28, 2008.

ual market. The share of the market accounted for by residual market plans, therefore, is one indicator of the extent to which rate regulation distorts the rate structure.

In fact, participation in residual market plans dropped sharply in both New Jersey and South Carolina after each state allowed more rate flexibility. For example, in 1998 over $468 million in written premiums were collected by the residual market plan in South Carolina, which accounted for 26 percent of all auto insurance premiums in the state in that year, the highest percentage in the nation. The following year, in 1999, that share dropped to 8.6 percent. By 2006 South Carolina's residual market premiums had fallen below $1 million and accounted for less than 0.1 percent of the state's auto insurance market. Likewise, in 2002 New Jersey's residual markets plan collected $423 million in premiums, representing 6.2 percent of all auto insurance premiums. By 2006 the residual market share in the state had declined to 2.9 percent.[20] Clearly, the deregulatory steps in both New Jersey and South Carolina reduced the distortions in rates that had previously caused large numbers of auto consumers to seek refuge in residual market plans. This is important because, as discussed further below, the evidence suggests that rate distortions can lead to higher overall claims losses and thus higher insurance premiums.

In sum, the evidence from both the South Carolina and New Jersey experiences with partial deregulation indicates that consumers in each state were not harmed by—and could well have benefited from—this change in the regulatory regime.

Revisiting California's Proposition 103: Did Consumers Really Benefit?

After climbing rapidly in the years preceding passage of Proposition 103, California auto insurance premiums essentially were flat in the following decade; in contrast, premiums nationwide continued to increase.[21] This result follows directly from the law itself, which froze most insurance premiums from late 1989 through 1994 and required all rate increases and decreases to be approved by the insurance commissioner before they could take effect. In addition, the proposition required a 20 percent rollback, or rebate, of insurance rates, as of late 1987.

But none of this means that Proposition 103 actually benefited consumers. To know if that was or was not the case requires at least an estimate of what rates

20. The data in this paragraph are from Automobile Insurance Plan Service Office (1999–2006).
21. Jaffee and Russell (2002).

would have been had competition been allowed to continue to set premiums. It is entirely possible that under a tougher prior approval regime, if insurer costs had been falling, the regulatory system may have inhibited insurers from lowering rates through normal forces of competition. If this had occurred, then the proposition would have harmed consumers.

How can this hypothesis be tested? One way is to compare what happened to the average loss ratio and to other measures of insurer profitability in the state before and after Proposition 103. The loss ratio (ratio of total losses incurred to premiums earned in a given year) can be viewed roughly as the inverse of an insurer's markup (think of the inverse of the loss ratio as being premiums divided by losses, which looks like a markup measure). It is a rough indicator, because in fact claims losses in any year are backward looking. In a market setting, insurers will set premiums by projecting what their future losses are likely to be. Nonetheless, the loss ratio for a given year is likely to affect projected future premiums. It also can be viewed as a measure of the competitive intensity in a state or, in the event of regulation, what kind of markup regulators are willing to approve. The average underwriting profit in any given year and the return on net worth also serve as other measures of competitive intensity.

Other things being equal, if auto claims losses fell after Proposition 103, as in fact happened, then the shift toward tighter regulation would have resulted in lower premiums than otherwise would have been the case only if the loss ratio increased or measures of insurer profitability declined. The opposite effect—that is, if the loss ratio declined (meaning more premiums collected for any given dollar of losses incurred) or insurer profitability increased—would suggest that consumers would have been better off if the normal forces of competition had been allowed to operate.

Table 6-3 provides the loss ratios and profit measures before and after Proposition 103. We include a number of years following 1989, the year in which the proposition first became law, because the proposition did not become fully effective until 1995 (due to delays resulting from litigation and further regulatory refinement of the proposition).

The numbers in the table tell a compelling story: whether by loss ratios (the inverse of the markup), underwriting profit, or return on net worth, insurers did far better after Proposition 103 was adopted and gradually implemented than in the immediately preceding years. The increase in insurer profitability occurred despite a flattening of insurance premiums themselves. How did this happen?

Jaffee and Russell discuss this issue extensively in their chapter of the Cummins study and report the obvious answer: incurred losses per insured vehicle in

Table 6-3. *Auto Insurance Loss Ratios and Profitability Measures, California,*
1985–98
Percent

Year	Loss ratio	Underwriting profit	Return on net worth
1985	75.4	. . .	3.0
1986	75.4	−10.7	5.6
1987	76.1	−12.2	2.6
1988	74.0	−9.4	4.5
		Postregulation	
1989	69.7	−4.8	9.6
1990	69.7	−5.4	9.0
1991	62.4	1.9	16.5
1992	60.3	6.5	21.2
1993	61.7	5.0	18.4
1994	62.5	5.9	16.7
1995	60.4	8.0	18.7
1996	58.2	9.7	19.3
1997	53.6	11.2	18.9
1998	57.0	3.9	12.4

Source: National Association of Insurance Commissioners (2003).

California fell substantially after Proposition 103 was implemented. By far the
most important reason for the drop in losses was the decline in collisions with
fatalities and injuries due to greater seat belt usage in the state. In addition, Jaffee
and Russell find that the California Supreme Court's ruling in *Moradi-Shalal*
v. *Fireman's Fund,* which significantly limited the exposure of insurers to bad-faith
claims arising out of third-party injury claims, also led to lower losses. Both of
these factors clearly had nothing to do with Proposition 103. Jaffee and Russell
suggest that two other factors, linked to the change in regulation, might have contributed to the decline in losses, although they do not quantify the impacts: the
mandated "good-driver" discount, which should have encouraged safer driving,
and the incentives the premium freeze should have given insurers to reduce fraud
and other expenses. At the same time, however, by requiring the prior approval of
rate changes, the proposition may also have discouraged insurers from filing rate
decreases in a timely fashion, thus increasing profit margins.

The bottom line from California's experience with rate regulation is that it is
not appropriate to infer that tighter regulation of insurance rates worked—in the
sense that it benefited California consumers—just because premiums remained
essentially flat after Proposition 103 went into effect. Had loss ratios stayed at lev-

Table 6-4. *Loss Ratios and Underwriting Profits, New Jersey and South Carolina, Various Years*
Units as indicated

State	Loss ratio	Underwriting profit (percent)
New Jersey		
2001	71.5	−9.1
2002	61.8	−1.0
2003[a]	57.9	4.3
2004[a]	57.2	4.7
2005[a]	60.2	2.5
South Carolina		
1997	79.1	−17.8
1998	75.7	−15.4
1999[a]	75.4	−13.5
2000[a]	77.7	−18.8
2001[a]	69.5	−5.7

Source: National Association of Insurance Commissioners (2007).
a. After partial deregulation.

els comparable to those before 1989, when rates were more market determined, given the decline in incurred losses for the reasons already noted, it is likely that auto insurance premiums in California would have been lower had Proposition 103 never been enacted.

A natural question one might ask is what would a similar before-after analysis of loss ratios and underwriting profits, as opposed to premiums, in New Jersey and South Carolina look like? Might it be the case that premiums would have fallen even further or increased less rapidly in each state had each state continued to regulate rates? The data shown in table 6-4 are mixed, but on the whole, in our view, they do not undermine the previous conclusion—that, at the very least, deregulation did not harm consumers in each state and conceivably could have benefited them.

It is true that for New Jersey the loss ratio fell modestly in 2003–05, compared to 2001–02 (although by 2005, the loss ratio had climbed back close to the 2002 level) and that underwriting profits after deregulation were positive, rather than negative, compared to the two years before deregulation. Nonetheless, profitability for auto insurers was already improving rapidly in the year before deregulation (whether measured by loss ratio or underwriting profits), or perhaps more precisely, was being allowed by the regulators to improve. Furthermore, in 2006, by which time partial deregulation had been in effect for some time, underwriting profits for insurers had fallen below zero again (0.3 percent). Broadly considered, these trends do not clearly establish that continued regulation would have kept average auto insurance premiums in New Jersey lower than they were when they were partially deregulated. This is especially true in light of the press report noted above, which indicates that many New Jersey customers were saving substantial sums on their auto insurance premiums following the change in the regulatory regime.[22]

As for South Carolina, table 6-4 shows no clear drop in the loss ratio or rise in underwriting profits in the two years immediately after the partial deregulation in that state, although by 2001 there is a marked rise in insurer profitability. Taken together, these data do not point to a clear conclusion either way about what average premiums might have been in South Carolina had its strict regulatory system remained in place. The premium data themselves, however, are quite clear: South Carolina consumers fared better than consumers nationwide in the years immediately following partial deregulation in the state.

Rate Regulation and Claims Losses

One of the consistent findings of prior research, including the study by the Cummins team, is that whatever the average of impact rate regulation may be, such regulation tends to distort rates so that low-risk drivers subsidize higher-risk drivers. Because individuals respond to economic incentives to at least some degree, in principle, higher-risk drivers in the most tightly regulated states therefore should drive less carefully relative to drivers of similar characteristics in the deregulated states, where higher-risk drivers face rates that are much more aligned with their accident risk propensities. In fact, several earlier studies find that, once other factors are controlled for, rate regulation indeed does elevate losses. This is the case both for workers' compensation and for auto insurance.[23]

The most recent study of this issue relates to the auto insurance market in Massachusetts, which perhaps until recently has been among the most tightly regulated in the country. Richard Derrig and Sharon Tennyson examine the regulation-loss linkage issue using two approaches. Both approaches clearly support the notion that regulation has increased total losses incurred.[24]

22. Treaster, "Car Insurance Rates Drop in New Jersey."
23. With regard to workers' compensation, see Danzon and Harrington (2001); and Barkume and Ruser (2001). For personal auto insurance, see Tennyson, Weiss, and Regan (2002); and Weiss, Regan, and Tennyson (2005).
24. Richard A. Derrig and Sharon Tennyson, "The Impact of Rate Regulation on Claims: Evidence from Massachusetts Automobile Insurance" (ssrn.com/abstract=1115377).

First, Derrig and Tennyson compare auto insurance loss costs in Massachusetts to those in other states over the 1972–95 period, controlling for differences in regulatory environment, traffic density, per capita income, the statewide average cost per day of staying in a hospital, and the amount of insurance coverage purchased. Using standard regression analysis techniques, the authors estimate that auto insurance losses were 44 percent higher than what one would have expected based on the state's demographic composition and its liability coverage.

Second, Derrig and Tennyson examine claims costs in different towns within Massachusetts, some of which benefited from subsidies in the state's average rating system and others that did not, over the "accident years" 1993–2004. Again, using standard statistical techniques, the authors find that auto insurance losses grew faster in towns that received subsidies. This finding too is consistent with the hypothesis that rating regimes that have the effect of subsidizing higher-risk drivers on balance entail higher claims costs, and thus higher overall premiums, than rates that are aligned with risk.

If the first result reached by Derrig and Tennyson, namely that rate regulation can lead to higher claims costs of as much as 44 percent, is anywhere near accurate, it suggests that average premiums in Massachusetts are most likely inflated by a similar amount. This makes it conceivable that even many high-risk drivers in Massachusetts—who under a more market-determined rating system would have to pay higher rates than low-risk drivers—may still pay less because rating freedom would substantially reduce the overall average, or base, premium to which any positive risk adjustment might be added. Perhaps we will soon know, since in 2007 Massachusetts began a process of modest reform of auto insurance that allows insurers greater freedom in setting rates.

Conclusions

The academic literature on the effect of auto insurance rate regulation makes it very clear that over the long run rate regulation does not benefit consumers. To the contrary, studies indicate that because such regulation can distort rates and thus incentives for prudent driving, rate regulation can lead to even greater losses and thus higher premiums, on average. The Massachusetts experience, in particular, lends support to this conclusion.

Much of the literature appropriately controls for nonregulatory factors in seeking to determine the impact of rate regulation. We use a different technique here to control for these other factors, borrowing from the "event study" literature. Specifically, we look at what happened to average auto insurance premiums in two states that partially deregulated rates: South Carolina and New Jersey. In each case we see that rates actually declined or did not increase as fast as the national average. This result supports the inference that, at the very least, consumers were not harmed by rate deregulation—and could well have benefited.

The California experience with Proposition 103 also indicates that it would be wrong to assume that consumers benefit from stricter rate regulation simply by looking at what happens to average rates. Because losses declined in that state after Proposition 103 went into effect, rates should also have declined (totally apart from the mandated rollback or rebate). The higher insurer profit margins that developed after the shift toward tighter regulation indicate that intensified prior approval of rates can have the counterproductive effect of discouraging insurers from reducing rates to match declining costs. This result is much less likely to occur when markets and competition, not regulators, govern rates.

Broadly considered, the evidence reviewed here should provide comfort to legislators considering the federal OFC legislation. Allowing market forces to determine insurance rates charged by federally chartered insurers would be in consumers' best interests.

References

Automobile Insurance Plan Service Office. 1999–2006. *AIPSO Facts* (various years). Johnston, R.I.
Barkume, A., and J. Ruser. 2001. "Deregulating Property-Casualty Insurance Pricing: The Case of Workers' Compensation." *Journal of Law and Economics* 44, no. 1: 37–64.
Cummins, J. David, ed. 2002. *Deregulating Property-Liability Insurance: Restoring Competition and Increasing Market Efficiency.* Washington: AEI-Brookings Joint Center for Regulatory Studies.
Danzon, Patricia M., and Scott E. Harrington. 1997. *Rate Regulation in Workers' Compensation: How Price Controls Increase Costs.* Washington: American Enterprise Institute.
———. 2001. "Workers' Compensation Rate Regulation: How Price Controls Increase Costs." *Journal of Law and Economics* 44, no. 1: 1–36.
D'Arcy, Stephen. 2002. "Insurance Price Deregulation: The Illinois Experience." In *Deregulating Property-Liability Insurance: Restoring Competition and Increasing Market Efficiency,* edited by J. David Cummins, pp. 248–84. Washington: AEI-Brookings Joint Center for Regulatory Studies.
Grace, Martin F., and Robert W. Klein. 2008. "The Past and Future of Insurance Regulation: The McCarran-Ferguson Act and Beyond." Working Paper. Georgia State University.
Grace, Martin F., Robert W. Klein, Richard D. Phillips. 2002. "Auto Insurance Reform: Salvation in South Carolina." In *Deregulating Property-Liability Insurance: Restoring Competition and Increasing Market Efficiency,* edited by J. David Cummins, pp. 148–94. Washington: AEI-Brookings Joint Center for Regulatory Studies.

Harrington, Scott E. 2002. "Effects of Prior Approval Rate Regulation of Auto Insurance." In *Deregulating Property-Liability Insurance: Restoring Competition and Increasing Market Efficiency,* edited by J. David Cummins, pp. 285–312. Washington: AEI-Brookings Joint Center for Regulatory Studies.

Jaffee, Dwight M., and Thomas Russell. 2002. "Regulation of Automobile Insurance in California." In *Deregulating Property-Liability Insurance: Restoring Competition and Increasing Market Efficiency,* edited by J. David Cummins, pp. 195–236. Washington: AEI-Brookings Joint Center for Regulatory Studies.

Tennyson, Sharon, Mary A. Weiss, and Laureen Regan. 2002. "Automobile Insurance Regulation: The Massachusetts Experience." In *Deregulating Property-Liability Insurance: Restoring Competition and Increasing Market Efficiency,* edited by J. David Cummins, pp. 25–80. Washington: AEI-Brookings Joint Center for Regulatory Studies.

Weiss, Mary A., Laureen Regan, and Sharon Tennyson. 2005. "Incentive Effects of Automobile Insurance Rate Regulation on Loss Costs and Accident Frequency." Paper prepared for the First Annual Meetings of the WRIEC, Salt Lake City, August.

Winston, Clifford D. 1993. "Economic Deregulation: Days of Reckoning for Microeconomists." *Journal of Economic Literature* 31, no. 3: 1263–89.

PART THREE

Insurance Regulation, Financial Convergence, and International Trade

7

Convergence in Financial Services Markets: Effects on Insurance Regulation

Peter J. Wallison

Convergence in financial services refers to two quite different developments, each of which is likely to have a different but cumulative effect on regulatory structure. The most obvious form of convergence is conglomeration among banks, securities firms, and insurance companies, an effect that is largely the result of banking organizations—freed to do so by the Gramm-Leach-Bliley Act of 1999 (GLBA)—acquiring insurance and securities affiliates. To a much lesser extent, insurance companies have acquired securities firms, and in even fewer transactions, securities firms and insurance companies have acquired banks. The second form of convergence is in products and services, in which industry members (banks, securities firms, and insurance companies) have developed products that directly compete with the products and services of the others.[1] Moreover, all three industries are currently engaged in some part of the rapidly developing derivatives business, which is both increasing competition among them and driving them to behave in similar ways.

1. The financial services industry is often described as consisting of four separate services: banking, securities, insurance, and futures. The futures industry, although growing, is still substantially smaller than the other three and is not covered in this chapter.

As noted in this chapter, convergence in the financial services industry is frequently reported in academic and government studies but is seldom separated into its component parts or described in detail. Yet cross-industry competition—the most significant element of the convergence phenomenon—is extensive across a range of products and has a profound influence on the competitive behavior of financial services companies. Understanding the scope and scale of this competition is necessary for a full assessment of the likelihood that the regulation of insurance will change significantly and the direction that any change would take. Accordingly, this chapter attempts to describe some of the most significant areas of cross-industry competition and to assess how this competition will drive regulatory restructuring in the future.

Although the implications of convergence have already resulted in major changes in regulatory structures in many developed and developing countries, the same is not true for the United States.[2] Under the U.S. regulatory structure, banks, securities firms, and insurance companies are separately regulated. Banks and other depository institutions are chartered at both the state and federal levels and regulated at the federal level by four separate agencies. Securities firms are ordinary business corporations, chartered under state law but largely regulated at the federal level by the Securities and Exchange Commission (SEC). Insurance companies are solely state chartered and regulated.[3] Combined, more than a hundred state and federal regulators have jurisdiction over one or more members of all three industries. Recently, the U.S. Treasury Department—citing industry convergence, among other things—recommended what it called an "optimal regulatory structure" for the future. The Treasury noted:

> The growing institutionalization of the capital markets has provided markets with liquidity, pricing efficiency, and risk dispersion and encouraged product innovation and complexity. At the same time, these institutions can employ significant degrees of leverage and more correlated trading strategies with the potential for broad market disruptions. Finally, the convergence of financial services providers and financial products has increased over the past

2. According to the Institute of International Bankers Global Survey (2001), by 2001 the following countries had established consolidated regulatory authorities for financial services: Australia, Canada, Colombia, Denmark, Ireland, Japan, Korea, Norway, Peru, Sweden, and the United Kingdom. According to the GAO, Germany should be added to this list. See U.S. Government Accountability Office (2004), p. 62.

3. A more complete summary of the current regulatory structure for financial services in the United States appears in Brown (2005), pp. 10–19.

MARKET CONVERGENCE AND INSURANCE REGULATION

decade. Financial intermediaries and trading platforms are converging. Financial products may have insurance, banking, securities, and futures components.

These developments are pressuring the U.S. regulatory structure, exposing regulatory gaps as well as redundancies, and compelling market participants to do business in other jurisdictions with more efficient regulation. The U.S. regulatory structure reflects a system, much of it created over seventy years ago, struggling to keep pace with market evolutions and, given the increasing difficulties, to anticipate and prevent financial crises.[4]

The Treasury's new structure (apart from an ill-defined role for the Federal Reserve as "market stability regulator") would consist of two agencies, one to perform the functions of a prudential, or safety-and-soundness, regulator and the other to act as a consumer protection or business conduct regulator for all three industries. This is a radical new idea for the United States, where the notion of functional regulation has always meant regulating separate industries separately (the type of regulation recognized by the GLBA), and advocates of consolidating the financial regulatory agencies often went only as far as to suggest that a single agency might regulate banks as well as securities firms. The insurance industry was not covered because it is not federally regulated. The Treasury's proposal, however, is broader; its "optimal regulatory structure" would regulate banks, securities firms, and insurance companies as though they were simply different ways of delivering essentially the same product: financial services. The Treasury calls this an "objectives-based regulatory structure," meaning that the regulatory purpose is the same for each of the industries and thus should emanate from a single agency. "The goal of establishing a [single agency for prudential regulation]," according to the Treasury, "is to create a level playing field among all types of depository institutions where competition can take place on an economic basis rather than on the basis of regulatory differences."[5]

Although some will argue that this is a bridge too far and unnecessary to bring about an orderly system of financial regulation in the United States, it is quite similar to the approach that has been adopted in the United Kingdom, where the Financial Services Authority (FSA) regulates banks, securities firms, and insurance companies as though they were one industry with three branches. Thus the FSA has three directorates, each covering all three industries: Regulatory Processes and

4. U.S. Department of the Treasury (2008), p. 4.
5. U.S. Department of the Treasury (2008), p. 18.

Risk; Consumer, Investment and Insurance; and Deposit Takers and Markets.[6]
This more flexible definition of functional regulation seems consistent with the
regulation of an industry in which each of the major components is in fact competing with each of the others. To be sure, the United Kingdom's move to an
FSA—a single, consolidated financial services regulator—was apparently stimulated by conglomerate mergers among financial services firms rather than by competition among the principal constituents of the financial services industry, but as
noted below, existing laws in the United States make the development of competitive financial conglomerates unlikely.[7]

As expected, the Treasury's recommendations were greeted with reactions
ranging from yawns to howls of opposition, but they provoked very little serious
discussion. Although convergence along several lines is obviously occurring in the
financial services industry, there was at the time of the conference in July 2008 very
little apparent interest in changing the overall U.S. regulatory structure to adapt to
this evolution. However, the financial turmoil that ensued during August and the
fall of 2008 caused renewed interest in a change in regulatory structure, including
consolidation. Still, if any significant structural change occurs in the near future,
it will be the authorization of an optional federal charter for insurance companies,
but that action will simply add another agency—for chartering and regulating
insurance companies—to the federal government's already rich palette. To be sure,
such a development will have profound effects on the insurance industry, but
the question addressed here is whether the convergence that is now occurring in
the financial services industry will, over the longer term, result in a substantial
change in the *way* insurance is regulated, not simply in *where* it is regulated.

As the Treasury's report suggests, convergence in the financial services industry is putting pressure on U.S. regulatory structures. These pressures will only
increase as changes in technology, government policies to encourage saving, financial innovations, and economic conditions encourage even more cross-industry
competition. I argue that convergence along the lines outlined below will eventually force a change in the U.S. financial services regulatory structure and that, in
that case, insurance regulation, of necessity, will be significantly affected.

In the following discussion, I review the different forms of convergence that
are occurring in the financial services industry and discuss how and why these
forms, over the longer term, will exert pressure on policymakers to change the reg-

6. Jackson (2005).
7. See for example Briault (1999).

ulatory structure. Because of the phenomenon of cross-industry competition, the eventual change in the U.S. regulatory structure is more likely to be something similar to the Treasury's "regulation by objective" than the more conventional approach adopted in the GLBA, in which the three principal industries that make up the financial services industry are regulated separately under a powerful consolidated federal regulator.

Conglomeration

Since the adoption of the GLBA, over 700 banking organizations have become financial holding companies (FHCs) by acquiring insurance companies or securities firms, or both. Because the participants in this expansion are for the most part the largest banking organizations in the United States, these 700-plus companies hold by far the major portion of all the assets in the banking industry.[8] The development of these conglomerate organizations has of course led to calls for a consolidated regulator with the authority to oversee the activities of consolidated financial services firms. To be sure, under the GLBA, the Federal Reserve Board has some limited authority to function as an umbrella regulator over all the subsidiaries of an FHC, but as a practical matter its scope of action is limited by the fact that the GLBA continued to recognize the states as the primary regulators of insurance companies and the SEC as the primary regulator of securities firms. For the Federal Reserve to break into this circle would entail a nasty turf fight.

The effect of conglomeration on regulatory structure is further limited by the fact that combinations among securities firms, insurance companies, and banks may be only a temporary phenomenon. It is noteworthy that within four years after it received approval to engage in both banking and insurance activities—the transaction that stimulated the enactment of the GLBA—Citigroup sold off its Travelers Insurance affiliate and has since also done the same with its mutual fund business. Periods of conglomeration, followed by periods of divestment, are common in the U.S. business community, and it remains to be seen whether combinations

---

8. Citing an International Monetary Fund study, the GAO reports: "Based on a worldwide sample of top 500 financial services firms in assets, the percentage of firms in the U.S. that are conglomerates—firms having substantial operations in more than one of the sectors (banking, securities and insurance)—increased from 42 percent of U.S. firms in the sample in 1995 to 61.5 percent in 2000; however, for the sample of U.S. firms, the percentage of assets controlled by conglomerates declined from 78.6 percent in 1995 to 73 percent on 2000." U.S. Government Accountability Office (2004), p. 50.

of banks, insurance companies, and securities firms really lend their parent companies any significant competitive advantages. Since the recent turmoil in the financial markets, there has been increasing discussion in the banking industry about divesting a lot of extraneous financial activities and refocusing on banks' core business.

In addition, without a change in current law, it is unlikely that conglomeration will extend much beyond its current level. This is because an insurance company or securities firm that acquires a bank will immediately become subject to regulation by the Federal Reserve as an FHC. In this event, in addition to becoming subject to the Federal Reserve's stringent and complex capital requirements for FHCs and bank holding companies, FHCs are not permitted under the GLBA to acquire companies or to engage in activities that are not "financial in nature." The term *financial* is not well defined in the GLBA, and its application can create severe restrictions on expansion into new businesses. For example, it is now nine years since the banking industry asked the Federal Reserve to declare that real estate brokerage is a financial activity. The board has not acted on the request largely because of opposition in Congress, an opposition stimulated by realtors, who fear bank competition. Under these circumstances, few companies that are not already subject to regulation by the Federal Reserve are likely to acquire banks and become FHCs.

A change in current law is not out of the question but must be considered highly unlikely. In its 2008 report, the Treasury recommends the elimination of holding company regulation by the Federal Reserve. The ostensible purpose of holding company regulation is to protect the bank subsidiary from overreaching or manipulation by its parents and affiliates. The Treasury correctly notes that this can be accomplished equally effectively by the regulator of the bank itself. A reform of this kind would permit the elimination of restrictions on ownership of banks by commercial companies and—more important from the perspective of this chapter—would permit securities firms and insurance companies to acquire banks and form conglomerate enterprises that combine all three major elements of the financial services industry. However, because holding company regulation, and the concomitant restrictions on the activities of holding companies, protects the banking industry against new entry and new competition and is also vitally important to the Federal Reserve as a source of its continuing control over the banking industry, it is unlikely to be changed in the near or even medium term.

Accordingly, although it is the most frequently cited reason for seeking regulatory consolidation, conglomeration among securities firms, insurance companies, and banks is not a likely source of pressure for fundamental changes in the structure of financial services regulation.

Product Convergence

In a 2004 report the Government Accountability Office (GAO) notes that convergence does not solely involve conglomerate mergers among financial services firms:

> While convergence has taken place among firms using similar products and derivatives to manage assets and risks, it has also taken place in product offerings by firms in different segments of the financial services industry. These firms are competing against each other to provide households, businesses, and governments with the same basic services. . . . Similarly, firms in different sectors compete by offering products that have similar ability to meet some business needs. Issuance of commercial paper can provide financing similar to commercial loans, and catastrophe bonds and reinsurance provide similar protections, as do surety bonds and standby letters of credit.[9]

The trend highlighted by the GAO has developed over the last quarter century. Unlike conglomeration, this development is driven by continuing advances in information technology, tax changes that encourage savings, and increasing amounts of disposable savings in the hands of consumers. As Elizabeth Brown writes in recommending a consolidated regulator for financial services:

> In the latter half of the twentieth century, market forces increasingly pushed banks to offer more securities and insurance products and pushed securities and insurance firms to devise new products that were in direct competition with banking products. The distinction between the banking, securities and insurance sectors began to blur because these new financial products were fungible. A consumer could choose to open a deposit account with a bank or a money market account with a securities firm. An investor could buy securities through a brokerage firm or a bank. As a result, pressure was brought to bear on Congress to move away from a system based predominantly on entity regulation to a system that employed a more functional regulation approach in order to create a level playing field. Functional

9. U.S. Government Accountability Office (2004), pp. 54–55.

regulation focuses on regulating based on the type of product being provided, instead of on the type of institution providing the product. Under a pure functional regulation scheme, the securities regulators would regulate securities regardless of whether they were sold by banks or securities firms.[10]

Because it is driven by government policies and long-term trends that are likely to continue, cross-industry competition in consumer and business products and services is likely to become even more intense. The relative size of the largest and most competitive products offered by the members of the financial services industry is shown in table 7-1.

Cross-Industry Competition

The following section outlines the major areas in which cross-industry competition is occurring. The list is illustrative rather than exhaustive; less important areas of cross-industry competition are not discussed.

Banks versus Securities Firms

Banks originally developed as intermediaries between the suppliers and users of capital.[11] Banks and securities firms are natural competitors because both perform the same general function of channeling capital from disparate and anonymous suppliers to specific users. The value of banks in this role rested on their superior information about borrowers, which could not be efficiently obtained by bank depositors acting on their own. However, with the development of standardized accounting and faster, cheaper, and more decentralized communications, financial and other information could be made available to investors. More borrowers were thus able to access a wider pool of capital through the less expensive securities market, where the intermediaries—securities firms—were usually acting as agents rather than buying and reselling as principals. Securities firms have been able to outcompete banks in this activity because, by acting as agents, they can

10. Brown (2005), pp. 11–12.
11. This section was written in July 2008, when four large securities firms functioned as both broker-dealers and investment banks. In September one of these firms, Lehman Bros., entered bankruptcy, two others, Goldman Sachs and Morgan Stanley, became financial services holding companies under the jurisdiction of the Federal Reserve Board, and one, Merrill Lynch, agreed to be acquired by Bank of America. It remains to be seen whether the surviving investment banks will continue to be competitive with commercial banks in some sectors of finance, but the investment banking business model is likely to survive, and over time other players will probably move into this space.

Table 7-1. *Financial Assets of Households and Nonprofit Organizations, 2003–07*
Units as indicated

Financial asset	2003		2004		2005		2006		2007	
	$ Billion	Percent	$ Billion	Percent	$ Billion	Percent	$ Billion	Percent	$ Billion	Percent
Deposits	5,327.7	15.6	5,706.3	15.4	6,087.9	15.4	6,732.7	15.6	7,388.5	16.3
Life insurance	1,013.2	3.0	1,060.4	2.9	1,082.6	2.7	1,163.7	2.7	1,204.8	2.7
Pension fund reserves	9,744.4	28.6	10,564.6	28.7	11,391.0	28.8	12,323.6	28.5	12,779.5	28.2
Corporate equities	5,767.5	16.9	5,938.1	16.0	5,874.9	14.9	6,178.3	14.3	5,446.6	12.0
Noncorporate equity	5,396.8	15.9	5,986.4	16.1	6,651.4	16.8	7,329.8	17.0	7,891.9	17.4
Mutual fund shares	2,904.3	8.5	3,417.4	9.2	3,839.7	9.7	4,536.0	10.5	5,081.9	11.2
Debt securities	2,929.7	8.6	3,213.0	8.7	3,449.8	8.7	3,666.9	8.5	3,977.0	8.8
Other	964.5	2.8	1,119.8	3.0	1,166.4	2.9	1,286.9	3.0	1,526.8	3.4
Total	34,048.1	100.0	37,096.0	100.0	39,543.7	100.0	43,217.9	100.0	45,333.0	100.0

Source: Federal Reserve, *Flow of Funds Accounts for the United States.*

perform their intermediary function less expensively than banks, acting as principals, can. This competition has forced banks to change their business model. As recounted by the GAO:

> Generally, financial services firms, especially banks, have had to adapt to the ease with which corporations can now directly access capital markets for financing, rather than depending on loans. For example, with the emergence of the commercial paper market, many large firms with strong credit ratings that had been dependent on bank loans were able to access capital markets more directly. As a result, those large banks that had been major lenders to these firms have had to find new sources of revenue. Banks are now relying more on fee-based income that is generated by structuring and arranging borrowing facilities, providing risk management tools and products, and servicing the loans they have sold off to other institutions as well as from fees on deposit and credit card activity, including account holder fees, late fees, and transactions fees. Many large banking institutions have moved into investment banking activities, including arranging OTC derivative transactions for their corporate customers.[12]

Technology has also provided advantages to securities firms. Fast data processing permitted the growth of mutual funds and made cash management accounts possible, thus allowing consumers to write checks on their mutual fund savings and making cash management accounts direct competitors with bank transaction deposits.

Bank deposits are so similar to securities products that litigation has been necessary to tease them apart. Without an express exemption from securities laws, bank deposits would be regarded as securities, and in numerous cases certificates of deposit (CDs) have been defined as securities when they were issued by uninsured banks or when a securities firm made a market in them.[13] The Office of the Comptroller of the Currency, the regulator of national banks, has ruled that banks can offer insured but unsecured notes with floating rates of interest.[14] These notes would compete directly with mutual fund shares or floating-rate corporate securities.

12. U.S. Government Accountability Office (2004), p. 51.
13. *SEC* v. *First American Bank & Trust,* 481 F. 2d 673 (8th Cir. 1973); *Gary Plastics Packaging Corp.* v. *Merrill Lynch,* 756 F.2d 230 (2nd Cir. 1985).
14. Office of the Comptroller of the Currency, Interpretive Letter 922 (December 13, 2001).

The competition, then, between banks and securities firms took the form of investment and savings products as well as payment vehicles and consumer lending. Interest-paying bank deposits and bank sweep accounts competed with money market mutual funds; bank CDs competed with mutual funds and the short-term notes sold by securities firms. Banks acquired stables of mutual funds that enabled them to offer their customers equity as well as fixed-income investments. Banks and securities firms both offer credit cards, and both create mortgage-backed and other asset-backed securities that facilitate consumer lending and compete for the funds of institutional investors. Banks have also established private banking sections and collective investment funds, which compete directly with the traditional investment advisory and asset-management functions of securities firms.

On the commercial side, commercial paper and longer-term debt securities sold by securities firms compete with short-term and long-term bank loans. The larger securities firms, although without the capacity to take deposits, gained access to the capital markets by using their securities portfolios as collateral. These firms are therefore able to offer short-term bridge loans to corporate clients, which use the cash to make acquisitions. In this way, these firms compete directly with banks, which have traditionally been the source of this form of financing. After the GLBA eliminated restrictions on affiliations between banks and securities firms, commercial banks acquired or established securities affiliates, which could and did underwrite securities in direct competition with securities firms. In addition, banks continue to offer participations in loans that they maintain on their books and also in syndicate loans to other banks. Securities firms privately place notes and bonds for corporate clients, notes and bonds that in substantial respects mimic banks' loan participations and syndications. Table 7-2 shows that one investment bank product—medium-term loans—has grown faster in recent years than the commercial and industrial loans traditionally offered by commercial banks.

Finally, both securities firms and banks are active competitors in the derivatives market. Derivatives of various kinds are synthetic instruments that can be designed to accomplish a number of risk-management purposes. Interest rate swaps, for example, in which two companies exchange fixed and floating payments on a notional principal amount, have been a prominent feature of capital markets for at least twenty-five years, and both banks and securities firms serve as both principal and agency intermediaries for interest rate swaps. Credit default swaps are an even more interesting development: in these swaps, banks and securities firms both compete on a principal or agency basis. In a credit default swap, any company can take on or divest risk by buying or selling protection against a third party's default on an obligation. The implications of this transaction for the future

Table 7-2. *Medium-Term and Commercial and Industrial Loans, by Issuer,*
1993–2006
Billions of dollars

	Medium-term loans			Commercial and industrial loans	
Year	All issuers	Financial issuers	Nonfinancial issuers	Commercial banks	Savings institutions
1993	210.9	125.4	85.5	538.6	9.8
1994	235.5	145.9	89.6	589.1	9.9
1995	267.5	171.1	96.4	661.4	12.2
1996	287.3	194.5	92.8	709.6	14.9
1997	302.1	221.2	80.9	795.0	16.2
1998	388.7	290.4	98.3	898.6	21.1
1999	420.6	320.2	100.4	969.3	27.1
2000	446.4	349.3	97.1	1,052.0	34.0
2001	479.2	384.9	94.3	981.1	38.8
2002	515.9	422.9	93.2	910.8	41.7
2003	556.1	470.6	85.4	869.5	51.6
2004	639.4	560.3	79.1	907.7	59.8
2005	712.9	641.3	71.6	1,019.6	66.0
2006	869.7	796.3	73.3	1,139.6	75.2

Source: Federal Reserve and Federal Deposit Insurance Corporation.

of convergence have not been fully assessed, but in principle it allows securities firms, insurance companies, and banks to trade exposures to different kinds of risks, including risks that they might not be permitted to acquire by the regulatory regime under which they function. For example, a securities firm can take on the risk of a long-term commercial loan by selling protection through a credit default swap with a bank that wants to continue to hold the loan in its portfolio but would like to divest all or a portion of the credit risk. In effect, the bank has off-loaded the credit risk on the loan to the securities firm while retaining the cash flow the loan provides. This can be a profitable transaction for the bank if the cash flows on the loan exceed the payment it is making to the securities firm. But it is noteworthy that in this transaction the securities firm has moved one step closer to being a commercial bank by assuming the credit risk on a traditional bank product. The fast-growing market for credit default swaps consists of about $62 trillion in notional amount of swaps today and is likely to grow considerably larger. The more mature interest rate swap market has a notional amount of $382.3 trillion outstanding.

Banks versus Insurance Companies

The effect of derivatives such as credit default swaps is particularly strong in the convergence of banking and insurance. One study notes that convergence between banking and insurance refers to the following:

—Insurers have developed tools and products that are increasingly substitutes for capital market instruments.

—Banks and the capital markets have developed tools and instruments that are substitutes for traditional insurance products.

—Customer companies increasingly go to both the capital markets and banks and to insurers to buy risk management products.[15]

There are two distinct types of insurance companies: life-health insurers and property-casualty insurers.[16] Life companies, which offer investment-based insurance policies to consumers, have generally been in competition with banks, but recently innovations in capital markets have also caused some of the products of property-casualty companies to converge with the products and services of banks.

Bank competition with life companies occurs on both the liability and the asset sides. Both entities are seeking investments and funding from the same sources. In this connection, life insurers offer guaranteed investment contracts (GICs), and banks offer bank investment contracts (BICs) and CDs. BICs and GICs are similar in that both offer investors (often pension funds and other institutional investors) the opportunity to add to or withdraw funds from the account without penalty while still receiving a rate of interest that is better than the ordinary CD. GICs can also be short term and thus competitive with CDs and interest-bearing bank accounts.

On the asset side, some of the competition between life insurers and banks revolves around the effort of banks to revise their deposit structures so they can function as fixed annuities. A long-term bank deposit like a CD already has some of the characteristics of an annuity. When it matures, it can be drawn upon in retirement. What it lacks is a tax-free internal buildup of value and an indefinite life. In an annuity, traditionally an insurance product, a consumer agrees to make

15. Baltensperger and others (2007).

16. Insurance companies are incorporated either as life-health companies or as property-casualty companies. For analysis purposes, the insurance industry is divided into three principal sectors: life, accident and health, and property-casualty insurance. See chapter 2 for an overview of the structure of the insurance industry.

Table 7-3. *Time and Savings Deposits and Annuities, Flow and Assets,*
1997–2006
Billions of dollars

	Time and savings deposits		Annuities	
Year	Flow	Total assets	Fixed deposited funds	Total reserves
1997	219.6	3,187.5	131.9	1,455.0
1998	244.5	3,432.0	166.5	1,608.5
1999	175.3	3,607.3	78.6	1,780.7
2000	309.1	3,916.4	288.9	1,819.7
2001	335.8	4,248.8	193.7	1,585.0
2002	321.5	4,570.2	324.1	1,619.1
2003	291.4	4,861.1	296.5	1,900.0
2004	470.4	5,381.6	439.1	2,105.9
2005	586.0	6,375.4	470.1	2,258.2
2006	608.2	6,997.0	507.4	2,415.2

Source: American Council of Life Insurers and Federal Reserve, *Flow of Funds Accounts.*

one or a series of payments to an insurer in exchange for the insurer's agreement to make a series of payments to the consumer for life or for a specified period of years. In the 1980s banks began to offer annuity deposits, in which the consumer would make a fixed deposit and receive a series of payments for life, and the Federal Deposit Insurance Corporation (FDIC) determined that a similar instrument, the retirement CD, which combines a bank deposit with an agreement by the bank to pay out the proceeds after maturity for the life of the holder, is insurable. Under pressure from the insurance industry, Congress removed the tax advantages of this instrument in 1996, but the ordinary time and savings deposit is a significant competitor with insurance companies' fixed annuities, since it offers FDIC insurance.

Table 7-3 shows the ebb and flow of funds into fixed annuities offered by insurance companies and the time and saving deposits offered by banks as they have competed for savings since 1997.

Property-casualty companies compete with banks principally on the product side. Among their products is the surety bond, which provides an insurance company's backing for a financial risk.[17] This product is matched by a bank's standby letter of credit, which performs the same function. Here is an area where credit

17. The primary issuers of different forms of financial guaranty insurance are primarily "monoline" insurance companies, which specialize in these products, but other property-casualty insurers are not precluded from offering such products.

default swaps are driving a convergence between banks and insurance companies. Both are able to buy and sell protection, and both are active in acquiring risks by swapping protection for cash flows. Insurance companies, in particular, are able to take on risks in the form of ordinary commercial loans that they would not ordinarily be able to acquire. With GICs as a funding source and a portfolio of commercial loan risks taken on through the market for credit default swaps, an insurance company can look a lot like a traditional commercial bank. At the same time, banks offering protection through credit default swaps are competing with the bond insurance offered by insurance companies.

Securities Firms versus Insurance Companies

Securities firms compete with life insurance companies on the investment, or asset, side. Mutual funds, for example, although not exclusively a product of securities firms, are competitive with universal life policies and with variable annuities. Variable annuities provide variable returns during the annuity period based on the performance of separate accounts within the annuity. Sometimes they are accompanied by a guaranteed level of return offered by the insurer with an additional amount paid if investments exceed a threshold level. In the sense that they pay off based on investment performance, variable annuities are very similar to mutual funds, but there are differences. Variable annuities are not liquid before maturity, while the investment in a mutual fund may be withdrawn at any time in whole or in part, generally without penalty. On the other hand, variable annuities have tax advantages in that the buildup in value in the annuity over time is tax free; taxes apply when the annuity payments begin. The relative growth of mutual funds and variable annuities is shown in table 7-4.

Life insurance companies have also established investment advisory units—like banks' wealth management groups—that seek to manage clients' funds in a comprehensive way, in competition with the traditional role of securities firms.

It is on the property-casualty side that some of the more interesting developments are occurring. There, the development of catastrophe bonds directly challenges the role of reinsurance. In a catastrophe bond transaction, an insurer typically contracts with a special-purpose vehicle, which agrees to pay all or a portion of the insurer's loss if a specified catastrophe, like a hurricane or an earthquake, occurs. The special-purpose vehicle sells bonds, which are entitled to receive the proceeds of the premium paid by the insurer to the special-purpose vehicle if the catastrophe does not occur during the time specified in the contract. If it occurs, the issuer is not required to repay the interest and principal of the bond

Table 7-4. *Mutual Funds and Annuities, Various Measures, 1997–2006*
Billions of dollars

| | Equity and hybrid mutual funds | | Annuities | |
Year	Net new cash flow	Total net assets	Variable deposited funds	Total reserves
1997	243.6	2,685.1	119.5	1,455.0
1998	167.2	3,342.9	126.0	1,608.5
1999	173.9	4,420.7	140.7	1,780.7
2000	278.6	4,308.2	165.9	1,819.7
2001	41.5	3,764.5	160.3	1,585.0
2002	−20.0	2,988.0	142.1	1,619.1
2003	184.2	4,114.6	163.1	1,900.0
2004	220.6	4,903.3	190.9	2,105.9
2005	160.8	5,507.1	197.5	2,258.2
2006	166.5	6,563.7	208.6	2,415.2

Source: Investment Company Institute and American Council of Life Insurers.

(depending on its terms and the amount of the issuer's losses), and the bondholders lose part or all of their investment. If it does not occur, the bondholders receive the premiums plus whatever has been earned on the funds through investment of the principal by the special-purpose vehicle. In this case, then, securities firms have developed a product that competes directly with reinsurance, although not with primary insurance. Nevertheless, for very large and specific risks, it is possible that catastrophe bonds could be a substitute for primary insurance.[18]

As in the case of banking, securities firms are also able to challenge insurance companies for financial guarantees such as surety bonds and bond insurance. This is done through credit default swaps that are bought and sold by securities firms acting as a principal or agent. At the time of its collapse in March 2008, Bear Stearns had approximately $40 billion in notional amount of credit default swaps on its books. Although there are few data on this, and no court decisions of which I am aware, it also appears that credit default swaps might enable securities firms and banks to cover losses in a way similar to the indemnities offered by insurance companies for the destruction of property. In that case, the products of securities firms and banks could be highly competitive with the traditional products of insurance companies.

18. While most catastrophe bonds have been issued by insurance and reinsurance companies, in a few instances noninsurance firms have issued catastrophe bonds to cover their exposure, effectively bypassing insurance and reinsurance markets to obtain this kind of protection.

Implications of Convergence for Regulatory Structure

Just as the touchstone of convergence is product competition among the banks, securities firms, and insurance companies that are the principal members of the financial services industry, so it is competition among these players that is likely to force serious consideration by Congress of changes in the current regulatory structure. As this competition comes to dominate the financial services industry, sound government policy should appropriately focus on ways to keep the playing field level. It is difficult to see how this could be done in a regulatory regime in which each of the competing industries is regulated in a different way. This thought is well expressed in a 2007 report of the GAO to the Senate Banking Committee:

> The [financial services] industry's trends, coupled with legislative changes, challenge regulatory agencies to provide adequate regulatory oversight while ensuring that regulation does not place any segment of the industry at a disadvantage relative to the others. The current structure—with its multiple regulators and charters—is further challenged by the need to recognize sector differences and simultaneously provide similar regulatory treatment for similar products. Regulatory agencies do collaborate to ensure consistent treatment of similar activities across institutional charters and legal entities, as well as in consolidated supervision of large complex organizations. However, our prior work . . . found instances where regulatory differences could lead to unequal treatment of firms.[19]

The GAO enlarges upon this idea later in the report:

> The federal financial regulatory agencies face challenges posed by the dynamic financial environment: the industry's trends of consolidation, conglomeration, convergence, and globalization have created an environment that differs substantially from the prevailing environment when agencies were formed and their goals set by legislation. In particular, the fact that different agencies have jurisdiction over large, complex firms that offer similar services to their customers creates the potential for inconsistent and inequitable treatment. Differences, even subtle ones, among the agencies' goals exacerbate the potential for inconsistency.[20]

19. U.S. Government Accountability Office (2007), pp. 25–26.
20. U.S. Government Accountability Office (2007), p. 36.

The GAO's views actually describe only a portion of the problem of inconsistent regulation. In reality, regulatory agencies—like other government agencies—actively resist collaboration that might reduce their own control. Such "turf" protection is rampant in government and is a constant source of friction among agencies with overlapping jurisdictions. The jurisdictional brawl between the SEC and the Commodity Futures Trading Commission over which agency has regulatory jurisdiction over securities derivatives is a classic case and is still not fully resolved. The current dispute between the Office of Thrift Supervision and the SEC over which agency has jurisdiction over the holding companies of both securities firms and thrift institutions is another salient example. Jurisdictional disputes between agencies with similar jurisdictions must be accepted as a fact of life in government, and pretending that they can be avoided is naïve.

The problem here is not simply that regulation will be inconsistent, as the GAO seems to assume, but rather that agencies will actively seek to advantage their regulated clients in their competition with other participants in the financial services industry. This is not a case of regulatory competition or the classic "race to the bottom." Instead, it reflects a tendency on the part of the regulatory agency to see the world from the perspective of the industry it regulates. This phenomenon is frequently called *regulatory capture*, in which a regulatory agency protects the interests of the regulated industry.[21]

As former Treasury Under Secretary Peter Fisher notes:

I take it as given that too much of our financial regulatory process is aimed at limiting rather than expanding effective competition. We have too much, rather than too little, regulatory arbitrage. Rules that expand competition are in the public interest. Rules that limit competition—directly by bestowing unique privileges on a narrow set of firms—are not in the public interest because they limit the forces that help us efficiently convert savings into investment.

In financial services this is not principally a function of "agency capture." Individual firms do have incentives to limit competition, and there may be some degree of agency capture. But in financial services a problem arises because the chartering regulatory authority has an incentive to promote the "soundness" of its particular form of intermediation by limiting competition. Each chartering regulatory authority has just a single corner or piece

21. Brown (2005), pp. 50–51.

of the total capital structure of financial intermediation and, thus, has an incentive to "protect" the revenue sources of its franchisees in order to assure their "soundness."[22]

Regulatory arbitrage is a particular problem associated with diversified financial services firms. Because many banking products and services can be duplicated as securities or insurance products or services, and vice versa, it is possible for a single conglomerate organization to shift its product offerings from a place where they are heavily regulated to a regulatory regime where they are not. This has good and bad points; less regulation may spur innovation and competition, but it may also confer a competitive advantage on a conglomerate firm that is competing with a firm that does not have this regulatory option.

Finally, the implications of derivatives have not been fully explored by those who study regulatory structure. The credit default swap, in particular, can easily elude the regulatory distinctions among securities firms, insurers, and banks by transferring the risks traditionally taken by each of these constituents of the financial services industry. Thus in a typical credit default swap an insurer can receive a stream of payments from a bank by promising to protect the bank against a default by one of its corporate borrowers. Although this looks like a simple indemnification arrangement, in reality the insurer is taking on the risk associated with a corporate loan: in a sense it is becoming a bank by taking on a typical bank risk. Similarly, a bank can sell protection to an insurer against a liability on a surety bond; in doing so, the bank has in effect taken on an insurance risk. The reason that these risk transfers do not provoke regulatory objections is in part because each transfer, by diversifying risk, adds to the safety and soundness of the participants. In effect, it is a hedging transaction.

There is no indication that credit default swaps will be suppressed or restricted in the future. The notional amount of these facilities—that is, the face amount of the obligations they are backing—is now $62 trillion. Most of the proposals for controlling credit default swaps are directed at making them more transparent or the trading in them more efficient. Meanwhile, their potential for turning insurers into banks and banks into securities firms will continue to confound efforts to maintain separate regulatory regimes for each of these industries.

22. Peter Fisher, "The Need to Reduce Regulatory Arbitrage," remarks, Brooklyn Law School Center for the Study of International Business Law (www.ustreas.gov/press/releases/po3444.htm).

To be sure, at this point the United States is not close to considering any significant change in the regulatory structure for financial services. Before that can even be considered by Congress, it will be necessary for one of the major components of the financial services industry—life and property-casualty insurers—to be chartered and regulated at the federal level. Legislation to create an OFC has been introduced in the Senate and the House of Representatives but is not under serious consideration at this time. Nevertheless, with the support of the largest insurance companies and their business associations, it is likely that an OFC will be authorized within a few years. At that point it will be possible to contemplate some form of consolidation of the federal financial services regulatory structure. Indeed, one of the driving forces for life insurers to support the OFC is the fact that they are placed at a disadvantage in competing with banks and securities firms because of the time required to gain the necessary approvals for new products from more than fifty regulators at the state level. (This issue and a number of others are covered in detail by Martin Grace and Hal Scott in chapter 3.)

It is accepted that Congress never acts on anything unless there is a crisis at hand, but it is possible that the turmoil in the financial services industry today will provide the spur for serious congressional consideration of regulatory restructuring. And even if it does not, the strong trends toward cross-industry competition—driven by changes in technology, tax laws, economic growth, and such leveling developments as credit default swaps—are very likely to continue. Eventually, unless Congress rationalizes the regulatory structure, it will be faced with unceasing requests to adjudicate jurisdictional disputes among agencies and industries. When industries are regulated separately but are competing directly, as they are today and will be increasingly in the future, there will be more frequent instances in which one agency has authorized a product or service that another agency and its regulated industry believe is not authorized by law. The resulting disputes will force Congress to adopt clarifying legislation. Any such reform will not be complete until the insurance industry is included.

In this case, the objective of Congress should be to create the most level playing field possible so that distinctions among the charters and the traditional functions of the component industries do not provide advantages to any one of them. With this standard in view, a reasonable way to accomplish this objective is to treat banks, securities firms, and insurance companies as a single industry and regulate them as Treasury has proposed, according to the objectives of regulation rather than the particular way their products and services were structured or delivered in the past.

References

Baltensperger, Ernst, and others. 2007. "Regulation and Intervention in the Insurance Industry—Fundamental Issues." Zurich: Reinsurance Co.

Briault, Clive. 1999. "The Rationale for a Single National Financial Services Regulator." Occasional Paper Series 2. London: Financial Services Authority,

Brown, Elizabeth. 2005. "E Pluribus Unum—Out of Many, One: Why the United States Needs a Single Financial Services Agency." *University of Miami Business Law Review* 14, no. 1: 10–19.

Institute of International Bankers. 2001. *Global Survey for 2001.* New York.

Jackson, Howell E. 2005. "An American Perspective on the U.K. Financial Services Authority: Politics, Goals & Regulatory Intensity." John M. Olin Discussion Paper 522. Harvard University (www.law.harvard.edu/programs/olin_center).

U.S. Department of the Treasury. 2008. *Blueprint for a Modernized Financial Regulatory Structure.* Washington.

U.S. Government Accountability Office. 2004. *Financial Regulation, Industry Changes Prompt Need to Reconsider U.S. Regulatory Structure.* GAO-05-61.

———. 2007. *Financial Regulation: Industry Trends Continue to Challenge Federal Regulatory Structure.* GAO-08-32.

8

U.S. Insurance Regulation in a Competitive World Insurance Market: An Evaluation

John A. Cooke and Harold D. Skipper

There are long-standing charges that U.S. insurance regulation acts as a barrier to entry and discriminates unfairly against foreign insurers, resulting in a less competitive and robust national insurance market. Simultaneously, many U.S. insurers believe that the U.S. regulatory system hampers them in international competition and that other countries cite it to justify their own trade barriers against them. This chapter addresses these and related issues in the context of the proposal for an optional federal charter (OFC) for insurance companies.

The OFC proposal needs to be examined in the context of insurance regulation at the national and international levels. We begin by reviewing global regulatory trends affecting financial services, with an overview of international insurance markets. We then examine international aspects of the U.S. market, with particular attention to features of the U.S. regulatory system that affect foreign-owned insurance providers in the U.S. market.

Drawing on this analysis, we conclude our discussion by suggesting how an OFC might bring competitive advantages for U.S. insurers and welfare benefits for U.S. insurance consumers in a competitive world insurance market. We highlight how a federal insurance presence could serve the cause of U.S. insurers and reinsurers seeking international expansion, provide global representation and advocacy for U.S. insurance interests, minimize international retaliation against them, and enhance the efficiency and competitiveness of the U.S. market, both in the global marketplace and for the benefit of U.S. insurance consumers.

Global Financial Markets

In recent decades, convergence among financial services providers (earlier operating in largely separate markets) has been a global phenomenon. Convergence has taken place both at the product level (for example, asset insurance through credit derivative swaps) and supplier level (for example, banks engaging in reinsurance or insurers in capital markets). At the center of this process is the growth of alternative risk-transfer techniques. Against this background, governments worldwide have accepted the need to foster greater competition. They have also acknowledged the need for regulatory integration that takes account of financial convergence while guarding against systemic risk.

Different approaches to supervision have emerged. Partly reflecting economic development, most are prudential while others remain more protective, with further divisions between principles-based and rules-based approaches. Given the convergence among financial services subsectors, growing numbers of countries (starting with Singapore in 1984) have adopted forms of integrated systems with a single regulatory agency. These include the two biggest insurance markets outside the United States (the United Kingdom in 1997 and Japan in 1998). Others, including India and China, retain functional regulatory regimes with forms of structured consultation to foster regulatory coherence. Still others, notably Australia, follow a so-called twin-peaks model of having one regulatory agency responsible for prudential matters and another responsible for consumer protection and market conduct functions.

From the U.S. point of view, the European Union approach seems particularly relevant. It has achieved a high degree of harmonization of prudential supervisory standards, and in addition there is a national regulator in each of the twenty-seven member states. The harmonized approach enshrined in EU law means that all member states must follow similar standards for insurance supervision, developed under the European Union's Financial Services Action Plan (FSAP) and based on mutual recognition. A striking effect of these common standards is that an insurer (whether EU-owned or foreign-owned) established and supervised in one member state has the legal right to establish and provide its services in any other member state without further prudential requirements.

This approach is being developed under the FSAP to cover all of the main areas of financial services and to provide coherence in prudential regulation (while market conduct regulation remains at the member-state level). Looking forward, the FSAP's ultimate goal is to ensure that supervisory best practices are followed uniformly throughout the EU's regulatory system so that the fullest extent of mutual recognition exists among EU regulators. A foreign-owned financial services provider wishing to enter the EU market need only be established and supervised in one member state to operate across the entire EU market.[1]

Overview of International Insurance

Like other financial services suppliers, insurers provide essential finance, risk transfer, and investment management tools to help economies grow, diversify, and become more competitive. Insurers offer functions and generic benefits to a national economy similar to those of other financial intermediaries. Insurers from overseas can contribute to financial market stability by providing locally unavailable pools of capital, innovative risk management, and new technologies. According to a World Bank report, countries with open financial services sectors grow an average of 1 percent faster than other countries.[2]

Today's world insurance market is characterized by increasing interdependencies both among insurance and other financial services and among previously distinct national markets. The post-9/11 world insurance market differs markedly from its pre-9/11 counterpart. Today's world insurance economy is truly global, with effects on all national and regional insurance markets. The global market is under unprecedented pressure to be both deep and broad, unconstrained by artificial or outdated supervisory practices that tend to fragment it or inhibit innovations. Such a global market requires national regulators to meet requirements of scale and standing that are proof against regulatory capture by protectionist interests and capable of holding their own in a world in which a degree of regulatory competition is inevitable and healthy.

The most commonly accepted measure of insurance market size is gross direct premiums written. Globally, these totaled more than $4,061 billion in 2007, representing a real average annual growth rate of 3.3 percent, below the long-term trend. Figure 8-1 shows the regional distribution of insurance premiums in 2007. Europe is the world's largest market, accounting for 41 percent (after rounding) of total direct premiums written. The U.S. and Canadian shares are 30 percent and 2 percent, respectively.[3]

1. This principle is unlikely to change, but current strands in EU thinking, such as those contained in the de Larosière report (2009) and the Turner Review (2009), suggest that there may be some revisions to its operation.

2. Mattoo, Rathindran, and Subramanian (2001).

3. International insurance premium data are from Swiss Re (2008).

Figure 8-1. *Insurance Premiums, by Global Region, 2007*

Percent

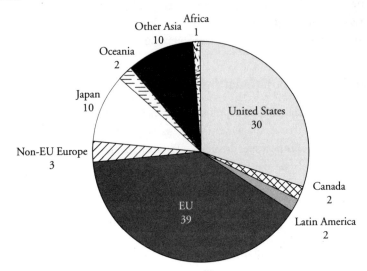

Source: Swiss Re (2008).

Europe's global significance is reflected in the international growth of its insurers and reinsurers. Of the world's twenty largest insurance groups based on revenues in 2007, eleven are European (nine being EU groups, including the world's top three). Six of the top twenty groups are from the United States; the other three are from Japan. Reinsurers also are vital to the insurance supply chain. Five of the ten largest reinsurance groups are European, including the top two, Munich Re and Swiss Re. The United States is home to three of the top ten reinsurance groups, and two are based in Bermuda.

Japan's share of the world market (10 percent) continues to shrink. Conversely, the world share of "other Asia" continues to rise, with double-digit growth in several markets. The thirty members of the Organization for Economic Cooperation and Development (OECD) accounted for 88 percent of worldwide premiums in 2007, a gradually declining share even with OECD enlargement.

The South and East Asian, Latin American and Caribbean, and Central and Eastern European emerging markets have experienced particularly strong growth in recent years. Indeed, emerging markets as a whole realized 11.6 percent real premium growth in 2007, contrasted with 2.5 percent growth for industrialized countries and 1.8 percent for the United States.

For U.S. insurers, these trends point to great opportunities in many markets worldwide but weaker growth in the United States and other advanced markets. Indeed, real growth in U.S. nonlife insurance premiums in 2007 was negative, at −1.3 percent. For the life sector, real growth of 3.6 percent was respectable, if still comparatively low. Driven chiefly by an aging population's demand for retirement and related products, this market will likely remain robust, as some 76 million baby boomers—one-quarter of the U.S. population—face retirement and along with it the need for additional retirement income, a Social Security program with fiscal problems, and the limits of defined contribution pension plans.

International Dimensions of the U.S. Insurance Market

We explore the international dimensions of the U.S. insurance market from three perspectives: first, cross-border insurance trade, both imports and exports; second, establishment (affiliate) insurance trade both by foreign interests in the U.S. market and by U.S. interests in foreign markets; and third, foreign non-life reinsurance, because of its importance to the U.S. insurance market and economy.

Cross-Border Insurance Trade

Surprisingly, the United States runs an overall deficit in its insurance trade with global partners. Exports of insurance by U.S. providers increased by 19 percent in 2006, to about $9.3 billion ($25.8 billion premiums and related income less $16.5 billion in losses).[4] Reinsurance accounts for 60 percent of the total. Canada accounts for 20.6 percent of the total, followed by the United Kingdom, Japan, and Bermuda, at 13.2 percent, 10.8 percent, and 9.2 percent, respectively. Imports into the United States increased by 18 percent in 2006, to $33.6 billion ($71.0 billion premiums and related income paid less $37.4 billion in losses). Reinsurance accounts for 90 percent of the total. Bermuda (with 37.8 percent) was the largest source of U.S. insurance imports, with Switzerland, the United Kingdom, and Germany, at 16.7 percent, 9.3 percent, and 9.0 percent, respectively.

---

4. Unless otherwise noted, the data cited are from the U.S. Department of Commerce (2007), pp. 114–15 and 132. Cross-border figures are on a net basis that includes smoothing for "normal" losses. Affiliate data reflect payment of premiums only, so the two data sets are not directly comparable.

Figure 8-2. *Insurance Exports and Imports, United States, 1995–2006*

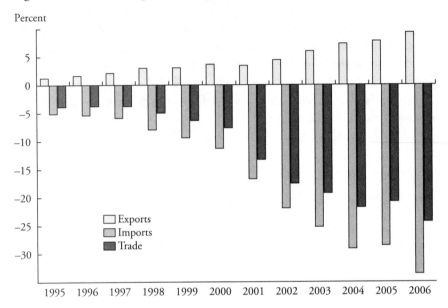

Percent

Exports
Imports
Trade

1995 1996 1997 1998 1999 2000 2001 2002 2003 2004 2005 2006

Source: U.S. Department of Commerce (2007).

Thus the United States ran a trade deficit on cross-border insurance business in 2006 of about $24.3 billion. Figure 8-2 shows the trend in U.S. insurance trade balances between 1995 and 2006.

Establishment Insurance Trade

Foreign-owned insurers and reinsurers play an important role in the U.S. market, and affiliates of U.S. firms do likewise in foreign markets. For 2006, data from the National Association of Insurance Commissioners (NAIC) indicate that foreign-owned, locally established insurers wrote $182.4 billion in premiums in the United States.[5] Life and nonlife insurance accounted for $117.1 billion and $65.3 billion, respectively, amounting to 23.1 percent and 13.6 percent of the U.S. market. European-owned insurers accounted for 64 percent of all such premiums.

As regards overseas affiliates of U.S. firms, the latest data available from the U.S. Department of Commerce show insurance sales in foreign markets totaling

5. National Association of Insurance Commissioners, calculation by authors.

$87.7 billion in 2005.[6] Europe was the largest market for U.S.-owned insurers, representing 24 percent of all such foreign writings, with the United Kingdom accounting for more than half of the European total.

NAIC data indicate that there were 969 U.S. domestic direct life insurer groups in 2006, of which 103 were foreign owned and 866 were locally owned. Individual and group annuities accounted for 76.2 percent and 44.4 percent of foreign-owned U.S. annuity writings, respectively. This means that foreign-owned providers wrote almost half of all annuity business in the United States, an increasingly important source of retirement security. Some 348 U.S. domestic direct nonlife insurers were foreign owned in 2006, with 2,433 owned locally.

Foreign Nonlife Reinsurance

As with other markets worldwide, the U.S. insurance market depends heavily on foreign reinsurers. The critical role that reinsurance plays can best be illustrated by noting that, after virtually every big U.S. catastrophe, reinsurers have been major contributors to recovery. For natural disasters, typically one-third of direct insurers' losses are reimbursed by their reinsurers. Figure 8-3 shows the share of losses paid by reinsurers after several recent disasters.

Some $54.7 billion in nonlife premiums were ceded by U.S. domestic insurers to 2,283 foreign-domiciled entities in 2006, accounting for 53.1 percent of total premiums ceded to professional reinsurers by U.S. nonlife insurers, with the balance ceded to U.S.-domiciled reinsurers.[7] The market share of U.S. reinsurers has been declining, having been 61.6 percent ten years earlier. Adding writings of locally established, foreign-owned reinsurers to cross-border writings reveals that foreign interests wrote some 84.5 percent of all U.S. nonlife reinsurance in 2006.

Effects of U.S. Insurance Regulation on Foreign Involvement in the U.S. Market

As countries began to recognize the welfare benefits of open financial services markets, liberalization progressed, but protectionist sentiments were never far below the surface. Merely agreeing that another nation's firms can enter your market need not bring a truly open market. The structure and nature of domestic regulation can thwart effective access.

---

6. U.S. Department of Commerce (2007).
7. Reinsurance Association of America (2008).

Figure 8-3. *Losses Paid by Reinsurers, U.S. Disasters, 1989–2005*

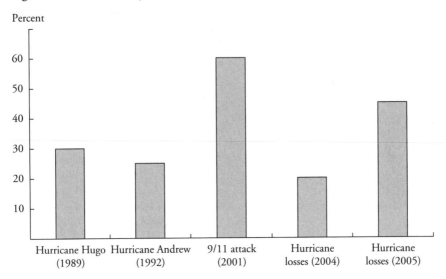

Source: U.S. Department of Commerce (2007).

Regulation exists to rectify market failures. A government ordinarily has many ways of addressing these. All may be adequate, but some will prove less burdensome on competition than others, and governments should prefer those to all others to minimize societal deadweight losses. It is for this principled reason that article 6 of the General Agreement on Trade in Services (GATS) provides that any measures involving qualification requirements, technical standards, and licensing procedures should be based on objective and transparent criteria that are *no more burdensome than necessary* to ensure the quality of the concerned service and that do not, in themselves, constitute restrictions on market access or national treatment (emphasis added).

We structure our examination around the trade concepts that have long been at the center of free trade thinking, particularly since World War II. In applying these concepts, we depart from some traditional U.S. insurance parlance. In U.S. parlance, a *domestic insurer* is one domiciled (incorporated) in the same state in which it sells insurance. A *foreign insurer* is one domiciled in a U.S. state different from that in which it sells insurance. In other countries, a *foreign insurer* is one domiciled in another country. In the United State, an *alien insurer* is one domiciled in a country other than the United States. International trade conventions use the terms *domestic* and *foreign* to denote the nationality of insurers. We follow those conventions here.

The trade concepts in question are embedded in innumerable trade agreements, including the North American Free Trade Agreement (NAFTA) and those of the OECD and the World Trade Organization (WTO). They are an accepted part of international trade negotiation.

—Market access is the right of a foreign supplier to enter a market via establishment or cross border. This principle is implicit in GATS article 16 for bound sectors.

—Most-favored-nation (MFN) treatment requires that no country's services or service suppliers shall be accorded more favorable treatment than any other country's services or service suppliers. GATS article 2 establishes the MFN principle for services. But even total adherence to the MFN principle says nothing about whether a market is truly open to foreign competitors or whether admitted foreign competitors are treated fairly.

—National treatment is intended to ensure equality of competitive opportunity for foreign entrants. It requires governments to apply domestic rules such that foreign suppliers receive treatment no less favorable than domestic suppliers in similar circumstances. GATS article 17 establishes the national treatment principle with regard to bound sectors, subject to national reservations (which must be explicitly declared).

—Transparency requires legal provisions regarding market access and domestic operation to be clearly set out, easily ascertainable, and openly administered. GATS article 3 mandates core transparency requirements from which no exemptions are permitted.

Proponents of the existing state-based insurance regulatory system contend that the U.S. insurance market treats foreign insurance providers fairly in terms of market access, MFN, national treatment, and transparency. This is reasonably accurate as regards any individual state's entrance requirements and operational regulations, with notable exceptions. However, two dubious assumptions underlie it.

The first is that the existing subnational regulatory regime is "no more burdensome than necessary" and does not, in itself, constitute a disincentive to entry, deny equality of competitive opportunity, or add opaqueness. Even if each of the

fifty states' insurance laws and regulations individually offered a full and unre-
stricted right of market access and national treatment, subject only to reasonable
prudential measures, one could not conclude that entry disincentives were non-
existent and national treatment assured. Attempting to do so is equivalent to
asserting that the number and variety of laws and regulations with which an existing provider or a potential entrant must comply are irrelevant to ease of entry and
operation. Complexity, in itself, is a disincentive to entry and efficient operation;
the more there is, the more significant the barrier.

The second is that an individual state with essentially the same entrance
requirements for all existing and aspiring out-of-state insurers (both overseas and
other states) ensures effective market access and national treatment for foreign
providers. Even if all of the states' laws and regulations had identical licensing and
operational requirements for out-of-state insurers, one could not conclude that
their collective effect would be to ensure effective market access and national treatment for foreign providers. Attempting to do so is tantamount to asserting that it
is acceptable for a state to maintain trade barriers and discriminatory regulation
against foreign insurers if similar barriers and regulation are maintained against
U.S. insurers domiciled in other states. The existence of interstate trade barriers
and discriminatory regulation does not, of itself, justify international trade barriers and discriminatory regulation, especially if they are "more burdensome than
necessary."

These two implicit assumptions can be viewed in another way. That the United
States has a domestic insurance regulatory regime under which regulation is delegated to the individual states does not mean that a trade-related evaluation of the
regime falls to the individual states alone. The totality of the regime should be
evaluated, requiring both a state-by-state and a national evaluation.

Market Access Problems

Thus consistent with the need for both a national and a state-by-state evaluation,
our discussion of market access is structured around two barrier classifications:
barriers relevant to both interstate and international insurance and barriers relevant primarily to foreign entrants. Most if not all of the issues examined below
have been raised by other nations with the U.S. Trade Representative (USTR) as
barriers to entry and often breaches of national treatment.[8]

---

8. The information presented on state practices draws mainly from U.S. Trade Representative
(2005).

Our examination begins with aspects of U.S. insurance regulation that have been identified as trade barriers to both interstate insurance commerce and foreign entry. We cover ten such aspects:[9]

—Insurer licensing requirements
—Monopoly insurers
—Government-owned or government-sponsored insurers
—Reinsurance cessions
—Extraterritorial application of state law
—Market exit
—Personnel licensing requirements
—Tax laws
—Retaliatory laws
—Regulatory exemptions and variations

Licensing requirements mean that an insurer wishing to conduct insurance business in all fifty U.S. states must qualify for and obtain fifty separate licenses.[10] Licensing standards vary significantly from state to state, and insurers seeking licenses in multiple states must comply with the different requirements of each as regards capital requirements, fit-and-proper standards, business plans, product lines, and processes for reviewing and approving policy forms. Some progress toward uniformity in licensing standards has been made, but unresolved issues persist, not least the failure to enact mutual recognition.

Obtaining fifty separate licenses with differing qualification requirements is costly and time consuming. While one study pegs the average direct costs of an additional state license at $8,673, a more realistic measure is their sales prices in the market.[11] The state licenses of "shell" insurance companies—those with little or no business—are reportedly valued at no less than $50,000 and as much as

9. Normally, states may not impose taxes or regulatory burdens that infringe upon interstate commerce, as such actions violate the commerce clause of the U.S. Constitution. However, in enacting the McCarran-Ferguson Act in 1945, the U.S. Congress effectively delegated authority over insurance commerce to the states, thus barring a commerce clause challenge of any state insurance law or regulation.

10. Add six to the number of jurisdictions if Washington, D.C., and the five U.S. territories (American Samoa, Guam, Marianas Islands, Puerto Rico, and the U.S. Virgin Islands) are included.

11. Bair (2004).

$200,000. An attorney specializing in insurance regulatory matters has mentioned a shell insurer licensed in forty-nine jurisdictions for a total sales price of $3,125,000, or $63,775 per license.[12]

Research has established a positive relationship between insurers' costs and the number of states in which they are licensed, despite economies of scale.[13] The United Kingdom's Financial Services Authority reports U.S. regulatory expenditures as a percent of premium income to be considerably higher than those of France, Germany, Ireland, Sweden, or the United Kingdom.[14]

It remains questionable whether the NAIC's planned reform measures will be fully adopted by the states. To date, the results are not promising for direct insurers, with some promise for reinsurers. Streamlining the U.S. state licensing system will be a decades-long project; and even in areas showing some convergence, there is no ratchet mechanism to guarantee against future divergence. State licensing requirements continue to be particularly significant market access barriers.[15]

Monopoly insurers are found in five states: North Dakota, Ohio, Washington, West Virginia, and Wyoming have monopolistic state workers' compensation funds.[16] State employers are required to purchase their workers' compensation insurance from them unless they self-insure. Fourteen other states operate state funds competing with private insurers. In the absence of market failures that would prevent a competitive market in this externality-laden line, and given that most U.S. states and many countries have competitive workers' compensation markets, the rationale for these monopolies seems weak. As such, they constitute entry barriers.

Government-owned or government-sponsored insurers is the third barrier. It is ironic that, while most states prohibit the licensing of government-controlled insurers and reinsurers (as discussed below), one of the largest states has created both a direct insurer and a reinsurer that compete with private companies. The Florida Hurricane Catastrophe Fund (FHCF) was established in 1993 to pro-

---

12. Joseph L. Cregan, e-mail to author, May 16, 2008.

13. See for example Grace and Klein (2000) and Pottier (2007).

14. Financial Services Authority (2004), appendix 5.

15. The European Union and likely other U.S. trading partners have formally requested action to remove or reduce this barrier and have made similar requests in the case of compulsory reinsurance cessions, surplus lines and large commercial risks restrictions, government ownership restrictions, initial entry license requirements, and citizenship or residency requirements.

16. Insurance Information Institute (2008). West Virginia is in the process of privatizing its fund after making provision to cover the fund's $3 billion deficit.

vide catastrophe reinsurance to property insurers in the state, and the Florida legislature further expanded its capacity in 2007. In Florida the Citizens Property Insurance Corporation, a state residual market mechanism for property insurance, was created in 2002 (merging previously existing property insurance residual market mechanisms), and its scope was also broadened in 2007. Both actions followed a tightening of the Florida direct and reinsurance property markets following catastrophic hurricane losses in 2004 and 2005.

The Citizens Property Insurance Corporation is now the second-largest homeowners' insurer in Florida and is also authorized to write commercial residential property insurance coverage. The consensus among private insurers is that both Citizens and the FHCF enjoy privileged regulatory treatment, enabling them to offer below-market rates and to operate with less capital than required of comparable private insurers. Existing insurers and those that would seek entry are at a competitive disadvantage.[17] Florida citizens and businesses are among the largest insurance consumers in the United States. Florida's actions hinder market access to private insurers.

Reinsurance cessions are yet another barrier relevant to interstate and international insurance. In Minnesota, for example, all self-insured and insured workers' compensation plans must reinsure with the Workers' Compensation Reinsurance Authority, a state-created association. Compulsory reinsurance cessions are commonly explained (in developing countries) as means of minimizing foreign exchange outflow and of safeguarding markets against possible reinsurance shortages. These rationales seem inapplicable to Minnesota, with the cession barring market access to this line for other reinsurers.

In addition, Nevada domestic insurers may purchase reinsurance only from a reinsurer admitted to Nevada. In Texas, mutual life insurance companies may not take out direct reinsurance with non-U.S. companies, and Maine may restrict reinsurance for workers' compensation. Such provisions are inconsistent with both market access and national treatment principles.

Extraterritorial application of state law is practiced by thirteen states in at least some elements of their laws. This means that the state applies its law not only to each licensed insurer's and reinsurer's in-state business but also to these providers' operations in other states. New York is best known for this and perhaps the state that applies its laws most broadly. Obviously, the more states that apply their laws in this fashion, the more confusion and opportunity for conflict are created.

17. Towers Perrin (2007), p. 2.

This is especially challenging for reinsurers, which often are licensed in all U.S. jurisdictions.

In economic terms, the application of extraterritoriality can be expected both to render regulatory compliance more complex (a transparency issue) and to discourage domestic and foreign insurers and reinsurers from entering such states' markets. Indeed, so onerous is the application of New York law that many large insurers opt to create New York–only subsidiaries rather than submit their entire group to such dual (at the least) oversight.

Market exit barriers can discourage market entry in the first place. If an insurer wishes to withdraw from a market or from a line of business, it is customary that the supervisor must be satisfied that the legitimate expectations of the insurer's existing policyholders will be met and that long-term contracts will be satisfactorily cared for. In current U.S. practice, the rule has been applied in arbitrary ways, going beyond existing policyholders' interests. For instance, in some states practicing price suppression, insurers have been known to threaten to cancel their licenses to write the suppressed line in the state. Often, regulators—including those in New Jersey and Florida—have responded by raising barriers to exit, such as requiring insurers to cease writing all lines if they withdraw from the objectionable line. Measures of this kind appear to go beyond ordinary prudential requirements or the protection of policyholders. Such punitive market-exit measures discourage market entry.

Additionally, several licensing issues affecting personnel of both interstate and international insurers' market access stand out:

—Prior out-of-state licensing requirements: Twenty-eight states issue nonresident licenses for individuals to engage in certain services auxiliary to insurance only if the individual is already licensed in another state. The services to which the prohibition applies vary, but most apply it to producers or to reinsurance intermediaries, while others extend it to consultants and adjusters.

—Residency requirements: Thirty-four states require in-state residency for surplus-lines brokers, and thirty-four require it for surplus-lines agents. Additionally, seventeen states will not issue licenses to nonresidents for various service functions that require licensure, such as adjuster, solicitor, services representative, bail bondsman, and customer representative.

—Producer license fees: Nonresidents may be charged higher fees for producer licenses in twenty-two states.

—Countersignature laws: Until recently, most states had countersignature laws requiring nonlife insurance contracts sold by a nonresident producer to be countersigned by a resident agent, who was entitled to share in the writing producer's commission. Almost all of these laws have recently been revoked, either after a successful legal challenge or through seemingly voluntary state action.[18] Nonetheless, they have been a fixture of state insurance regulation for decades, favoring "home team" producers over those from elsewhere. This and the previous three restrictions restrain market access.

Most tax laws historically have applied differentially as between insurers domiciled in the state and those domiciled in other states and nations. For decades before 1981, thirty-four states provided for higher taxes on out-of-state companies than on companies domiciled in the state. In 1985 the U.S. Supreme Court, in a five-to-four ruling, rejected Alabama's two arguments in support of its discriminatory tax law, ruled the law in violation of the equal protection clause of the U.S. Constitution, and remanded the case to the Alabama courts for a further hearing on other purposes proffered by the state.[19] Most states thereafter eliminated most of the discriminatory elements of their tax laws, although nine states still levy higher taxes on out-of-state, including foreign, insurers than on their domestic insurers. The economic effect is the same as a tariff—that is, it is an obvious entry barrier. Second, neither the pre-1985 nor the present discrimination by the states would have been legally permissible in any financial sector except insurance because of the McCarran-Ferguson Act.

Retaliatory laws constitute another market access hindrance for both interstate and international insurers. Typically, a host state imposes a premium tax on both out-of-state and domestic insurers. Under retaliatory laws, further taxes are imposed on an out-of-state insurer if that insurer's domiciliary jurisdiction imposes taxes and fees on the business in that jurisdiction of the host state's insurers that are higher than those of the home state. It is difficult to assign an exact cost to this system, but its very complexity imposes costs. State tax rates and fee schedules vary, so that retaliatory laws entail complicated rate and fee calculations for any insurer transacting business in multiple states, raising questions about the transparency of the costs of doing business and insurers' ability to ascertain these costs. Despite the system's complexities and the element of double taxation, individual

18. The cases have been won through equal protection clause challenges, which are far more difficult to sustain legally than commerce clause challenges. However, the latter are impossible to bring because of the McCarran-Ferguson Act.

19. *Metropolitan Life Insurance Company* v. *Ward,* 105 S.Ct. 1676.

states are unlikely to make unilateral changes. Retaliatory laws are barriers to entry into insurance markets.

Regulatory exemptions and variations are the tenth market access barrier applicable to both interstate and international insurers. They arise from the need to facilitate insurance for large commercial risks. The classic model of state-by-state insurance supervision evolved from a perceived need to protect local interests and policyholders by insisting that risks be covered locally. The general effect of the adaptations is to alter the overarching requirements that insurance should be placed with admitted insurers, in three broad ways:

—Economic needs test: Where it can be proved that the admitted market has declined to take on a risk (declinature), the risk may be placed with surplus-lines insurers. These placements are subject to an additional premium tax and have to satisfy certain other rules.

—Exemption of certain insureds: Some states exempt from compliance with state laws certain large commercial insureds that meet certain criteria; such exemption enables these insureds to make direct placements of both licensed and surplus-lines business (including with their own captives). Such placements are subject to additional reporting and taxation requirements.

—Exemption of certain insurance lines: Some states exempt certain insurance lines from their laws. The most common exemption (variable in scope from state to state) relates to marine, aviation, and transport (MAT) insurance.

Common to all three approaches is the recognition that a state's admitted market may be unable to cater to all large risks and that large commercial insureds are likely to be least in need of the full protection of the state supervisory system. Although the surplus-lines regime is common to virtually all states (albeit with varying declinature rules), the other exemptions are not applied consistently across the states, and the definitions of large industrial insureds and MAT business vary from state to state, requiring complex analysis by insurers before accepting such risks.

Furthermore, some states do not recognize these exemptions or grant only partial or conditional exemptions. Finally, most states require surplus-lines insurers to keep trust funds in the United States as a precondition for surplus-lines eligibility. Despite the degree of partial flexibility applying to large commercial risks, the pattern of continuing restrictions means that overseas insurers' market access to the large commercial risks market remains heavily circumscribed and, where higher premium taxes apply, subject to fiscal penalties.

Six aspects of U.S. insurance regulation have been identified as being market access trade barriers relevant primarily to foreign entrants.[20]

—Government ownership restrictions
—Initial entry licensing
—Citizenship and residency requirements
—Seasoning requirements
—Reciprocity laws
—Trusteed surplus-funds requirements

At least twenty-seven states bar government-owned or government-controlled insurers and reinsurers from securing licenses, whether for cross-border or establishment purposes. Control is presumed to exist if any government or government agency directly or indirectly owns the voting securities, controls them, or holds the power to vote shares or proxies representing 10 percent (5 percent in Alabama) or more of them. The policy concern with such insurers is said to revolve around the potential for unfair competition by invoking sovereign immunity, by subsidizing prices, or by using confidential information. Only three states (California, Colorado, and Pennsylvania) allow a government-controlled insurer to demonstrate that it will not engage in prohibited activities and, thereby, to obtain a license.

Even if the policy concern were justified, less burdensome approaches exist. Such prohibitions restrict market access and deny the U.S. insurance market additional capacity. Such insurers and reinsurers have competed fairly for years in other national markets and presumably in the twenty-three U.S. states with no prohibitions.

Initial entry licensing varies among states. Four states (Maryland, Minnesota, Mississippi, and Tennessee) provide no mechanism for licensing the initial entry of a non-U.S. direct insurer or reinsurer as a subsidiary unless the company is already licensed in another U.S. state. An additional eleven states provide no

20. We do not cover the U.S. federal excise tax (FET) on premiums, as the subject of this chapter is state regulation and taxation, not federal taxation. This tax is 1 percent of premiums on life insurance and reinsurance and 4 percent on nonlife insurance premiums paid to foreign-domiciled insurers (that is, cross-border trade) on U.S. risks. A recent ruling by the IRS holds that such taxes are to be assessed each time business is retroceded, thus resulting in a cascading effect. Under double-taxation treaties between the United States and some countries, those countries' insurers and reinsurers may be FET exempt. As the FET is levied on a gross basis and only on foreign insurers, it is essentially an ad valorem tariff on cross-border services.

mechanism for licensing initial entry of a non-U.S. direct insurer or reinsurer as a branch, unless that company is already licensed in another state. No economic logic has been found for these market access restrictions. They appear to be free riding by these states, effectively denying direct access to their markets.

Citizenship and residency requirements also vary among states. U.S. citizenship is required of all incorporators of insurance companies in Hawaii, Idaho, South Dakota, and Washington. For an additional eleven states, either two-thirds or a majority of incorporators must be U.S. citizens or state residents for all or most forms of insurers. Sixteen states, including New York, have various forms of U.S. citizenship or residency requirements for membership on the board of directors. Additional or different citizenship or residency requirements are found in several more states for various specialty forms of insurers, such as reciprocals and farm mutuals.

The justification offered for their existence centers on the desirability that board members and company executives have local knowledge and commitment when forming or operating insurance businesses and that state authorities be able more easily to assert jurisdiction over them. The first argument—redolent of paternalism (if not protectionism)—is not sustainable: local residency is no guarantee of market knowledge, and professional knowledge of the market is in any case required of directors, controllers, and senior staff of an insurer as "fit and proper persons."

The jurisdiction contention too seems unsustainable. Formerly, it was common worldwide, but its incidence is now declining. U.S. states with such requirements are progressively fewer. It does not follow that such requirements will be eliminated, but if they remain, they will continue to be both barriers to entry and national treatment inconsistencies.

Seasoning requirements prevent a foreign insurer from becoming licensed in jurisdictions until it has been in business for a minimum period. Certain states have traditionally applied seasoning requirements. These requirements do not apply to insurers domiciled in another U.S. state. As with countersignature laws, they appear to have market access and national treatment implications under the GATS.

Reciprocity laws exist in thirteen states. These laws enable insurance commissioners to retaliate against perceived unfair insurance trade rules in other countries.

Trusteed surplus funds are required in twenty-five states. Under this requirement, U.S. branches of non-U.S. firms must maintain surplus funds in excess of deposits. These trusteed surplus funds are usually held in trust by either a state or a U.S.-incorporated trustee, such as a bank, and are barriers to market access.

Most-Favored-Nation Treatment Problems

No MFN inconsistencies seem to attach to state insurance regulation and taxation. (FET is another matter.) Stated differently, the U.S. insurance regulatory regime, whether viewed nationally or at the individual state level, appears to apply all of the market access restrictions discussed above equally to all trading partners. The position may change in the future, in ways that would be permitted under GATS, if the expanding web of U.S. bilateral trade agreements were to accord special treatment to certain countries' services or providers.

National Treatment Problems

The concept underlying national treatment is that foreign and domestic companies are treated equally after they have entered the market. The economically correct way to examine the U.S. situation is from both individual state and national perspectives. We follow the same generic bifurcation for national treatment analysis as we did for barriers to market access.

Most national treatment inconsistencies in the United States relevant to both interstate and international insurance are identified in the market access discussion. These include the following:

—Compulsory and restrictive reinsurance cessions that apply differentially to domestic and out-of-state reinsurers.

—Extraterritorial application of state laws, which can create differential requirements for insurers and reinsurers.

—Producer and other licensing issues, which can be administered inconsistently.

—Domestic preference tax laws, that create differential burdens between a state's domestic insurers and those domiciled in other jurisdictions.

—Commercial insurance treatments, which often impose differential burdens between domestic and out-of-state insurers.

Inconsistencies relevant primarily to foreign insurers are also identified previously. The U.S. government has notified the OECD of insurance exceptions that it is taking in the OECD national treatment instrument. Three areas are covered:

—Nonadmission of foreign-government-owned and -controlled insurers in states that prohibit licenses for such insurers. Only thirteen states are notified to the OECD, whereas the USTR lists twenty-seven. Of course, such prohibitions are inconsistent with national treatment.

—Reciprocity laws. These can amount to withholding national treatment if the relevant measure is directed against foreign providers.

—Trusteed surplus fund requirements. These funds are required irrespective of whether they are justified under the GATS prudential carve-out, and they imply unfair national treatment since they are specifically directed against foreign providers.

Three other areas have national treatment effects, as noted in the market access discussion:

—Initial entry licensing. This licensing—in which states provide no mechanism for licensing initial entry of a non-U.S. direct insurer, reinsurer, or individual engaged in business auxiliary to insurance unless first licensed in another state— constitutes discrimination against non-U.S. providers.

—Citizenship or residency requirements for incorporators and board members. These requirements are inconsistent with national treatment.

—Seasoning requirements for foreign but not domestic insurers. These constitute discrimination against affected non-U.S. providers.

Another national treatment inconsistency relevant primarily to foreign insurers is current U.S. regulatory policies governing the treatment of reinsurance provided by foreign reinsurers. For a U.S. insurer to receive credit for reinsurance, the assuming reinsurer must be authorized or must post security to cover its obligations to the cedant. For authorization, a reinsurer must be licensed in at least one state and meet the relevant capital and surplus requirements. A reinsurer doing business across borders is not authorized and must post security in the United States through trust funds, letters of credit, or other collateral. Regulators' prime concern in requiring such situs funds is ease of securing recoverables (amounts due) from reinsurers beyond the state's reach. The resulting system bears down most on foreign insurers and reinsurers (although the United States has taken no reservation in GATS).

The reinsurance and collateralization system is at odds with virtually all other major insurance markets, which have safely relied on domestic primary insurers' capacity to assess for themselves whether to require collateral in a business-to-business contract, without interposing state requirements, with their attendant costs for reinsurers, primary insurers, and insurers' clients. We are unaware of any damage to these markets from such a procompetitive practice. Even so, substantial opposition exists to changes in this practice.

Collateralization is costly. Both letters of credit and trust funds carry direct costs and compliance burdens. The New York State Insurance Department estimates that "foreign reinsurers had an estimated $120 billion in collateral posted in the US in 2005 . . . on which they pay about $500 million a year in transaction costs."[21] There are also indirect costs through forcing reinsurers to segment investment portfolios on a noncommercial and localized basis, thus harming their scope for optimum portfolio management to secure the highest expected rate of return consistent with safety and geographical diversification. Unless all these costs are absorbed (which is unlikely), they are borne by direct insurers and their customers.

After many years of negotiations trying to modify the system have proved inconclusive, U.S. insurance regulators are now proposing a system that would allow a single state with the appropriate regulatory capacity to be the sole U.S. regulator to supervise all of a national reinsurer's or a port-of-entry reinsurer's U.S. reinsurance business.[22] The proposal would partially address collateralization by easing its burden for the world's most financially secure reinsurers. But market distortions would remain, and a range of unlicensed non-U.S. reinsurers could still need to post collateral.

What is the system's effect on the global insurance economy? The U.S. market accounts for about one-half of total reinsurance premiums worldwide. In 2005 U.S. gross reinsurance premiums to offshore reinsurers accounted for almost 39 percent of the world's total gross reinsurance premiums. Thus 39 percent of all ceded reinsurance premiums worldwide was potentially subject to U.S. collateralization requirements. On such a scale, the market-distorting implications must be significant, and they raise several questions. To what extent does the continuous collateralized guarantee for U.S. cedants (equivalent to 70 percent of global gross reinsurance premiums in 2005) impose negative spillover effects on the world reinsurance market by raising reinsurance costs, aggravating cycles in the supply of insurance and reinsurance, increasing the cost of capital, and cramping expansion of worldwide reinsurance capacity? Further, what is the effect especially on emerging markets without other risk-sharing options, since the burden of increased volatility and higher insurance and reinsurance costs is likely to fall here most heavily? Should the United States feel a responsibility for taking corrective action?

21. New York State Insurance Department, press release, "New York Modernizes Regulation on Reinsurance Collateral," October 2007.
22. Connolly (2008).

Transparency Problems

It cannot be said that the U.S. insurance regime is not transparent, in the strict sense of GATS article 3. The United States is a positive law country, and all relevant federal and state laws are published and are available in hard copy and on the Internet. Court and other interpretative findings are similarly easy to access. On these grounds, U.S. insurance regulation as viewed on a state-by-state basis suffers no meaningful transparency problems.

However, when viewed from a national perspective, transparency becomes more ambiguous. From an economic viewpoint, the U.S. system is opaque, as it requires trading partners to take account of dozens of parallel sets of changing laws and regulations. From a GATS viewpoint, the notification rules of GATS article 3 then become important: the more complex a regime for a significant services market, the greater a WTO member's duty to notify all regulatory changes promptly (and at least annually) to the WTO Council for Trade in Services.

An Optional Federal Charter in a Competitive World Insurance Market

Both opponents and proponents of an OFC approach to federal insurance regulation acknowledge that the current state-based insurance regulatory system has serious problems, among them

—The need for more efficient, effective, and timely product reviews and improved time to market.

—Improvement in producer licensing with an eye toward reciprocal licensing in all jurisdictions and greater uniformity.

—The need to streamline company licensing.

—The need for more effective and coordinated market conduct oversight.

—The elimination of price controls that reduce competition and consumer choice.

—The need for a means of reducing or eliminating some or all reinsurance collateral requirements.

—The need to eliminate the extraterritoriality aspect of state insurance laws, especially with respect to reinsurance.

Proponents of an OFC contend that their approach is the most effective and efficient means of addressing not only these problems but also those identified earlier. They also argue that an OFC would bring about some regulatory parity between insurance and other regulated financial services, provide an effective voice in support of the U.S. insurance industry's interests internationally, and ultimately, through a more procompetitive regulatory environment, allow a more competitive, innovative domestic insurance industry to emerge, in which international players enjoy strong market access and national treatment.

Opponents of an OFC contend that such a charter would spur a regulatory race to the bottom, expand federal bureaucracy, lead to lower state tax revenues, cause legal and regulatory conflicts, and fail to take account fully of local needs and preferences. They also contend that the agreed benefits could be secured by a combination of new, targeted federal laws and by the NAIC and the states being more attuned to the problems. Opponents have not explained whether or how all of the international trade problems identified earlier would be rectified. Both opponents and proponents agree that the states cannot alone solve the problems listed above and that federal legislation is necessary to tackle at least some (opponents) or all (proponents) of them.

Below we examine the international implications of an OFC from two perspectives: first, its possible implications for U.S. insurers and reinsurers seeking international expansion and, second, its implications for foreign insurers and reinsurers in the U.S. market.

U.S. Insurers and Reinsurers in International Expansion

Future insurance demand in numerous markets worldwide is expected to far outstrip demand in the United States, as a consequence of higher long-term economic growth and a low level of insurance density and penetration. A greater international presence by U.S. insurance specialists holds the potential for high rewards, aiding the U.S. economy and balance of payments, assisting U.S. multinationals worldwide, and helping other nations and their businesses and citizens to achieve the greater growth and wealth creation that will permit them to buy more U.S. goods and services. Yet a recent study by J. François Outreville suggests that U.S. insurers and reinsurers have fallen behind European insurers in exploiting such opportunities.[23]

In his study, Outreville examines the largest forty-five insurers and reinsurers worldwide in terms of premiums written in 2003, the latest year for which relevant data were available. At that time, twenty-two companies were European (eighteen from the European Union), fifteen from the United States, seven from Japan, and one from Korea. Outreville first compares this list with one developed

23. Outreville (2008).

in 1986, taking only the top twenty in each listing. In 1986 eight companies were from the United States, with six each from Japan and Europe. For 2003, the top twenty comprised twelve companies from Europe, five from Japan, and only three from the United States. The story here is that, comparatively, U.S. insurance providers did not grow as rapidly as those in Europe.

This leads to Outreville's second examination, which involves paring down the 2003 listing of forty-five to the thirty "most international" companies, using weighted measures of the concept of international. The number of U.S. companies falls by more than one-half, to seven. Japan has but a single company. All twenty-two of the European companies from the listing of forty-five are among the top thirty, and they occupy the top five positions, with a U.S. company (the American International Group, or AIG) ranking sixth. The ranking of the next U.S. company is eighteenth. Leaving aside definitions and research methodology, it seems that U.S. insurers are falling behind European insurers in international expansion. This is borne out by current surveys: "Global insurance industry acquisitions in 2007 were driven by non-U.S. insurers—primarily Western European firms—who clearly see value in this market. In fact, only 20 percent of primary and reinsurer transactions involved a U.S. entity at all. . . . We expect that U.S. firms will continue to be domestically focused in their acquisitions."[24] The obvious question for both federal policymakers and U.S. insurance executives is, Why?

Many observers place much of the blame on the absence of a U.S. insurance regulatory presence at the strategic federal level, coupled with reliance on a system of state-based regulation with nineteenth-century roots that demands disproportionate amounts of executive time. As if to reinforce this point, EU Commissioner Charlie McCreevy, introducing the Solvency II proposal to the European Parliament, said, "Financial services is one of Europe's great success stories globally. European insurers are world leaders. If we are to maintain our position and to build on it, Europe needs to be prepared to step up its game and take the lead globally when it comes to the regulation of financial services. One cannot achieve this without being ambitious."[25]

He could have been writing about the United States when he observed, "National differences distort and undermine the Single Market, as well as hinder effective competition. This results in increased costs for EU insurers, and higher

24. Sherry Manetta, director, quoted in Conning Research and Consulting, press release, Hartford, Conn., May 28, 2008.

25. Among other things, Solvency II will provide for consolidated supervision of insurance firms at the financial holding company level and a risk-based approach to capital requirements. McCreevy (2007), pp. 2 and 4.

premiums for European consumers and businesses, thus hampering growth." And finally, "There is growing nervousness in the US about the EU surging ahead while the US itself is stuck with a highly fragmented insurance regulation." Proponents of an OFC contend that it would, in effect, step up the U.S. game by, among other things, assisting international expansion efforts through representation and advocacy, enhancing insurer efficiency, and minimizing retaliation.

The right to enter into international agreements, relations, and trade negotiations rests exclusively with the U.S. federal government. Neither state insurance regulators nor the NAIC has the constitutional authority to enter into international agreements of mutual recognition or joint supervision on behalf of the United States. Similarly, while regulators and the NAIC may represent their own perspectives within the International Association of Insurance Supervisors (IAIS), they cannot represent the U.S. government. Nor can they do so in the Insurance Committee of the OECD, the Joint Forum, WTO negotiations, or any other bilateral or multilateral forum or negotiation.[26] No insurance supervisor or the NAIC has the legal mandate to represent the government or the interests of the U.S. insurance industry in responding to an international crisis or maintaining stability.

This lack of formal representation has always been a challenge for federal authorities and U.S. insurance interests with an international orientation, especially in international trade negotiations. The practical effect, since the USTR has no authority to bind the states, is a constraint on the USTR's capacity to reach negotiated settlements on matters touching on insurance regulation. Thus the USTR cannot promise any U.S. insurance market opening in return for market opening by a trading partner. Indeed, the USTR can only "bind the status quo" in state insurance regulation, to the great frustration of U.S. trading partners (and the USTR).[27] Having a federal insurance supervisory authority would solve these

26. Hearing such observations from informed foreign experts who are friends can reinforce their effects. Two former U.K. regulators recently wrote, "In the absence of a federal regulator there is no strong American voice in the International Association of Insurance Supervisors. Nor is there a centre of research and expertise on the financial stability implications of developments in insurance markets." This last observation seems especially prescient in view of the current economic crisis. Davies and Green (2008), p. 167.

27. Of course the USTR and other relevant federal officials consult with the NAIC and key state regulators in formulating and negotiating U.S. positions, and state officials often serve as advisory members of U.S. delegations. Even so, no state regulator (and certainly not the NAIC) can bind even his or her own state to recommended positions, let alone bind other states. Moreover, the high turnover in state insurance regulators (some twenty-three were new to their offices last year) greatly inhibits meaningful "learning by doing" in international forums.

problems of representation. Both the U.S. insurance industry and national economic interests would then be more effectively represented in any future economic crises and in the growing collaborative interactions of global financial services regulators covering broad economic, fiscal, regulatory, and trade matters, removing what has been characterized as "a distinct competitive disadvantage" for U.S. insurers.[28]

Moreover, state insurance regulators are not tasked with promoting global regulatory cooperation or the international expansion of their domestic insurers, and their budgets typically fund such activities only to a limited extent. Indeed, were state funds regularly deployed for such activities, one could expect criticism from state legislators and citizens for "wasting" state resources on nonstate matters. A state-based system provides little or no incentive and no legal locus standi for regulators to heed the international impact of their actions or to leave their state oversight duties to travel internationally. A federal regulator, by contrast, could assume such responsibilities.

Regarding efficiency, U.S. insurers and reinsurers are said to be at competitive disadvantage vis-à-vis their international competitors. The direct and indirect costs of U.S. insurance regulation are high, as noted; these costs deflect financial and managerial resources that otherwise could be used for competitive purposes. The global competitors of these companies, in contrast, can operate in more efficient regulatory environments and explain (and cost) their national and international business plans and strategies to a single home regulator possessing informed expertise in global insurance issues.

Increasing numbers of U.S. businesses have exposures that transcend both state and national boundaries. Globalization of business is a reality. Greater U.S. insurer international expansion should make for more efficient risk management services to U.S. and other countries' multinational corporations, reducing costs to both users and suppliers and allowing a client's global business risks to be covered seamlessly. This reality differs markedly from that of the nineteenth century, when the U.S. insurance regulatory pattern was set, with the view that risks and insurance markets were small and local. As the former Maine insurance commissioner and president of the NAIC testified in 2007, "The need to operate within the state patchwork of regulation in the US means that insurers with customers with worldwide operations are hindered in their efforts to keep

28. Condron (2007), p. 8.

pace with the complex risk issues confronting clients doing business on a national and international basis."[29]

Moreover, a federal insurance regulator could be recognized internationally as strengthening the U.S. financial services regulatory framework, currently perceived as fragmented and lacking effective consolidated conglomerate supervision. A single agency responsible for maintaining high and uniform standards of supervision and leading global best practice could enhance the competitiveness of U.S. insurers with global operations by altering that perception. A state-based regulatory system seems, on its face, incompatible with increasingly integrated and global financial markets and customers. Arguably, the U.S. insurance industry should have an insurance supervisory system capable of matching its global reach and future potential.[30]

There is also the issue of retaliation against internationally oriented U.S. insurers and reinsurers by countries that see the fragmented U.S. regulatory system as a barrier to effective market access. The most pressing risks of retaliation today come from the EU, where U.S. interests face two possible areas of retaliation.

The first relates to the "equivalence" provision of Solvency II. This provision requires a non-EU-owned insurer with operations in the EU to show that the country in which its parent undertaking's head office is located has a supervisory system meeting an EU equivalence test; if it does not, the insurer faces unspecified measures. Large U.S. insurers operating in Europe fear that the EU will find the U.S. insurance supervisory regime not equivalent and that they will then be unable to count group-level capital against their European liabilities (unlike their EU competitors), resulting in higher capital costs.

The second relates to the EU's *Reinsurance Directive,* which has a reciprocity provision. Under this provision, EU member states reserve the right to "mirror" the regulatory requirements to which EU reinsurers are subject in any non-EU reinsurer's domiciliary country. Thus if U.S. regulators require EU

29. Iuppa (2007), p. 4.

30. In his recent remarks before dozens of CEOs of the world's most important insurers and reinsurers, the CEO of the Bermuda Monetary Authority defended Bermuda's looking to the EU and not the United States as a model for the future of dynamic insurance regulation. He observed: "I hope it is not too undiplomatic to state the obvious truth that the requirements to operate by consensus [in the United States] and then hope for changes at the state level inhibits dynamism. The disappointing pace of change on reinsurance collateral rules is an obvious case in point." Matthew Elderfield, remarks at the meeting of the Geneva Association, May 28, 2008, p. 1 (quoted with permission).

reinsurers doing business on a nonadmitted basis to post collateral for their U.S. liabilities, EU regulators could insist that unlicensed U.S. reinsurers doing business in the EU must do likewise for their EU liabilities (currently not required).

The EU Commission has engaged in an informal bilateral dialogue with state regulators for some ten years in an effort to resolve these and other issues. Little seems to have been accomplished. Additionally, in an effort to resolve insurance-related regulatory matters, the EU has for five years sent representatives to meetings of both the NAIC and NCOIL (National Conference of [State] Insurance Legislators). One has the distinct impression of frustration among EU officials at U.S. state insurance regulators' inability to progress their own reform agenda, the more so as reform of reinsurance collateralization has been discussed on the U.S. side for so many years without resolution.

Foreign Insurers and Reinsurers in the U.S. Market

An OFC seems to offer the potential—and the institutional mechanism—for rectifying all trade inconsistencies identified earlier and for opening the U.S. market. U.S. insurance buyers and sellers and the U.S. economy as a whole could then reap benefits. Both individuals and businesses should benefit from a stronger U.S. insurance industry and a stronger international presence in the U.S. insurance market.

Additional penetration should produce more competition, lower prices, new operational techniques, and more innovative services and products, including techniques and products successfully tested in other markets worldwide. Commercial insurance customers should benefit from easier access to the business risks market, matched by lower premiums and greater flexibility (but with the corresponding need to check insurers' financial security carefully). Both personal and commercial products offered by life insurers should become more competitive with products offered by other financial institutions.

A deeper foreign involvement in the U.S. insurance market also has the potential to help the market become less volatile for consumers because of increased capacity. This could be especially true if federal supervision introduced premium deregulation that allowed for more accurate risk-based pricing and avoided politically motivated redistributive pricing that distorts consumers' insurance costs. Similarly, international reinsurers, already important to the U.S. nonlife market, could bring increasing capacity to bear, both in catastrophe-prone areas, such as along the U.S. coasts, and in fields with special insurance problems, such as terrorism insurance.

An OFC also holds the potential to benefit the larger U.S. economy in ways going beyond gains to buyers, an inflow of additional insurance capital, and enhanced tax revenues. By creating a federal body, an OFC should serve as a mechanism for facilitating dialogue, cooperation, and coordination among various federal agencies and departments. This should facilitate the federal government's proper task of monitoring the economy and attendant risk trends in financial markets. Until the recent economic crisis, the conventional consensus was that the insurance sector (unlike banking) was unlikely to present systemic risks. This view had been questioned by many, as global insurance entities grew in size and global asset values became more volatile. The recent justification for bailing out AIG should put this conventional consensus to rest.[31] A state-based insurance supervisory system cannot be robust against such risks.

U.S. insurance industry data are either not timely or are oriented toward monitoring solvency rather than possible systemic effects. Neither the state regulators, the Treasury Department, nor any other federal entity routinely gathers relevant data. Finally, a federal insurance presence would enhance the ability to coordinate overall financial regulation where coordination is warranted (with respect to, for example, data security, privacy, Patriot Act compliance, and financial conglomerate oversight).

The benefits of an OFC to the U.S. insurance market are also evident. Every business decides how much capital to commit to each of its markets. This decision is influenced by innumerable factors, regulatory burdens and costs being important among them. Entry barriers, national treatment inconsistencies, and transparency issues all penalize market capacity building and lessen competition. If regulation is perceived as being unnecessarily strict, rigid, complex, or irrelevant to the market issues needing to be addressed, insurers and reinsurers can be expected to position their capital elsewhere or demand higher returns, or both.

Inappropriate regulatory requirements can result in difficulties in establishing optimum global group structures, leading to unnecessary costs and constraints for insurance business managers and insurance buyers. Moreover, given the nature of insurance as a risk business, these constraints may interact in unforeseen ways with other hazards of globalization, particularly exposure to new risks.[32] Naturally,

---

31. While AIG's financial problems originated at the holding company level because of credit derivative swaps issued by an investment subsidiary (insurance on assets but not historically subject to insurance regulation) and not at any of its many insurance companies, the belief was that the failure of AIG would have created systemic risks for both the United States and the world financial and insurance markets.

32. See De la Martinière (2003), in which these issues are examined in detail.

global businesses avoid such constraints when they can. That the present U.S. regulatory regime might discourage new foreign direct investment into the U.S. insurance market is supported by the observation that most new insurance and reinsurance capacity aimed at the U.S. market has recently been located in Bermuda, not the United States.

The current environment is a spur to regulatory forum shopping, and insurers and reinsurers can be expected to continue in their efforts to avoid or at least minimize interaction with the existing U.S. regulatory system through new reinsurance capital investment outside the United States, more offshore captives, and enhanced use of the surplus-lines market and pure cross-border trade. Conversely, another kind of forum shopping—the growth of U.S. domestic captive markets in several states—is encouraging. This is directly attributable to those states lowering captives' tax burdens, easing formation requirements, and allowing form and pricing freedom, as enjoyed for example in Bermuda. There could be similar positive reactions by commercial and personal insurance suppliers if adopting the OFC proposals heralded a more attractive on-shore environment.

An OFC, with federal institutional underpinning, could benefit the domestic U.S. insurance market by facilitating convergence of international and U.S. insurance accounting and solvency standards. The International Accounting Standards Board (IASB) is advancing toward international accounting standards, including standards for insurers, and the IAIS is moving toward less ambitious harmony in solvency standards. These are increasingly pressing matters, as financial markets become less isolated. As with international trade negotiations, state insurance regulators' lack of authority to represent or commit the United States or, in some instances, to present a clear, unified position on attendant issues, means that U.S. national and insurance industry interests are not advanced effectively.

In all these areas, a state-based insurance regulatory system leaves the U.S. insurance industry at a competitive disadvantage against other segments of the financial industry. More than ever, insurers compete directly with other forms of financial intermediation, as reflected in the repeal of the Glass-Steagall Act and the greater competitive freedoms conferred under the Gramm-Leach-Bliley Act. This intraindustry competition in investment, savings, and retirement products can be expected to intensify as the 76 million baby boomers approach retirement. Other U.S. financial markets operate under less fragmented, less costly, and more efficient regulatory systems, usually with a single federal regulator. This translates into marketplace advantages, which could be made equally open to insurers.

Conclusions

The United States knows from painful experience that terrorism, floods, hurricanes, earthquakes, wildfires, economic crises, and other risks respect no state's borders. Today's risks are regional, national, and global. A regulatory structure needs to be capable of readily adapting to this reality. The OFC proposal addresses several of these challenges. It would establish a federal competency in insurance that should strengthen U.S. insurance interests in international forums and trade negotiations while simplifying federal policymaking as regards international financial issues. Further, the United States should be better able to grasp and respond quickly and effectively to both national and international financial crises and to international regulatory developments.

An OFC should facilitate the beneficial internationalization of the U.S. financial markets because of improved coordination of federal financial regulation across financial sectors, with better assessment of overall financial risk, the creation of a level playing field among financial institutions, and the establishment of a U.S. federal competency for insurance within financial conglomerates. An OFC should also facilitate establishment of mutual recognition while avoiding retaliation, especially between the EU and the United States and likely other jurisdictions as well, allowing greater regulatory efficiency and less costly insurance and reinsurance.

The extent to which state insurance regulation restricts foreign entry and operations in the United States and impedes U.S. insurer involvement in international markets ultimately is an empirical question. Evidence and testimony from both actual and potential foreign entrants and large U.S. firms with existing or potential international operations provide almost unanimous support for the proposition that the existing system is unnecessarily costly, acts as a barrier to effective market access, fails to provide true equality of competitive opportunity, and fails to effectively advance U.S. insurance interests internationally. Economic logic supports this point of view.

Finally, long experience with the state-based regulatory system provides little reason for optimism that the states can achieve workable mutual recognition or can reform the existing system meaningfully and successfully. Its problems seem to be systemic. As in the past, the threat of federal action has already spurred moves toward reform in some key areas. But even with the most optimistic take on reform, the trade barriers and restrictive practices would largely persist. So too would their costly and time-consuming burdens on insurance providers (whether U.S. or foreign) and their U.S. customers.

References

Bair, Sheila. 2004. *Consumer Ramifications of an Optional Federal Charter for Life Insurers.* University of Massachusetts Isenberg School of Management.

Condron, Christopher M. 2007. "The Need for US Insurance Regulatory Reform. A Life Insurance Perspective." *PROGRES Newsletter,* no. 46 (December): 5–8.

Connolly, Jim. 2008. "NAIC Approves 'Framework' to Revise Reinsurance Collateral." *National Underwriter,* December 8 (www.propertyandcasualtyinsurancenews.com/cms/nupc/Breaking%20News/2008/12/08-REINSURANCE-jc).

Davies, Howard, and David Green. 2008. *Global Regulation: The Essential Guide.* Cambridge, U.K.: Polity Press.

De la Martinière, Gérard. 2003. "The Complexity of Managing a Global Company: Regional Exposure vs. Global Exposure." *Geneva Papers on Risk and Insurance* 28, no. 1: 87–93.

De Larosière, Jacques. 2009. "Report of the High Level Group on Financial Supervision in the EU," chaired by Jacques de Larosière. Brussels: European Commission, February.

Financial Services Authority. 2004. *Annual Report 2003–04.* London.

Grace, Martin F., and Robert W. Klein. 2000. "Efficiency Implications of Alternative Regulatory Insurance Structures." In *Optional Federal Chartering and Regulation of Insurance Companies,* edited by Peter J. Wallison, pp. 89–131. Washington: American Enterprise Institute.

Insurance Information Institute. 2008. "Workers Compensation." New York (www.iii.org/media/hottopics/insurance/workerscomp [May 2008]).

Iuppa, Alessandro. 2007. Statement before the House Financial Services Subcommittee on Capital Markets, Insurance, and Government Sponsored Enterprises. October 30.

Mattoo, Aaditya, Randeep Rathindran, and Arvind Subramanian. 2001. "Measuring Services Trade Liberalization and Its Impact on Economic Growth: An Illustration." Policy Research Working Paper 2655. Washington: World Bank.

McCreevy, Charlie. 2007. " 'Solvency II' Launch Event." European Parliament.

Outreville, J. François. 2008. "Foreign Affiliates of the Largest Insurance Groups: Location-Specific Advantages." *Journal of Risk and Insurance* 75, no. 2: 463–91.

Pottier, Steven W. 2007. "State Insurance Regulation of Life Insurers: Implications for Economic Efficiency and Financial Strength." Report to the ACLI, University of Georgia.

Reinsurance Association of America. 2008. "Offshore Reinsurance in the US Market—2007 Results." Washington.

Swiss Re. 2008. "World Insurance in 2007: Emerging Markets Leading the Way." Study 3. *Sigma.* Zurich.

Towers Perrin. 2007. "Weathering the Next Storm: Insurance Industry Perspectives on Florida Law." Stamford, Conn.

"Turner Review: A Regulatory Response to the Global Banking Crisis." 2009. London: Financial Services Authority, March.

U.S. Department of Commerce. 2007. *Survey of Current Business* (October).

U.S. Trade Representative. 2005. *Revised Financial Services Offer* (www.ustr.gov/Trade_Sectors/Services/2005_Revised_US_Services_Offer/Section_Index.html).

Contributors

John A. Cooke
International Financial Services,
London

Robert Detlefsen
National Association of Mutual
Insurance Companies

Martin F. Grace
Georgia State University

Robert W. Klein
Georgia State University

Robert E. Litan
Ewing Marion Kauffman Foundation
and Brookings Institution

Phil O'Connor
PROactive Strategies

Hal S. Scott
Harvard Law School

Harold D. Skipper
Georgia State University

Peter J. Wallison
American Enterprise Institute

Index

System for Electronic Rate and Form Filing (SERFF), 36
Systemic risks, 28, 94–95

Take-all-comers laws, 137
Taxes: and global markets, 203; and national treatment problems, 207; state taxation of insurers, 46
Technology and securities markets, 176
Ten-firm concentration ratio (CR10), 18, 24
Tennessee, licensing in, 205
Tennyson, Sharon, 160–61
Terrorism insurance, 216
Texas: and licensing model law, 70; reinsurance requirements in, 201
Third-party injury claims, 158
Total adjusted capital (TAC), 39
Trade agreements, 197, 207
Trade barriers, 198–99
Transparency problems, 197, 210, 217
Travelers Insurance, 171
Treasury Department: and AIG loan, 94; and OFC, 3, 46, 79, 97–98, 104, 107; optimal regulatory structure recommended by, 168–70, 172; and residual market mechanisms, 88
Troubled Asset Relief Program (TARP), 94
Trusteed surplus funds requirements, 206, 208
Twin-peaks model, 190

Underwriting: and market conduct regulation, 41, 135–38; and OFC, 111, 114; for property-casualty insurance, 99; restrictions on, 107–10

Unfair trade practices rule (NAIC), 70
Uniform Certificate of Authority Application (UCAA), 36, 112
Uniformity: cost savings from, 93; and NAIC, 58; and rate regulation, 29–30; in state-based regulatory system, 66–71
United Kingdom: and cross-border insurance trade, 192, 193; independence of FSA in, 75; principles-based regulation in, 120; regulatory model of, 77, 79, 169–70, 190
U.S. Trade Representative (USTR), 198–99, 213

Variable annuities, 181

Wallison, Peter J., 9–10, 167
Washington (state): citizenship requirements in, 206; workers' compensation monopoly in, 200
Wealth distribution, 103
West Virginia, workers' compensation monopoly in, 200
Wilson, James Q., 106–07
"Workable competition" standard, 26
Workers' compensation insurance: compulsory reinsurance cessions for, 201; and OFC, 93; rate regulation for, 40–41, 131, 160–61; and residual market mechanisms, 88, 132
World Bank, 191
World Trade Organization (WTO), 197, 210, 213
Wyoming, workers' compensation monopoly in, 200